Understanding China's Path to Modernization

Wang Xianqing
Editor

Understanding China's Path to Modernization

Scientific Insights and Development Path

中信出版集团
CITIC Press Group

palgrave
macmillan

Editor
Wang Xianqing
National School of Development
Peking University
Beijing, China

Translated by
He Leyun
Guangzhou, China

ISBN 978-981-96-7050-5 ISBN 978-981-96-7051-2 (eBook)
https://doi.org/10.1007/978-981-96-7051-2

Jointly published with CITIC Press Corporation
The print edition is not for sale in China (Mainland). Customers from China (Mainland) please order the print book from: CITIC Press Corporation

This Palgrave Macmillan imprint is published by the registered company Springer Nature Singapore Pte Ltd.
The registered company address is: 152 Beach Road, #21-01/04 Gateway East, Singapore 189721, Singapore

Contents

Contributors

Fang Cai Chinese Academy of Social Sciences, Beijing, China

Xiaohong Chen Enterprise Research Institute, Development Research Center of the State Council, Beijing, China

Caihui Fu Institute of New Structural Economics, Peking University, Beijing, China;
Institute of South-South Cooperation and Development, Peking University, Beijing, China

Yuzhen Gong National School of Development, Peking University, Beijing, China

Jikun Huang New Rural Development Institute, Peking University, Beijing, China;
China Center for Agricultural Policy, Peking University, Beijing, China;
Academy of Sciences for the Developing World, Trieste, Italy

Qifan Huang China Finance 40 Forum, Beijing, China

Yiping Huang National School of Development, Peking University, Beijing, China;
Institute of Digital Finance, Peking University, Beijing, China

Xiaoyan Lei National School of Development at Peking University, Beijing, China

Justin Yifu Lin Institute of New Structural Economics, Peking University, Beijing, China;
Institute of South-South Cooperation and Development, Peking University, Beijing, China;
National School of Development, Peking University, Beijing, China

Shouying Liu School of Economics, Renmin University of China, Beijing, China

Xiaochun Liu Shanghai Finance Institute, Shanghai, China

Jun Ma Macro & Green Finance Lab, National School of Development, Peking University, Beijing, China;
Institute of Finance and Sustainability, Beijing, China

Gaoning Ning National School of Development, Peking University, Beijing, China

Zhiping Song National School of Development, Peking University, Beijing, China

Hao Wang National School of Development, Peking University, Beijing, China

Min Wang Department of Economics, National School of Development, Peking University, Beijing, China;
China Center for Environmental and Energy Economics, Peking University, Beijing, China

Gao Xu BOC International (China) Co., LTD, Shanghai, China;
National School of Development, Peking University, Beijing, China

Jintao Xu Department of Economics, National School of Development, Peking University, Beijing, China;
China Center for Environmental and Energy Economics, National School of Development, Peking University, Beijing, China

Yang Yao National School of Development, Peking University, Beijing, China;
Beijing International MBA, Peking University, Beijing, China;
Institute of South-South Cooperation and Development, Peking University, Beijing, China

Miaojie Yu Liaoning University, Shenyang, China;
National School of Development, Peking University, Beijing, China

Weiying Zhang National School of Development, Peking University, Beijing, China;
Center for Market and Network Economy, Peking University, Beijing, China

Bo Zhao National School of Development, Peking University, Beijing, China

Yaohui Zhao Department of Economics, National School of Development at Peking University, Beijing, China

Anji Zhou National School of Development, Peking University, Beijing, China

How to Understand Chinese Path to Modernization

The Blueprint, Connotation, and Primary Task of Chinese Path to Modernization

Justin Yifu Lin and Caihui Fu

At a critical moment, as Party members and people of all ethnic groups nationwide embark on a new journey to build a modern socialist country in all respects and strive toward the second centenary goal, the 20th National Congress of the Communist Party of China (CPC) convened successfully. The report delivered during the 20th National Congress of the Communist Party of China (CPC) presents a great action plan for national rejuvenation; its overarching theme can be summarized as follows: Promoting the central task of advancing the great rejuvenation of the Chinese nation through Chinese path to modernization on all

This article was published in the sixth issue of *Economic Commentary* in 2022 under the original title: "The Blueprint, Connotation, and Primary Task of Chinese Path to Modernization—An Interpretation through the Lens of New Structural Economics."

J. Y. Lin (✉) · C. Fu
Institute of New Structural Economics, Peking University, Beijing, China

Institute of South-South Cooperation and Development, Peking University, Beijing, China

J. Y. Lin
National School of Development, Peking University, Beijing, China

W. Xianqing (ed.), *Understanding China's Path to Modernization*,
https://doi.org/10.1007/978-981-96-7051-2_1

fronts and building a modern socialist country in all respects by pursuing high-quality development under the guidance of the theoretical innovation of Marxism adapted to the Chinese context and the needs of the times. Through the lens of new structural economics and the historical trajectories of other countries' modernization endeavors, we will scrutinize Western modernization paradigms and theories, interpreting the report to the 20th CPC National Congress across three dimensions: the blueprint, connotation, and primary task of achieving Chinese path to modernization.

Deconstructing Western Modernization

In the vast tapestry of human development, modernization remains a relatively fleeting and localized phenomenon; only a select few countries have achieved modernization in the past two centuries. Viewed through the lens of new structural economics, grounded in the theory of social form rooted in endowment structures, the diversity of human civilization stems from the differences in endowment structures worldwide. The essence of modernization lies not in blind emulation of Western superstructural models that came after Western modernization, but in reshaping the production structure determined by one's own endowment structure that governs societal change, which then triggers corresponding adjustments in superstructure models. While Western developed countries took the lead in completing the Industrial Revolution, escaping the Malthusian trap, and establishing superstructure models that align with their economic structure, their early endeavors were markedly influenced by warfare, colonization, and capitalist exploitation—essentially a route of uncivilized modernization. In contrast, after enduring over a century of bloody struggles for national sovereignty and under the leadership of the CPC, China, with nearly one-fifth of the world population, has created a new form of human civilization within just over 70 years by embracing a socialist system domestically and advocating equitable, peace-oriented economic engagements internationally.

The Era of Post-Western-Centric Modernization Has Arrived

There is no denying that prevalent theories of modernization, and even broader conceptions thereof, are predominantly shaped by Western-centric perspectives. Even global historians, who strive to mitigate

Western-centric biases, still equate global modernization with the spread of the European triumvirate of revolutions—scientific, industrial, and political—casting the Western post-modernization superstructure as the epitome and conduit of modernity. The emergence and global popularity of the Western-centric modernization worldview can be attributed to three primary factors: the long-term economic and military supremacy of the West following the Industrial Revolution, the deliberate construction of a popular narrative depicting the "Western story" with beguiling and pacifying undertones, and the inclination of intellectuals and the general population in non-Western countries (the developing world) to seek enlightenment from the West. For example, the share of Europe and America in global manufacturing output increased from less than one-fourth in 1750 to over four-fifths in 1900. However, the Western world deliberately obscured its own ascent in historical chronicles and theoretical frameworks, haughtily deeming itself superior. On many occasions, this belief further reinforced their pre-existing notion of Christian superiority. Concurrently, the non-Western world subscribed to the narrative of Western ascendancy, mimicking it to a certain extent but with limited effect, akin to the folly of imitating others without understanding the essence.

Despite efforts by global historians such as Arnold Joseph Toynbee and Leften Stavros Stavrianos to break free from Western-centric historiography and highlight the diversity of human civilizations, the absence of a resurgence in non-Western civilizations has hindered scholars and the general public from fully escaping the grip of Western cultural supremacy. Consequently, they have been unable to objectively examine the origins of human civilizational diversity and move beyond the framework of Western-centric modernization. China's unique path to modernization, anchored in its rich civilization, has given rise to a new form of human civilization, challenging the prevailing Western-centric worldview. This holds profound theoretical significance, as evidenced by General Secretary Xi Jinping's characterization of the current era as one of "major changes unseen in a century." An illustrative example is the transformation of global economic dynamics. The Eight-Nation Alliance, invading Beijing at the beginning of the twentieth century, represented the world's major powers and advanced industrialized countries, which collectively contributed 50.4% of global gross domestic product (GDP) by purchasing power parity (PPP). In 2000, a similar group of eight countries emerged, also comprising the most advanced industrialized countries, accounting for 47% of global GDP. However, by 2018, their aggregate economic output, measured by PPP, had declined to only 34.7% of the global total. Meanwhile, in 2000, China's economic output, measured by market exchange rates, constituted only 3.6% of the global total and 11.8% of the United States. Yet, by 2021, China's economy made up 18.5% of the global total, surpassing 70% of the United States' economy. If measured by PPP, China had surpassed the United States in 2014 to become the world's largest economy. For the first time since the New Culture Movement, it has become possible for Chinese to re-examine the frame of reference for modernization with confidence.

The Essence of Modernization Lies in Structural Transformation Rather Than Westernization

The ascendancy of Western countries, in reality, is a relatively brief episode in humanity's extensive historical narrative, spanning just the past two centuries. Consequently, modernization should not be defined within the scope of Westernization. While this perspective gains traction, there exists a spectrum of viewpoints regarding the definition of modernization. Scholars across diverse fields—ranging from development economics, transformation economics, and development sociology to transformation sociology, development politics, and transformation politics—have explored this concept from different perspectives. Drawing from the paradigm of new structural economics, which finds its roots in Marxist historical materialism, we advocate for a definition of modernization that transcends comparisons with developed countries, but instead centers on a country's own economic base (its endowment and production structures, i.e., industries and technologies) and the corresponding superstructure (finance, education, politics, culture, etc.) that adapts accordingly. We contend that modern society should be identified in relation to its relative position compared to pre-modern societies, which means, from the perspective of human developmental history, escaping the Malthusian trap of pre-modernization.

Humanity's journey as a species originated in the Middle Paleolithic period, roughly between 250,000 and 50,000 years ago. During that time, humans primarily relied on gathering activities to secure food and essential resources vital for survival. Subsequent milestones in human history witnessed the advent of agriculture across various regions and timeframes, marking a groundbreaking transition in human history from hunting and gathering to food production. Influenced by distinct natural environments across continents, agricultural structures evolved differently worldwide due to varying endowment structures, species origins, and challenges in domesticating plants and animals, thus contributing to the formation of diverse ancient civilizations. However, constrained by limited natural resources shaping agricultural endowment structures, endeavors in pre-modern societies to expand into new territories, develop new farming techniques, or understand natural laws were often insufficient to improve living standards in tandem with population growth. This dynamic, famously encapsulated as the Malthusian trap, dictated societal trajectories during pre-modern eras. It was not until the onset of the Industrial Revolution that countries like Britain managed to break free from the Malthusian trap and paved the way toward human modernization.

Western Expansionary (Aggressive) Modernization and Its Theoretical Critique

The established Western capitalist countries embarked on a path of modernization through brutal colonial campaigns and harsh wartime capitalism, accumulating primitive capital and catalyzing the scientific and industrial revolutions. These efforts led to continuous industrial upgrades and technological advancements, resulting in heightened productivity. Concurrently, various facets of modernization within the superstructure—society, politics, and culture—continued to progress. This trajectory enabled those Western countries not only to escape the Malthusian trap but also to assert global dominance, creating a profound disparity with Asian, African, and Latin American countries, which often found themselves subjected to colonial or semi-colonial subjugation and exploitation. By 1800, Europeans controlled approximately 35% of the world's land area, a figure that ballooned to 67% by 1878 and exceeded 84% by 1914. In the early 1800s, Americans were already growing opium in Türkiye, fueling the opium trade to support universities on the East Coast and Bell's invention of telephone. However, historical research indicates that the West did not always hold an initial advantage over the East before the Industrial Revolution. In fact, in 1750, China accounted for 33% of global manufacturing output, while India contributed 25%. However, as Prof. Wen Yi revealed in his work, the West spent over a century fabricating a highly deceptive narrative of the popular historical view known as the "Western story," stating that "it is the unique democratic system and rational thinking of ancient Greece and the legal legacy of ancient Rome and Germanic tribes that laid the institutional foundation for the emergence of modern Western scientific and industrial civilization." This subsequently evolved into a post-Renaissance democratic parliamentary system and rule of law society, distinguishing it from Eastern despotism. This inclusive parliamentary systems and rule of law paved the way for an inclusive capitalist economic system, characterized by principles such as contractual integrity, individual liberation, safeguarding of property rights, and checks on autocratic power, thereby effectively reducing transaction costs across various markets, including intellectual and commodity exchanges, fostering wealth accumulation, spurring scientific innovation, and triggering both scientific and industrial revolutions.

China's remarkable economic growth within its distinctive socialist framework has astonished and perplexed the world. Many believe that sustaining such growth miracle hinges on the rapid adoption of Western political systems, yet Zhang Xiazhun challenges this notion, asserting that the so-called advanced systems prevalent in developed countries today, such as democratic processes, bureaucratic structures, intellectual property rights, corporate governance practices, financial systems, welfare policies, and labor regulations, are primarily outcomes of the Industrial Revolution or superficial aspects of modernization rather than fundamental catalysts. Despite this, Western theories, such as new institutional economics, which propagate the "Western story," continue to gain prominence even though they tend to conflate cause and effect. On the other hand, the Marxist narrative that "the base largely determines the superstructure, but the superstructure also has an influence back upon the base," which aligns with the facts of human historical development, is experiencing diminishing influence in various theories, especially mainstream economic theories. Therefore, there arises a pressing need to infuse social sciences, particularly economics, with a more distinctly Marxist lens drawn from China's modernization experiences. Such an approach can cultivate a Chinese-centric paradigm in social sciences and economics, effectively guiding China's socialist modernization endeavors and offering insights for other developing countries navigating the path to modernization.

Few Successful Modernizers Emerged Under the Colonial Rule of Western Modernization Theories

On January 23, 1826, the Spanish flag came down at the Callao Port of Peru, marking the end of Spain's more than 300 years of colonial rule over Peru and the overall independence of Latin America. Subsequently, on December 30, 1922, the Soviet Union was established, becoming the largest country in the world at that time. Between 1944 and 1985, a significant wave of independence swept through 96 countries, representing about one-third of the global population. However, among the nearly 200 original developing economies, only China's Taiwan and South Korea have transitioned from low-income to middle-income economies and subsequently high-income economies. The Chinese mainland was soon to join their ranks, emerging as the only large country to achieve this progression. Even among the 101 middle-income economies in 1960, a staggering 87% struggled to break free from the middle-income trap and ascend to high-income levels over the ensuing half-century. Among the 13 economies that did break through, eight were either Western European neighboring countries with initially small gaps or oil-producing nations, with the remaining five including Japan and the Four Asian Tigers. The dissolution of the Soviet Union in 1991 came on the heels of its ambitious claims of constructing an advanced socialist society at the 24th Congress of the Communist Party of the Soviet Union. According to World Bank figures from 2017, a significant portion of the global population lived below the international poverty line of USD 1.9 per day, totaling 6.99 billion individuals, representing 9.3% of the global population. Notably, sub-Saharan Africa alone harbored a staggering 433 million individuals living below this extreme poverty line. The frustrating modernization journey of late-developing countries indicates that, whether in developed or developing nations, most of the past modernization theories have largely proven to be futile. As of today, countries across Africa, South Asia, and Eastern Europe have not yet successfully found a path to modernization, facing challenges such as the poverty trap in Africa, the middle-income trap in Latin America, and the transition trap in Eastern Europe.

In the pursuit of building a modern socialist country in all respects, China must uphold the "Four-sphere Confidence" (i.e., confidence in the path, theory, system, and culture of socialism with Chinese characteristics) and formulate a modernization theory tailored to our distinctive national conditions. As the report to the 20th CPC National Congress highlighted, "Since the 18th National Congress, with the courage to make theoretical explorations and innovations, our Party has, from an entirely new perspective, deepened its understanding of the laws that underlie governance by a communist party, the development of socialism, and the evolution of human society. It has achieved major theoretical innovations, which are encapsulated in the Thought on Socialism with Chinese Characteristics for a New Era." Just as there are no bounds to practice, there is no end to theoretical innovation. To keep advancing theoretical innovation on the basis of practical experience, we must, first of all, gain a good command of the worldview and methodology of the Thought on Socialism with Chinese Characteristics for a New Era and adhere to and make good use of its stances, viewpoints, and methods. This involves putting people first, maintaining self-confidence, independence, and originality, alongside innovation, problem-solving, systemic thinking, global perspective, and a people-centered approach that respects their needs, ingenuity, and wisdom. We must remain firm in our conviction in Marxism and socialism with Chinese characteristics and strengthen our confidence in the path, theory, system, and culture of socialism with Chinese characteristics. By consistently proposing new ideas, perspectives, and methods, we can effectively address challenges, offer scientifically grounded approaches, and propel the endeavors of both the Party and the state. Our overarching objective is to devise solutions deeply rooted in our distinctive national context, comprehensively planned, and tailored to our unique circumstances, ultimately fostering sustained progress and prosperity.

Blueprint for Chinese Path to Modernization

The Quest for Chinese Path to Modernization

From the Opium Wars to the First Sino-Japanese War, and from the Second Sino-Japanese War to the War to Resist US Aggression and Aid Korea, the Chinese people have valiantly fought for over a century to secure national independence and establish the modern China we see today. Under the leadership of the CPC for just over 70 years, nearly one-fifth of the world's population has been lifted out of poverty. Notably, after embracing the policy of reform and opening-up, China swiftly got out of the Malthusian trap within a few decades, steadfastly upholding and refining the socialist system with Chinese characteristics. This has ushered in a transformative era of modernization within the rich tapestry of China's five-millennia civilization. The escape from the Malthusian trap represents a shared aspect of modernization itself, as well as between modernization in China and the West. However, unlike Western methods involving warfare, colonization, and the imposition of capitalist exploitation systems, China opted for a transformative approach by embracing socialism internally and, on the global stage, fostering peaceful and equitable economic and trade exchanges. For instance, China has never sought overseas colonies or maintained military bases with colonial intentions. It stands as the primary trading partner for over 120 countries and regions, and the second-largest for more than 70 others. Remarkably, China ranks either first or second in trade partnerships for over 90% of countries and territories globally. Therefore, at the crux of the distinct trajectories of modernization between China and the West lies the stark contrast between civilized and aggressive paths toward progress. China has, in essence, charted a pioneering course, contributing a unique chapter to the mosaic of human civilization.

China's successful transition toward a civilized path of modernization stems not only from the cultural inclinations of the Chinese nation toward peace but also from the assimilation of experiences and the adoption of a pragmatic and tailored approach to modernization that suits national conditions. This concept, initially introduced by Deng Xiaoping, the chief architect of China's socialist reform and opening-up, aimed to caution against hasty actions and instead set realistic developmental goals that resonate with China's distinctive national conditions. This involved rejecting the wholesale adoption of Western models and championing a self-determined path for development. Since 1978, China's economic transformation has diverged from the *Washington Consensus*. Under the leadership of the CPC, China embarked on gradual reforms that advocate for emancipating the mind and seeking truth from facts. While many economists initially doubted this method would be less than ideal compared to planned economies, fearing it would exacerbate corruption and reduce economic efficiency, the outcomes proved otherwise. Through this transitional strategy, struggling enterprises received protective subsidies, ensuring economic stability. Concurrently, opening up entry to industries with comparative advantages and competitive strengths accelerated economic development and capital accumulation. Formerly non-competitive, capital-intensive industries gradually realigned with comparative advantages, paving the way for future reforms. In contrast, countries strictly adhering to the *Washington Consensus* experienced economic collapses, stagnation, and prevalent issues such as corruption and wealth inequality. Today, successful countries that have effectively transitioned have followed an unconventional path—one characterized by a gradual, dual-track approach to transition, initially deemed illogical by mainstream economists.

Great Changes in the New Era

The report to the 20th CPC National Congress highlighted notable accomplishments in reform and opening-up and socialist modernization, as well as great advancements in Party building. These achievements have established a robust foundation, facilitated favorable conditions, and ensured essential support for further progress. However, there exist long-standing and pressing issues, both, demanding immediate attention. In response, the CPC Central Committee has shown strategic foresight, decisive decision-making, and unwavering resolve in tackling challenges. Through a series of strategic measures and transformative initiatives, the CPC has achieved breakthroughs and obtained landmark results, weathering risks and tests across political, economic, ideological, and environmental domains. As a result, the country witnesses historic achievements and profound changes, propelling China into a new phase of building a modern socialist country in all respects. The past decade marked three major events of great immediate importance and profound historical significance for the cause of the Party and the people: We embraced the 100th anniversary of the founding of the CPC; we ushered in a new era of socialism with Chinese characteristics; and we eradicated absolute poverty and finished building a moderately prosperous society in all respects, thus completing the First Centenary Goal.

The great changes of the new era have established a solid groundwork for propelling the great rejuvenation of the Chinese nation through the comprehensive advancement of Chinese path to modernization. Over the past decade, China's economic prowess has witnessed a remarkable leap. Per capita GDP doubled from RMB 39,800 to RMB 81,000, while the total GDP surged from RMB 54 trillion to RMB 114 trillion in 2022. China's share in the global economy stood at 18.5% in 2021, marking a substantial increase of 7.2 percentage points and consolidating its position as the world's second-largest economy. Meanwhile, the manufacturing industry's value-added accounted for over 28% globally, maintaining its position as the world leader. In 2021, China led global charts for international patent applications for three consecutive years, reaching over 69,500 applications. In the same year, it also led in total merchandise trade and foreign investment attraction, with total imports and exports reaching USD 6.1 trillion and actual foreign investment utilization hitting USD 173.5 billion. Over the years, China has built the world's largest education, social security, and healthcare systems, establishing a robust human capital foundation for modernization endeavors. In 2020, China witnessed the graduation of 8.7 million students from regular universities, with STEM disciplines (related to science, technology, engineering, and mathematics) constituting 62% of the total. China has also made significant strides in its ecological endowments, institutional frameworks, and security conditions. As the report to the 20th CPC National Congress proposed, we have acted on the idea that lucid waters and lush mountains are invaluable assets. We have persisted with a holistic and systematic approach to conserving and improving mountain, water, forest, farmland, grassland, and desert ecosystems. China's ecological conservation systems have been improved. This has led to historic, transformative, and comprehensive changes in ecological and environmental protection. Through decisive political initiatives, China has undertaken sweeping reforms, resulting in transformative changes across diverse sectors. Socialism with Chinese characteristics has matured and evolved, substantially augmenting the country's national governance capacity and modernization endeavors. Guided by a holistic perspective on national security, China remains steadfast in safeguarding its sovereignty, security, and developmental interests, leading to a notable overall enhancement of its national security posture.

Mission and Tasks in the New Era

In the report to the 20th CPC National Congress, it was solemnly declared that, "From this day forward, the central task of the Communist Party of China will be to lead the Chinese people of all ethnic groups in a concerted effort to realize the second centenary goal of building China into a great modern socialist country in all respects and to advance the rejuvenation of the Chinese nation on all fronts through a Chinese path to modernization." As General Secretary Xi Jinping pointed out in the report to the 19th CPC National Congress, "The original aspiration and the mission of Chinese Communists is to seek happiness for the Chinese people and rejuvenation for the Chinese nation. This original aspiration, this mission, is what inspires Chinese Communists to advance."[1] In 1921, the 1st CPC National Congress laid out a manifesto outlining the Party's ultimate goal of achieving complete liberation for the Chinese people and all of humanity, presenting the grand ideal of communism. Later, the 2nd CPC National Congress adopted the Party's core programmatic principles, with the highest aim being the realization of communism and the lowest aim being the execution of democratic revolution. In 1925, Mao Zedong expressed in the inaugural issue of the journal *Political Weekly*, "Why do we need revolution? To liberate the Chinese nation, to establish governance by the people, and to ensure economic prosperity for all."[2] At the 7th CPC National Congress, the principle of "wholeheartedly serving the people" was enshrined in the Party Constitution, emphasizing the CPC's commitment to advancing the interests of the Chinese nation and its people. After 28 years of strenuous endeavor, the CPC led the Chinese people to achieve comprehensive national independence and liberation, culminating in the founding of the People's Republic of China (PRC). Following the PRC's founding, the Party Constitution was amended at the 8th National Congress, emphasizing that the fundamental objective of all Party endeavors is to fulfill the material and cultural needs of the people to the greatest extent possible.

Following the initiation of reform and opening-up, the 12th CPC National Congress highlighted the imperative of advancing socialism with distinct Chinese characteristics and the strategic goal of building a moderately prosperous society. From 1978 to 2021, China's GDP saw an average annual growth rate of 9.2%, surpassing the duration and pace observed of the East Asian miracle witnessed during the period of rapid growth, thereby marking an unprecedented feat in human history. To accomplish the historic mission of poverty alleviation and the realization of a moderately prosperous society in all aspects, the 18th and 19th National Congresses of the CPC prioritized the building of a moderately prosperous society in all respects and securing definitive triumph in this

[1] Editor's note: "Secure a Decisive Victory in Building a Moderately Prosperous Society in All Respects and Strive for the Great Success of Socialism with Chinese Characteristics for a New Era–Delivered at the 19th National Congress of the Communist Party of China" (Reference: http://www.gov.cn/zhuanti/2017-10/27/content_5234876.htm).

[2] Editor's note: Reference: http://dangshi.people.cn/n1/2021/0715/c436975-32158396.html.

pursuit. On July 1, 2021, General Secretary Xi Jinping declared during the centenary celebration of the CPC that we have built a moderately prosperous society in all respects.[3] The transformative shifts witnessed over the past decade in the new era serve as monumental milestones in the annals of the Party, the PRC, the era of reform and opening-up, socialist development, and the progress of the Chinese nation. With steadfast conviction, the CPC and the Chinese people are steering the nation toward a momentous transition, progressing from standing tall, attaining prosperity, to becoming stronger as a nation. As reforms progress and socialist modernization deepens, the realization of the great rejuvenation of the Chinese nation has embarked on an irreversible historical journey. The comprehensive objectives outlined in the report to the 20th CPC National Congress have set forth a precise blueprint for achieving the great rejuvenation of the Chinese nation through a Chinese path to modernization.

The Blueprint for Modernization

Achieving the great rejuvenation of the Chinese nation stands as the paramount aspiration of the Chinese people in modern times. The Party's second centenary goal calls for building China into a great modern socialist country that is prosperous, strong, democratic, culturally advanced, harmonious, and beautiful by 2049, the centenary of the People's Republic of China. China aims to basically realize socialist modernization by 2035, with overall developmental goals listed as follows:

- Significantly increase economic strength, scientific and technological capabilities, and composite national strength; substantially grow the per capita GDP to be on par with that of a mid-level developed country
- Join the ranks of the world's most innovative countries, with great self-reliance and strength in science and technology

[3] Editor's note: "The Grand Celebration of the Centenary of the Founding of the Communist Party of China Held With Xi Jinping Delivering an Important Speech" (Reference: http://www.gov.cn/xinwen/2021-07/01/content_5621846.htm).

- Build a modernized economy; form a new pattern of development; basically achieve new industrialization, informatization, urbanization, and agricultural modernization
- Basically modernize the system and capacity for governance; improve the system for whole-process people's democracy; build a law-based country, government, and society
- Become a leading country in education, science and technology, talent, culture, sports, and health; significantly enhance national soft power
- Ensure that the people are leading better and happier lives; bring per capita disposable income to new heights; substantially grow the middle-income group as a share of the total population; guarantee equitable access to basic public services; ensure modern standards of living in rural areas; achieve long-term social stability; make more notable and substantive progress in promoting the people's well-rounded development and prosperity for all
- Broadly establish eco-friendly ways of work and life; steadily lower carbon emissions after reaching a peak; fundamentally improve the environment; largely accomplish the goal of building a Beautiful China
- Comprehensively strengthen the national security system and national security capabilities; achieve basic modernization of national defense and the armed forces.

In his report to the 20th CPC National Congress, General Secretary Xi Jinping underscored the significant strides made by the CPC in advancing a Chinese path to modernization, built upon extensive exploration and practical experience tracing back to the founding of the PRC, particularly during the era of reform and opening-up. Since the convening of the 18th CPC National Congress, the Party has witnessed innovative breakthroughs in both theoretical understanding and practical applications. The central theme in the report to the 20th CPC National Congress can be succinctly summarized as follows: the full implementation of Xi Jinping Thought, which serves as the guiding principle for accomplishing two major tasks: leading the Chinese people as the Party's central task to achieve comprehensive socialist modernization and fostering high-quality development as the primary task in building a modern socialist country. The report delivered at the 20th CPC National Congress delineated specific directives across 12 key domains, all centered around the Party's central mission. These include:

1. accelerating the creation of a new development pattern and pursuing high-quality development;
2. invigorating china through science and education and developing a strong workforce for the modernization drive;
3. advancing whole-process people's democracy and ensuring that the people run the country;
4. exercising law-based governance on all fronts and advancing the rule of law in China;
5. building cultural confidence and strength and securing new successes in developing socialist culture;
6. improving the people's well-being and raising quality of life;
7. pursuing green development and promoting harmony between humanity and nature;
8. modernizing china's national security system and capacity and safeguarding national security and social stability;
9. achieving the centenary goal of the People's Liberation Army and further modernizing national defense and the military;
10. upholding and improving the policy of One Country, Two Systems and promoting national reunification;
11. promoting world peace and development and building a human community with a shared future; and
12. exercising full and rigorous self-governance and advancing the great new project of Party building in the new era.

The Connotation of Chinese Path to Modernization

Distinctive Features of Chinese Path to Modernization

Chinese path to modernization, guided by the CPC, amalgamates common attributes found in modernization endeavors worldwide with distinct Chinese characteristics rooted in its national conditions. The report to the 20th CPC National Congress highlights five key features defining Chinese path to modernization: the modernization of a huge population, the modernization of common prosperity for all, the modernization of material and cultural-ethical advancement, the modernization of harmony between humanity and nature, and the modernization of peaceful development. These features are emblematic of China's historical legacy, natural endowment, strategic objectives, and global significance in the realm of modernization. Given the country's profound historical background, expansive territory, and substantial populace, the essence of its rejuvenation and progress lies in upholding the principles of dialectical materialism, seeking truth from facts, rooting in national conditions, and forging its own path. Modernization cannot be limited to select demographics, locales, or societal facets—it necessitates adherence to and the development of socialism with Chinese characteristics, the promotion of common prosperity for all, ensuring synchronized modernization nationwide, and the holistic advancement progress across material, political, spiritual, social, and ecological dimensions of civilization. In contrast to the historical trajectory of established capitalist countries, which often pursued modernization through exploitative means such as colonialism, imperialistic dominance, and environmental degradation at the expense of other countries, Chinese path to modernization prioritizes peaceful development and harmonious coexistence with nature, embodying a more civilized approach to modernity. Just as the West goes to great lengths to cover up its history of colonial exploitation, it also vigorously champions extreme environmentalism to mask its own exploitation of nature. They unjustly criticize developing countries for the pollution issues inherent in their developmental phases. A case in point is carbon emissions: when assessing per capita cumulative emissions since 1900, the global average stands at 209 tons per person. Comparatively, China registers only 157 tons per person, whereas the United States records a substantially higher figure of 1218 tons per person, far surpassing China. Similarly, other major developed countries also exceed China by a considerable margin. In contrast, Chinese path to modernization follows a path of peaceful development and harmonious coexistence with nature, epitomizing a civilized approach to modernization. *The Resolution of the Central Committee of the Communist Party of China on the Major Achievements and Historical Experience of the Party Over the Past Century* underscored this stance, stating that "the Party has led the people in pioneering a uniquely Chinese path to modernization, creating a new model for human advancement, and expanding the channels for developing countries to achieve modernization. This has offered a new option for countries and nations who want to accelerate development while preserving their independence."

The advancement of the Chinese nation toward its great rejuvenation through Chinese path to modernization will bring about a new form of human civilization with profound historical implications on a global scale. The unique nature and immense importance of Chinese path to modernization in the global modernization process are undeniable. During the second plenary session of the 19th CPC Central Committee, General Secretary Xi Jinping highlighted that China is working to achieve modernization for more than 1.4 billion people, a number larger than the combined population of all developed countries in the world today. This transformation will fundamentally reshape the global modernization landscape, marking a monumental event in human history.[4] Envisioned within the framework of basically achieving modernization by 2035, as outlined in the report to the 20th CPC National Congress, China's per capita national income will notably exceed the threshold for high-income levels by that time, firmly placing the country among high-income economies, and signifying that the proportion of the global population residing within high-income economies will rise from the current 16% to approximately 35%. At that point, not only will the living standards of China's 1.4 billion population see significant improvement, but it will also unlock expanded market prospects and enhanced technological resources for over 50 billion individuals in low- and middle-income countries. Furthermore, it will afford greater access to China's developmental experiences to assist these countries in navigating their own development trajectories, thereby greatly propelling global modernization efforts forward.

Essential Requirements for Chinese Path to Modernization

The report to the 20th CPC National Congress has also articulated the essential requirements for Chinese path to modernization, which include upholding the leadership of the CPC and socialism with Chinese characteristics, pursuing high-quality development, developing whole-process people's democracy, enriching the people's cultural lives, achieving

[4] Editor's note: "The Establishment of a New Development Paradigm Is Inevitable for Implementing the New Developmental Philosophy in the New Developmental Phase" (Reference: https://www.ccps.gov.cn/xtt/202208/t20220831_154802.shtml).

common prosperity for all, promoting harmony between humanity and nature, building a human community with a shared future, and creating a new form of human advancement. These essential requirements are grounded in the distinctive characteristics of Chinese path to modernization. Central to Chinese path to modernization is the upholding and advancement of socialism with Chinese characteristics, with the paramount importance attributed to the leadership of the CPC. The foremost point highlighted in the historical experience of the CPC's endeavors over the past century, as summarized in the *Resolution of the Central Committee of the Communist Party of China on the Major Achievements and Historical Experience of the Party Over the Past Century*, is the "upholding of the Party's leadership," explicitly stating that "the CPC is the central leading force of our cause. The strong leadership of the Party is the fundamental reason why the Chinese people and Chinese nation have been able to transform their fate in modern times and achieved the great success we see today." In the report to the 20th CPC National Congress, General Secretary Xi Jinping unequivocally stated that "Our Party has a pivotal role in building China into a modern socialist country in all respects and in advancing the rejuvenation of the Chinese nation on all fronts"; and emphasized that "as the largest Marxist governing party in the world, we must always stay alert and determined to tackle the special challenges that a large party like ours faces, so as to maintain the people's support and consolidate our position as the long-term governing party." He also called on that "all of us in the Party must bear in mind that full and rigorous self-governance is an unceasing endeavor and that self-reform is a journey to which there is no end. We must never slacken our efforts and never allow ourselves to become weary or beaten. We must persevere with full and rigorous self-governance, continue to advance the great new project of Party building in the new era, and use our own transformation to steer social transformation."

The specific strategy for Chinese path to modernization encompasses the following elements: pursuing high-quality development, developing whole-process people's democracy, enriching the people's cultural lives, achieving common prosperity for all, promoting harmony between humanity and nature, building a human community with a shared future, and creating a new form of human advancement. This strategy integrates China's unique context with the principles of historical materialism and dialectical materialism, emphasizing the notion that the economic base shapes social structure, while social structures reciprocally influence the economic base. The report to the 20th CPC National Congress expressly identifies high-quality development as the foremost priority in the comprehensive building of a modern socialist country, stressing the importance of promoting the economy both qualitatively and quantitatively. China was a low-income country before 1996, and it firmly joined the ranks of lower middle-income countries in 1999 and then the ranks of upper middle-income countries in 2010. In the years 1990, 1995, 2000, 2005, 2010, and 2016, China's per capita national income reached 4.3%, 5.8%, 10.1%, 16.4%, 35.4%, and 67.5% respectively of the corresponding high-income threshold values for those years. This demonstrates a rapid convergence of China's per capita national income toward the high-income threshold at an almost exponential rate. Therefore, it is of paramount importance to effectively implement The Outline of the 14th Five-Year Plan for Economic and Social Development (2021–2025) and Long-Range Objectives through the Year 2035 of the People's Republic of China, which aims to double China's per capita income level or economic aggregate by 2035 compared to its 2020 level, as part of its development objective.

Strategic Steps for Chinese Path to Modernization

The strategic blueprint for building China into a great modern socialist country in all respects unfolds in two stages: basically realizing socialist modernization from 2020 through 2035; building China into a great modern socialist country that is prosperous, strong, democratic, culturally advanced, harmonious, and beautiful from 2035 through the middle of this century. This strategic framework for China's modernization, known as the "Two-step Strategic Plan" in the new era, is formulated based on historical experience and lessons, current developmental realities, and a commitment to adhering to both the objective laws of development and proactive strategic deployments, which will delineate specific guidelines and policies.

The *Resolution on Certain Questions in the History of Our Party Since the Founding of the People's Republic of China*, adopted at the sixth plenary session of the 11th CPC Central Committee in 1981, underscored the importance of conducting economic development in accordance with China's unique circumstances, progressively and in stages, to achieve the goal of modernization. Over the past 40 years, the CPC has steadfastly adhered to the guiding principles set forth in the *Resolution on*

Certain Questions in the History of Our Party Since the Founding of the People's Republic of China. At the 13th CPC National Congress, a Three-Step Approach was identified as the economic development trajectory: the first step was to double the gross national product (GNP) from 1980, ensuring the fulfillment of people's basic needs; the second step aimed to double the GNP again by the end of the twentieth century, achieving a moderately prosperous society; and the third step was to reach the level of moderately developed countries by the mid-twenty-first century, significantly improving people's living standards and essentially achieving modernization. By 2000, China's GNP had increased more than fourfold compared to 1980. Following this, the 15th CPC National Congress further subdivided the Three-Step Approach into three phases and outlined specific timelines, notably emphasizing the Two Centenaries. The 20th CPC National Congress segmented the second centenary goal into two stages for implementation. In the report to the 20th CPC National Congress, China's overarching developmental goal by 2035 was once again clearly defined, along with the aim to build a great modern socialist country grounded on basically realizing modernization.

China's 14th Five-Year Plan for the national economic and social development marks a groundbreaking alignment with the long-range objectives through the year 2035. The next five years will be crucial for getting our efforts to build a modern socialist country in all respects off to a good start. Our main objectives and tasks for this period are as follows:

- Make breakthroughs in promoting high-quality economic development; achieve greater self-reliance and strength in science and technology; make major progress in creating a new pattern of development and building a modernized economy
- Make new strides in reform and opening-up; make further progress in modernizing China's system and capacity for governance; further improve the socialist market economy; put in place new systems for a higher-standard open economy
- Further enhance the institutions, standards, and procedures of whole-process people's democracy; improve the system of socialist rule of law with Chinese characteristics
- Enrich the intellectual and cultural lives of our people; enhance the cohesion of the Chinese nation and the appeal of Chinese culture
- Ensure personal income grows basically in step with economic growth and pay rises in tandem with increases in productivity; ensure

much more equitable access to basic public services; develop a better multi-tiered social security system
- Substantially improve urban and rural living environments; make notable progress in building a Beautiful China
- Further consolidate national security; fulfill the goals for the centenary of the People's Liberation Army in 2027; make solid progress in building a Peaceful China
- Further increase China's international standing and influence; enable China to play a greater role in global governance

Theoretical Connotation of Chinese Path to Modernization

Marxism is the foundational guiding ideology upon which the CPC and China are founded and thrive. The report to the 20th CPC National Congress marked an elevation of theoretical innovation to an unprecedented position. In the second part, General Secretary Xi Jinping systematically expounded on opening up new horizons for Marxism tailored to China's conditions and contemporary demands, emphasizing that the adaptation of Marxism to China's conditions and contemporary demands is a process of seeking, revealing, and applying truth. Just as there are no bounds to practice, there is no end to theoretical innovation. Chinese Communists are keenly aware that only by amalgamating the fundamental principles of Marxism with China's unique realities and rich traditional culture and by applying dialectical and historical materialism can we offer accurate solutions to the major questions presented by our times, identified through practical experience, and ensure the perpetual vigor and relevance of Marxism. Through continuous theoretical, practical, and institutional innovation, the CPC has effectively propelled and broadened the process of Chinese path to modernization, consistently enhancing and advancing Xi Jinping Thought.

Chinese path to modernization also embodies a generalized theoretical essence. Viewed through the lens of new structural economics, it can be encapsulated as "one center, three basic points." "One center" is anchored in the endowment structure, reflecting a country's specific conditions and the foundational principles of Marxist dialectical materialism, serving as the basis for advancing modernization. In essence, Chinese modernization harmonizes the core tenets of Marxism with China's unique realities and its rich traditional culture. Meanwhile, the "three basic points" are a country's development, transformation, and operation based on its endowment structure. This underscores the historical materialist principle that "the economic base shapes the superstructure, which then in turn influences the economic base," within the context of a country's distinct social form. This is exemplified by the 10 affirmations, the 14 commitments, and the 13 areas of achievement that were articulated at the 19th CPC National Congress and the Sixth Plenary Session of the 19th CPC Central Committee. Contrary to mainstream modernization theories originating from Western developed countries, which draw primarily from the experiences of those countries and idealize the economic base and superstructure of developed countries as the pinnacle of modernization, this theory treats the disparities between developed and developing countries merely as quantitative differences, overlooking any qualitative distinctions, and considering the differences between developing and developed countries as deviations to be rectified. However, developing and developed countries exhibit both quantitative differences and qualitative distinctions. Marx's historical materialism reveals the differing "economic bases" arising from these distinctions, which subsequently shape the corresponding "superstructures." These distinctions should not be simplistically viewed as mere deviations to be rectified. Owing to inherent structural differences in industry, technology, physical infrastructure, and institutional arrangements arising from their endowment structures, the transition from a lower to a higher structural level is central to the matters related to development. Similarly, transitioning from a distorted structure to an undistorted one pertains to the matter of transformation, or reform. Moreover, countries at different developmental stages exhibit unique modes of economic and social operation based on their respective structural conditions.

The Primary Task of Chinese Path to Modernization

Prioritizing High-Quality Development as the Key to Achieving Chinese Path to Modernization

The central task of the CPC is to lead the Chinese people of all ethnic groups in a concerted effort to realize the second centenary goal of building China into a great modern socialist country in all respects and to advance the rejuvenation of the Chinese nation on all fronts through a Chinese path to modernization. In this regard, prioritizing high-quality development stands as the foremost objective in the comprehensive building of a modern socialist country. The CPC has consistently emphasized that development is the paramount focus of governance and national revitalization and has also soberly acknowledged that without a robust material and technological foundation, the comprehensive building of a strong modern socialist country is unattainable. The report to the 20th CPC National Congress elaborately explains the principal aspects, critical junctures, and areas requiring attention in achieving high-quality development within the historical framework of Chinese path to modernization. In summary, high-quality development means fully, accurately, and comprehensively implementing the new development concept in the new developmental stage, maintaining the course of reform in the socialist market economy, upholding high-level openness, and accelerating the establishment of a new development paradigm with domestic circulation as the core, complemented by mutually reinforcing domestic and international circulations. The effectiveness of high-quality development is directly related to whether the great endeavor of modernization can be realized as scheduled.

The report to the 20th CPC National Congress also elaborated on the priorities for high-quality development across five dimensions.

First, it underscored the imperative of concurrently advancing both the public and non-public sectors within the economy, emphasizing the synergistic fusion of an efficient market and a capable government, deemed essential for building a high-standard socialist market economy, stating that "We must uphold and improve China's basic socialist economic systems. We must unswervingly consolidate and develop the public sector and unswervingly encourage, support, and guide the development of the non-public sector. We will work to see that the market plays the decisive role in resource allocation and that the government better plays its role. In pursuing economic growth, we must continue to focus on the real economy. We will advance new industrialization and move faster to boost China's strength in manufacturing, product quality, aerospace, transportation, cyberspace, and digital development."

Second, it emphasized that the continuous development of productive forces is fundamental to the building of a strong modern socialist country. Therefore, the Chinese nation should modernize the industrial system, stating that "In pursuing economic growth, we must continue to focus on the real economy. We will advance new industrialization and move faster to boost China's strength in manufacturing, product quality, aerospace, transportation, cyberspace, and digital development."

Third, it acknowledged that rural modernization is the most challenging and arduous task within the comprehensive endeavor of building a modern socialist country. Therefore, the Chinese nation must comprehensively promote rural revitalization, "put agricultural and rural development first, and consolidate and expand the achievements in poverty alleviation, move faster to build up China's strength in agriculture and steadily promote the revitalization of businesses, talent, culture, ecosystems, and organizations in the countryside." The nation must also "reinforce the foundations for food security on all fronts, ensure that China's total area of farmland does not fall below the redline of 120 million hectares, and that China's food supply remains firmly in its own hands."

Fourth, it delineated that coordinated development serves as the linchpin for achieving socialist modernization, stating that "We will thoroughly implement the coordinated regional development strategy, major regional strategies, the functional zoning strategy, and the new urbanization strategy. We will improve the distribution of the major productive forces and develop a regional economic layout and a territorial space system that complement each other's strengths and promote high-quality development."

Fifth, the process of opening-up remains an inexhaustible driver for the development of socialist modernization. Therefore, we must "promote high-standard opening-up; steadily expand institutional opening-up with regard to rules, regulations, management, and standards; accelerate China's transformation into a trader of quality; promote the high-quality development of the Belt and Road Initiative; and endeavor to preserve the diversity and stability of the international economic landscape and economic and trade relations."

Understanding High-Quality Development Through the Lens of New Structural Economics

The 19th CPC National Congress has emphasized the importance of high-quality economic development. Nonetheless, several sectors hold misconceptions regarding the essence of such development. One common misconception is the belief that high-quality development contradicts the necessity for maintaining reasonable rates of economic growth. Another prevalent misconception is the narrow perspective on high-quality development, failing to connect it to the modernization endeavor. Positioned as the primary task in building a modern socialist country in all respects, high-quality development encompasses facets of a new developmental phase, an innovative mindset, and a pioneering framework for progress. It calls for enhancing the quality and efficiency of economic growth while ensuring a reasonable increase in quantity. The pursuit of socialist modernization by 2035, as outlined in the plan since 2020, underscores the imperative of maintaining steady growth rates. General Secretary Xi Jinping, in elucidating the formulation of *The Central Committee's Suggestions on The Outline of the 14th Five-Year Plan for Economic and Social Development (2021–2025) and Long-Range Objectives through the Year 2035 of the People's Republic of China*, explicitly stated, "After careful research and analysis, the drafting group believes that China's economy has the potential to sustain long-term stable growth based on its economic development capacity and conditions. By the end of the 14th Five-Year Plan period, achieving the current standard of a high-income country and doubling economic output or per capita income by 2035 is entirely feasible."[5] This underscores the need to maintain an approximate economic growth rate of 4.7% between 2021 and 2035, with prospects for sustaining this trajectory over the next 15 years.

Since the initiation of the reform and opening-up, China has seen significant changes in its comparative advantages, leading to a noticeable shift in its developmental trajectory. President Xi Jinping highlighted in 2013, during the APEC CEO Summit, that China's economy had entered a new developmental phase characterized by profound transformations and structural adjustments.[6] Subsequently, General Secretary Xi Jinping introduced the new developmental philosophy at the fifth plenary session of the 18th CPC Central Committee in 2015, which later formed the

[5] Editor's note: "Explanation on The Central Committee's Suggestions on The Outline of the 14th Five-Year Plan for Economic and Social Development (2021–2025) and Long-Range Objectives through the Year 2035 of the People's Republic of China"(Reference: https://www.qinfeng.gov.cn/info/1022/135345.htm).

[6] Editor's note: Speech by President Xi Jinping at the 2013 APEC CEO Summit(Reference:http://www.xinhuanet.com//world/2013-10/08/c_125490697.htm).

foundational framework for the country's 13th Five-Year Plan.[7] Given that there arises a necessity for the new developmental philosophy to adapt effectively as the developmental stage and the primary contradiction evolve, with the realization of the historic mission to build a moderately prosperous society in all respects, the primary contradiction facing Chinese society has evolved. What the Chinese nation now faces is the contradiction between unbalanced and inadequate development and the people's ever-growing needs for a better life, as stated at the 19th CPC National Congress. Guiding the transition of the development paradigm through the application of the new developmental philosophy is a strategic choice.

Furthermore, as China's primary contradiction shifts, the international contradiction within the global development landscape also evolves. With China's economic scale growing (representing about 18.5% of the global economy) and witnessing an enhanced economic structure (e.g., the service industry accounting for over 50% of the total share in 2015), the external impulse from the dual circulation model of markets and resources outside China is diminishing, and economic growth increasingly hinges on domestic economic cycles. The strategy to boost domestic demand, accompanied by the deepening of supply-side structural reforms and the establishment of a new development paradigm, reflects the prevailing economic development trends and represents a strategic imperative for the current stage. Therefore, in 2020, General Secretary Xi Jinping first proposed to build a new development paradigm during the seventh meeting of the Central Commission for Financial and Economic Affairs (CCFEA).[8]

Leveraging Advantages and Reinforcing Key Elements for High-Quality Development

As China progresses through its developmental stages, with evolving comparative advantages and upgraded industrial structures, education, science and technology, and human resources become the foundational and strategic pillars for building a modern socialist country in all respects.

[7] Editor's note: Reference: http://theory.people.com.cn/n1/2022/1010/c40531-32542078.html.

[8] Editor's note: Reference: http://theory.people.com.cn/n1/2022/1027/c40531-32553053.html.

The Chinese nation must regard science and technology as the primary productive force, talent as the primary resource, and innovation as the primary driver of growth. China will fully implement the strategy for invigorating the country through science and education, the workforce development strategy, and the innovation-driven development strategy. China will open up new areas and new arenas in development and steadily foster new growth drivers and new strengths.

In the pursuit of fostering common prosperity for a population exceeding 1.4 billion, China's prospects for high-quality development are vast and brimming with potential. Therefore, it is essential to fully capitalize on three core strengths (the late-mover advantage, the merit of overtaking through lane changes, and the benefits of a new system for mobilizing resources nationwide), so as to reinforce the three crucial aspects of high-quality development, i.e., narrowing socioeconomic disparities, spearheading innovation, and fostering self-reliance and empowerment. By prioritizing breakthroughs in the primary objective of building a strong modern socialist country, we can pave a clear path to success.

China must capitalize on the late-mover advantages in its new developmental phase to narrow the gap with developed countries. While China's income level approaches that of high-income countries, there remains a significant gap with those in Europe and America, presenting ample potential for introduction, digestion, absorption, and re-innovation. Despite potential obstacles, our path to catching up is clear. This form of innovation comes with relatively low costs and minimal risks, facilitating swift catch-up by leveraging the late-mover advantages during our development process. Moreover, China's endowment conditions upon entering the new developmental phase inherently possess a comparative advantage for high-quality catching up. The key to utilizing the late-mover advantages lies in fostering high-level openness. The report to the 20th CPC National Congress underscores the importance of leveraging the strengths of China's enormous market to attract global resources and production factors with our strong domestic economy and amplify the interplay between domestic and international markets and resources. This will position us to improve the level and quality of trade and investment cooperation. The report advocates for making appropriate reductions to the negative list for foreign investment, protecting the rights and interests of foreign investors in accordance with the law and fostering a world-class business environment that is market-oriented, law-based, and internationalized.

In the new developmental phase, it is crucial to accelerate the utilization of our advantages in overtaking by changing lanes to achieve leading breakthroughs. In the emerging economy centered on human capital investment and data resource development, China stands on par with developed countries and possesses unique advantages such as abundant human capital, a large domestic market, a diverse array of industries, and extensive application scenarios, as evidenced by the emergence of a large number of unicorn companies and the rapid rise of the digital economy in China. According to *the White Paper on China's Digital Economy Development (2020)*, as of the end of 2020, the proportion of China's digital economy in GDP had reached 38.6%. The key to leveraging the opportunity to overtake through lane changes lies in implementing the workforce development strategy. The report to the 20th CPC National Congress stressed the need to speed up work to build a strong educational system, greater scientific and technological strength, and a quality workforce. China will continue efforts to cultivate talents for the Party and the country and comprehensively improve our ability to nurture talents at home. All this will see us producing first-class innovators and attracting the brightest minds from all over.

During the new developmental phase, it is also imperative to accelerate the utilization of a new system to mobilize resources across the nation, thereby fostering self-reliance and bolstering capabilities, addressing critical bottlenecks, and ensuring national development security. The report to the 20th CPC National Congress emphasized that, setting our sights on the global frontiers of science and technology, national economic development, the country's major needs, and public health and safety, efforts must be accelerated to achieve greater self-reliance and strength in science and technology. Aligned with China's strategic needs, there is a need to concentrate resources on original and pioneering scientific and technological research to achieve breakthroughs in core technologies in key fields. Additionally, China should improve the system in which the Party Central Committee exercises unified leadership over science and technology work and improve the new system for mobilizing resources nationwide to make key technological breakthroughs. China will boost its strength in strategic science and technology and better allocate innovation resources.

Prioritization in Addressing Weak Links in High-Quality Development

The tensions between China and the United States, stemming from unprecedented changes in a century, are likely to persist for a long period. However, despite facing challenges such as U.S. containment and strategic suppression, there is no need for undue pessimism, and the key lies in upholding our strategic resolve for sustained development. China harbors the potential to sustain an average annual growth rate of about 8% from 2020 to 2035. If the country can sustain an annual growth rate of 5% to 6%, then socialist modernization can, to a large extent, be basically achieved by 2035. Subsequently, between 2035 and 2050, China will still maintain an estimated growth potential of around 6%. Should a growth rate of 4% be attained, China's per capita GDP could reach half that of the United States by 2049, with a total GDP being twice that of the United States.

In this context, the per capita GDP, economic scale, industries, and technology levels of the "three cities and five provinces" (i.e., Guangdong Province, Jiangsu Province, Zhejiang Province, Fujian Province, and Shandong Province, along with municipalities of Shanghai, Beijing, and Tianjin) in economically developed regions, suggesting that the United States will no longer hold a technical advantage over China. This shift could lead to a new balance in China–U.S. relations. In fact, as of 2020, the aggregate economic output of the seven most modernized coastal provinces, led by the Yangtze River Delta, the Guangdong–Hong Kong–Macao Greater Bay Area, and the Beijing–Tianjin–Hebei region, exceeded 40% of the national total. Similarly, the aggregate economic output of the 35 most modernized provincial capitals and sub-provincial cities, led by Shanghai, Beijing, Shenzhen, Guangzhou, Chongqing, and Chengdu, also surpassed 40% of the national total. The current overall level has, in fact, reached that of a moderately developed country.

On the journey of building a modern socialist country in all respects, China faces the real challenge of addressing our own weaknesses. At present, the monthly disposable income of the poorest 40% of households remains below RMB 1000 per person, encompassing approximately 600 million people. The majority of this low-income demographic is concentrated in rural areas across the central and western regions, among migrant workers, and a small portion of low-income households in some cities. China still accommodates over 500 million rural residents and nearly 300 million migrant workers, with more than 60% of the employed populace possessing education levels at or below junior high school. The economic disparities are evident, with regions like Hebei, Guizhou, Guangxi, Heilongjiang, and Gansu having per capita GDP that is below 30% of Beijing's. Similarly, the per capita regional GDP in Ningxia, Xinjiang, Henan, Yunnan, Xizang, Qinghai, and Jilin is less than 35% of Beijing's. Beyond the developed urban clusters, over 350 million people live in remote areas. The most challenging and arduous tasks in realizing a comprehensively modern socialist China persist within our rural landscapes. Therefore, rural revitalization, employment opportunities for people's livelihood, and coordinated regional development are the three weak links of high-quality development. They also represent the potential for comprehensive modernization.

The report to the 20th CPC National Congress stressed that China should advance rural revitalization across the board and continue to put agricultural and rural development first and pursue integrated development of urban and rural areas. To this end, China should implement an employment-first strategy, fostering high-quality and full employment. Thorough implementation of the coordinated regional development strategy, major regional strategies, the functional zoning strategy, and the new urbanization strategy is also essential. China will improve the distribution of its major productive forces, fostering a regional economic layout and territorial spatial system that complement each other's strengths and facilitate high-quality development. Leveraging the influence of urban clusters and metropolitan areas, the country will foster coordinated development among large, medium, and small cities, advancing urbanization centered on county seats. To achieve nationwide socialist modernization by 2035, a concerted effort at both national and regional levels that prioritize modernization for high-quality growth and ensure a harmonious spread of modernization is imperative.

Empowering National Rejuvenation Through Theoretical Innovation

In his article "Development Economics and Economic Development of Developing Countries–On the Theoretical Reference of Development Economics in the Development of Socialist Market Economy," General Secretary Xi Jinping advocated over two decades ago for the exploration of a Chinese path to modernization theory, stating that "We seek theoretical reference from development economics based on Western economics not only to gain insights into the trajectory of the socialist market economy but, more importantly, to establish a socialist development economics rooted in China's unique economic, political, cultural, historical, and philosophical contexts. This imperative aligns with the historical trajectory and the demands of the times. We hope that socialist development economics can 'blossoms on its branches and even outside the wall.'"[9] New structural economics, guided by Marxist principles, aims to amalgamate modern economic methods, summarize Chinese modernization experiences, and establish an independent theoretical framework to develop a generalized modernization theory concerning national development, transformation, and operation. This pioneering endeavor has been emulated and proven effective by several other developing and transitioning countries, symbolizing the metaphorical "blossoming outside the wall." The imperative now lies in expediting the assimilation and application of the spirit delineated in the 20th CPC National Congress, under the guidance of Xi Jinping Thought, which involves hastening autonomous theoretical breakthroughs in economics to support the dual objectives of Chinese path to modernization and high-quality development, thereby contributing to the great rejuvenation of the Chinese nation.

[9] Editor's note: Jinping Xi, "Development Economics and Economic Development of Developing Countries On the Theoretical Reference of Development Economics in the Development of Socialist Market Economy," *Academic Review* 9 (2001): 4–6.

Chinese Path to Modernization and China's New Economic Journey

Yang Yao

Why the Term "Chinese Path to Modernization"?

To understand the essence of Chinese path to modernization, one must first grasp why the term "Chinese path to modernization" rather than "modernization with Chinese characteristics."

A parallel can be drawn to the early 1980s when the concept of socialism with Chinese characteristics was introduced in response to the prevailing Soviet-style socialism. As China embarked on rural and urban reforms different from the Soviet model, it termed this approach socialism with Chinese characteristics. In 1987, China positioned itself in the primary stage of socialism to propel reforms forward.

This article is derived from the speech delivered by the author during the 73rd EMBA Forum hosted by the National School of Development at Peking University on November 17, 2022.

Y. Yao (✉)
National School of Development, Peking University, Beijing, China

Beijing International MBA, Peking University, Beijing, China

Institute of South-South Cooperation and Development, Peking University, Beijing, China

W. Xianqing (ed.), *Understanding China's Path to Modernization*,
https://doi.org/10.1007/978-981-96-7051-2_2

However, it is different this time around. Instead of labeling it as modernization with Chinese characteristics, it is termed Chinese path to modernization. This indicates that modernization does not adhere to a direct comparative framework; rather, the Chinese path to modernization serves as a model in itself. It signifies confidence in China's trajectory and theoretical beliefs, marking another stride forward.

Chinese path to modernization represents not only a historical trajectory but also a new theory. While its completeness remains open to further discussion, there exist many aspects worthy of refinement. Nevertheless, this conceptual framework alone serves as a great starting point, warranting deeper discussions and research.

The Origins and Early Stages of China's Modernization Journey

Given the nomenclature "Chinese path to modernization," let us delve into China's modernization process. The first stage, which I define as spanning from 1860 to 1978, or tracing back even further, encompasses over 100 years known in history as the Westernization era. Many people pinpoint the onset of Chinese modernization to 1840, coinciding with the First Opium War. Despite the cession of Hong Kong Island following the war, national awakening did not transpire at that time. It was only after the Second Opium War and the destruction of the Old Summer Palace that the elite class became aware and embarked on a journey of over 100 years of Westernization.

The second stage, spanning from 1978 to 2017, characterized by the emancipation of the mind, alongside a paradigm of reform and opening-up, which endured for a duration of 40 years.

Since 2017, we have entered a new era.

Reflecting upon historical trajectories yields an inquiry: Why the term Westernization? This reflection is beneficial, as it unveils the interplay of civilizations, amalgamating conflict and integration.

Delving into the interplay of civilizations, an exploration harks back around 2000 years ago, pinpointing the Northern Song dynasty, established in the year 960, as a key turning point. Before Northern Song dynasty, China witnessed a millennium of burgeoning national strength, asserting global eminence. However, the subsequent millennium after the dynasty bore witness to stagnation and even regression within China's trajectory.

Foreign cultural influences were evident even before the Northern Song dynasty, notably with the advent of Buddhism. It was not until the time of Zhu Xi in the Southern Song dynasty that Buddhism assimilated into Chinese civilization, taking nearly 1000 years. Chan Buddhism persisted as the predominant form, bearing similarities with the traditional philosophical tenets of Laozi and Zhuangzi,[1] resulting in a unique amalgamation. Today, the foreign origins of Buddhism are often overlooked, having integrated into China's traditional culture.

China is still currently under the influence of Western culture, yet to achieve complete assimilation.

After the Second Opium War, a burgeoning awakening among China's intellectual elites ensued. However, they believed that Chinese culture and institutions harbored no inherent deficiencies; rather, it was simply a matter of deficiency in technological advancement. The First Opium War showcased British supremacy with the conquest of China using merely one warship. Subsequently, during the Second Opium War, Anglo-French forces penetrated Beijing, and burned down the Old Summer Palace.

During this juncture, both the intellectual elite and the Qing government advocated for emulating the West as a means to surpass them. Thus emerged the Self-Strengthening Movement, spanning three decades. By the time of the First Sino-Japanese War, significant progress had been made through this movement, with the Qing government establishing the largest navy in Asia. However, this navy proved to be powerless against the Japanese. In fact, despite the Qing Navy's superiority over its Japanese counterpart and the formidable Qing garrison in Korea, the Beiyang Fleet was completely annihilated at Liugong Island in Weihai, Shandong in 1895, signaling the collapse of the Qing Dynasty's desire to strengthen itself through Westernization as part of the Self-Strengthening Movement.

Subsequently, the Chinese elites turned their attention to Japan's meteoric rise, attributing it to the Meiji Restoration, which involved institutional reforms. Inspired by this example, the elites also sought to reform the Chinese institutions, leading to the Hundred Days' Reform in 1898. Regrettably, this reform was short-lived, lasting merely 100 days and

[1] Daoism boasts two eminent figures: Laozi, who wrote the *Tao Te Ching*, and Zhuangzi, renowned for the eponymous *Zhuangzi*. Both thinkers are believed to have lived between the sixth and fourth centuries BCE. However, the narratives surrounding their lives are imbued with legend, making it difficult to separate between fact and myth.

ending in failure. The only lasting achievement of this endeavor was the establishment of the Imperial University of Peking, the predecessor of Peking University.

Faced with resistance to reform within the existing system, it became necessary to overthrow it. Therefore, impassioned intellectuals coalesced into political factions and united military forces to seek revolution. Finally, the Revolution of 1911, spearheaded by Sun Yat-sen, succeeded in overthrowing the Qing government and heralded the establishment of Asia's first republic.

In theory, China's transition to a stable and prosperous era seemed imminent. However, reality diverged from this trajectory. The ambitions of figures such as Yuan Shikai, who sought to reinstate monarchy, coupled with persistent conflicts among warlords, thwarted the country's prospects for stability. This made people realize that institutional reforms alone were insufficient; a concurrent transformation of underlying cultural and ideological paradigms was also necessary, as well as the exploration for a more stable path of development.

During this period, the outbreak of World War I plunged the whole of Europe into despair, leading European intellectuals to believe that Western civilization had reached its end. Similarly, certain Chinese intellectuals doubted the vitality of their own culture, and called for a deep excavation of cultural roots, giving rise to both the New Culture Movement and the May Fourth Movement of 1919. At the core of the New Culture Movement was a movement against feudal culture, with some proponents even advocating for the rejection of Confucianism.

During a period marked by explorations of alternative ideologies, a revolution erupted on the outskirts of Western capitalist civilization in Russia, transforming a previously underdeveloped country into a thriving one seemingly overnight. The October Revolution in Russia gave hope to both Western and Chinese intellectuals, fostering a belief that Western culture could be salvaged and that China had found a new way toward progress.

Prominent voices within China, exemplified by scholars like Li Dazhao and Chen Duxiu, saw the October Revolution and the principles of Marxism as catalysts for a paradigm shift in China's path, envisioning a comprehensive societal transformation through their adoption.

In response to the evolving landscape of the Chinese revolution, the Communist Party of China (CPC) was founded in 1921, aligning

Marxism with the Chinese workers' movement (the May Fourth Movement of 1919). A crucial factor contributing to the eventual success of the Communist Party of China lay in its adeptness at adapting to prevailing circumstances and navigating the unprecedented social changes taking place within China at the time, coupled with its continual process of self-renewal.

From its inception, the CPC consciously positioned itself as an entity that would drive China's progress, leading the country toward modernization through incremental steps.

Given the proximity to the revolutionary twentieth century, many find it challenging to evaluate this matter from a historical perspective. Nevertheless, it is worth noting that nearly every European society underwent significant revolutions during this era, all unfolded across protracted periods of unrest, including the English, French, Russian, and Spanish revolutions. Notably, the English Revolution lasted at least half a century, while the French and Russian Revolutions caused even longer periods of turmoil.

The arduous task of bridging the gap between ancient and modern societies was particularly pronounced in China, given its extensive historical background marked by relative stability and stark disparities in lifestyle compared to modern society. Consequently, the dismantling of antiquated structures and modes of thought proved to be a formidable challenge, as entrenched powers did not yield without resistance. Therefore, multiple movements and even revolutions became necessary to catalyze transformative change.

Following the complete assumption of political authority by the CPC in 1949, it initiated the implementation of its revolutionary ideals. Therefore, understanding the socialist revolution in China requires contextualizing it within the broader narrative of its modernization journey.

First Phase of Modernization Since the Founding of the People's Republic of China

A revolution is not a dinner party; it is the process of removing old forces from the historical stage and writing a new chapter.

After the founding of the PRC, the country witnessed significant revolutionary changes, which, based on personal observation, can be summarized as follows:

First, there were concerted efforts to dismantle the existing hierarchical social structure. Huang Renyu, a former military officer in the Kuomintang who later transitioned into a well-known historian, noted the Kuomintang's approach as top-down, whereas the CPC's as bottom-up, which aimed at fundamentally reshaping society from its grassroots through initiatives such as land reform, leveling the playing field for everyone, abolishing distinctions between capitalists and officials, and ultimately striving for equality. A prime example is the emancipation of women. Professor Zhang Dandan from the National School of Development at Peking University conducted insightful research comparing women born in Beijing in 1958 with their counterparts born in Taipei, as well as women born in Beijing in 1976 with their counterparts born in Taipei, while also including males from the corresponding period. Interestingly, it was found that women born in Beijing in 1958 exhibited exceptional competitiveness, even surpassing their male counterparts, driven by the era's advocacy for women's liberation and the prevailing belief in women's capacity to excel across diverse roles.

Second, there were concerted efforts to foster a unified sense of national identity. Despite the common perception of Chinese culture as inherently collectivist, a Japanese sociology student studying at Peking University argued that the Chinese society exhibits more individualistic than collective tendencies. This viewpoint came as a surprise to us. He pointed out that while Japanese individuals pass the ball in soccer games, Chinese players often prefer to dribble the ball themselves until they shoot for goal, rarely opting for passes. Over a century ago, Sun Yat-sen stated that Chinese people somewhat resemble scattered sand, underscoring the lack of cohesive national identity. To foster a unified sense of national identity, the CPC initiated forceful political measures that permeated every aspect of society, ushering us into a modern society rooted in a shared national identity.

Third, there were concerted efforts to direct the country's collective focus toward industrialization, an aspect that holds personal significance for me. I spent two years working in a factory in Xi'an, where both my parents and parents-in-law dedicated their entire careers. Established in 1956 as one of the 156 projects aided by the Soviet Union, this factory was a microcosm of society, attending to all aspects of life, including healthcare; the same doctor who delivered me later brought my son into the world. Today, the company continues to thrive, albeit with its headquarters relocated to Shanghai, emerging as a major state enterprise specializing in power transmission equipment. China's current achievements in industrialization are inseparable from the groundwork laid before the era of reform and opening-up, including the essential factors of skilled technicians and a dedicated workforce.

Fourth, there were concerted efforts to elevate the human developmental level. Amartya Sen, an internationally renowned Indian economist who currently works at Harvard University and a Nobel laureate in economics, advocates for the human development index comprising three key indicators: per capita income, life expectancy, and educational attainment. In the early stages following the founding of the PRC, China's healthcare and education systems outperformed those of many developing countries. Amartya Sen noted that after the initiation of reform and opening-up policies, China performed much better than India, owing to effective preparatory measures. For instance, China had a lower per capita GDP than India in 1978, only surpassing it in 1992; China's per capita GDP was five times that of India in 2022. In 1978, despite being poorer than India, China had an adult literacy rate of around 65%, whereas India's stood at approximately 40%. Concurrently, China had attained a life expectancy of 67 years, compared to less than 60 years in India. Meanwhile, China's infant mortality rate was as low as 54‰, half that of India's. While India also prioritized the development of heavy industry, its endeavors did not yield significant success. Even today, India's industrial output contributes just over 20% of its GDP, whereas China's once exceeded 40%, with the subsequent decrease attributed to transitioning into a post-industrialization phase—a natural progression during developmental upgrades.

During the initial 30 years following the founding of the PRC, Western influences were introduced. From 1977 to 1979, China experienced a period known as the "Western Leap," during which it imported machinery and equipment from developed countries. Entities such as Sinopec Yanshan Petrochemical Company, Sinopec Qilu Petrochemical Company, and Baoshan Iron & Steel Co., Ltd. that we recognize today were established during that phase.

Some argue that China's reform and opening-up began only after 1979, it should be noted that while accurate, it marked a comprehensive and fundamental emancipation of productive forces. Before 1978, China had already initiated the emancipation of the mind, a requisite and foundation for unleashing productive forces.

Second Phase of Modernization Since the Founding of the People's Republic of China

The third plenary session of the 11th CPC Central Committee in 1978 marked a significant turning point for China's reform and opening-up, setting the stage for a new phase of modernization. In my opinion, the period from 1978 to 2017 can be best described as Deng Xiaoping "leading the CPC back to China."

Deng Xiaoping once famously stated that he was merely a son of the Chinese people,[2] a statement carrying profound implications, underscoring his deep connection to his fellow citizens. Known for his pragmatic approach to problem-solving, Deng Xiaoping played a crucial role during that era, recognizing that socialism could not coexist with poverty. In retrospect, one of his major achievements was essentially repositioning the CPC within China at a higher level.

From my perspective, Deng Xiaoping spearheaded major shifts for both the CPC and the country as a whole:

The first major shift is a departure from radicalism and class struggles. The CPC's goal transitioned from revolutionary ideals aimed at creating a new China to leading toward the great rejuvenation of the Chinese nation. The concept of the great rejuvenation of the Chinese nation emerged in the early 1980s, emphasizing unity and progress toward a modernized, prosperous China, instead of focusing on class divisions and conflict.

The second major shift is embracing pragmatism in China. Chinese culture is known for its pragmatic approach, emphasizing the importance of living in the present moment. This practical mindset had several notable aspects: Chinese people value practical knowledge gained through experience over abstract truths—a belief deeply ingrained in Chinese proverbs. They uphold the notion that practice serves as the ultimate arbiter of truth, encouraging continuous engagement to uncover, challenge, and reveal new insights. Furthermore, Chinese society places a strong emphasis on results-driven approaches. For instance, in Silicon Valley, Chinese professionals often occupy technical roles such as chief engineers, while Indians predominantly assume managerial positions.

[2] Editor's note: Quoted from the preface written by Deng Xiaoping in February 1981 for the English edition of *Selected Works of Deng Xiaoping*, published by the Pergamon Press, Ltd.

Engineering epitomizes tangible work, embodying the principle of pragmatism. Guided by this pragmatic principle, many reforms in China have progressed steadily by incrementally dismantling barriers and effecting tangible change. Otherwise, navigating unseen constraints within abstract systems would have proved exceedingly challenging.

The third major shift is returning to the theme of meritocracy. It is notable that Chinese society upholds a deeply ingrained reverence for merit and competence. The assessment of an individual's merit and competence holds great significance. For example, the concept of common prosperity accentuates the importance of enhancing people's ability to generate income rather than solely relying on welfare provisions. The Chinese government strongly opposes direct cash disbursements, viewing them as potentially fostering a culture of indolence. The epitome of this belief is reflected in the CPC's cadre selection system. In a collaborative research effort spanning from 1994 to 2017, my colleagues and I examined data on government officials, encompassing their professional trajectories, subsequent transfer and promotions. Our findings revealed that there is a strong correlation between the economic performance of a city during an official's term and the probability of their promotion.

The fourth major shift is embracing the market economy. While traditionally viewed by many Chinese as a Western concept, Deng Xiaoping had long ago proposed that the market economy transcended capitalism and could be integrated into socialist frameworks. It should be noted that the market economy is not solely a Western construct but has its roots in China. Reflecting on the Northern Song dynasty, contemporary restaurants pale in comparison with the standards set back then. Additionally, China invented paper currency during the Song dynasty, making it the world's pioneer in this regard—and it is smoothly operational. China also pioneered tradable securities, showcasing significant financial innovation.

Key Points of Modernization in the New Era

Before the analysis of modernization in the new era, let me introduce a book by American scholars William Strauss and Neil Howe in the mid-1990s. Titled *The Fourth Turning: An American Prophecy—What the Cycles of History Tell Us About America's Next Rendezvous with Destiny*, this book discusses an 80-year cyclical pattern within the United States, starting from the Revolutionary War in the 1770s through subsequent pivotal events such as the Civil War in the 1860s and World War II in the 1930s and 40s, up to the present day. Essentially, it posits an 80-year cyclical pattern within the United States, with smaller cycles occurring every 20 years.

The period from World War II to the assassination of John F. Kennedy marks the first small cycle within the recent 80-year span in the United States. During that period, the country thrived, characterized by widespread ideological conformity. The subsequent two decades post-1960s witnessed an era of intellectual emancipation. Following Ronald Reagan's presidency, the next 20 years unfolded as an era of unraveling, coinciding with the timeframe during which William Strauss and Neil Howe wrote their seminal work. They anticipated that by 2005, the United States would enter the final 20 years, termed the crisis era, predicting almost accurately the financial crisis of 2008. The book speculates on how the period from 2005 to 2025 in the United States will conclude, envisioning either internal discord or external confrontation, heralding the genesis of a new historical epoch.

This seminal work challenged my perception of linear historical progression, particularly the notion of unidirectional advancement. It posits that history evolves in cyclical patterns, encompassing both large and small repetitive cycles. Later, I realized that this theoretical framework could also be applied to China.

The four generations of CPC leaders can be similarly categorized as four stages: founding, growth, unraveling (prosperity), and regeneration. Mao Zedong represents the founding generation, while Deng Xiaoping represents the era of rapid growth, and Jiang Zemin and Hu Jintao the unraveling generation, during which China's economy rose to second globally and held a substantial global influence. Starting from 2017, China entered the final small cycle within the broader 80-year span: the regeneration generation, symbolizing the advent of a new era.

What does this new era entail? Drawing upon the theoretical framework proposed by the aforementioned American scholars, the new era corresponds to two major events.

Firstly, it necessitates a rectification. During the preceding developmental phase in China, significant strides were made in terms of the emancipation of the mind and the implementation of reform and opening-up policies. However, this period also brought about numerous issues, notably the pervasive issue of corruption. In certain regions, corruption has become alarmingly normalized, despite thorough anti-corruption endeavors initiated since the 18th CPC National Congress.

Even subsequent to the 19th CPC National Congress, there persist individuals daring to engage in corrupt practices. This unusual circumstance calls for an approach that involves political rectification efforts against corruption, dissuasion of individuals from partaking in corrupt behaviors, and the establishment of a new ethical milieu.

Secondly, there is a pressing need to invigorate the Party organizations. Any waning or dissolution of Party organization's vitality could potentially lead to inappropriate alliances between the political and economic spheres, posing threats to long-term sustainable economic growth, especially in the pursuit of high-quality development. The convergence of political and business interests often results in the commercialization of governmental power, potentially enabling interest groups to co-opt the government, which, in turn, creates unjust market barriers that stifle fair competition and market dynamism, ultimately undermining China's international competitiveness. Drawing from my studies in developmental economics, I have conducted on-site research in various developing countries and delved into the historical trajectories of many developing countries. It is evident that the primary issue in the underdeveloped developing countries lies in the entrenched alliance among intellectual elites, business magnates, and political figures, which obstructs the emergence of healthy social competition.

Another critical concern demanding attention is inequality. According to surveys conducted biennially by the National School of Development, China's Gini coefficient peaked at 0.52. This figure is even comparable to those observed in sub-Saharan African and South American countries known for their huge wealth gaps. Notably, the poorest 10% of our population command only 0.5% of the total national income, often resorting to borrowing to meet basic needs and sustaining negative assets. In contrast, the wealthiest 10% control 70% of total national assets and 40% of total income, highlighting vast wealth inequalities. Therefore, it is imperative to make rectifications to address these disparities.

After years of rectification, the anti-corruption campaign is nearing its conclusion, and the Party organizations has been invigorated. However, the issue of inequality remains unresolved and necessitates further attention.

Looking toward the future, to realize Chinese path to modernization, several important aspects warrant further reconstruction.

First, it is paramount to restore the authority of the CPC, including organizational, theoretical, and popular authority. It will take a very long time for to achieve this goal.

Secondly, there is a need to reconstruct theoretical frameworks. Continuing to adhere to class struggle is untenable, yet orthodox political economy persists in its reliance on the labor theory of value, which posits that only labor generates value. This perspective implies that value creation is solely attributable to workers, excluding capital. However, in reality, workers often receive a small portion of total income, with the surplus designated as surplus value, i.e., exploitation. Where there is exploitation, there exists class conflict and struggle. Within this theoretical framework, the CPC remains aligned with the interests of the working class and can thus only serve as its vanguard, making it challenging to represent the entire nation. Failure to update the concept of the vanguard of the working class prompts the question: does the state, led by the CPC, maintain a class attribute? Therefore, this critical theory needs reconstruction. To do so, it is indispensable to re-examine the book *Das Kapital*. Historically, we have approached the text as an empirical work, but it is crucial to recognize that the labor theory of value, which forms its essence, is fundamentally an assumption rather than an empirically validated fact. Therefore, *Das Kapital* is a typical philosophical work rather than a conventional work of political economy. With this understanding, we can construct new theories grounded in empirical observations. Marxism and *Das Kapital* originate from the labor theory of value, suggesting the existence of class and exploitation, effectively justifying the legitimacy and necessity of the proletarian revolution. But what if the labor theory of value is merely a conjecture, particularly if this assumption proves to be weak or erroneous? Hence, there arises a compelling need to reconstruct our theoretical frameworks. Regarding the widely discussed concept of common prosperity today, the crux must center on enhancing the income capacity of the populace through strategic investment, transcending mere redistribution of existing wealth. Otherwise, the essence of common prosperity risks conflicting with the core values cherished by the common people, implying that certain individuals could accrue gains without commensurate effort. Therefore, it is imperative to heed the directive articulated in the report to the 20th National Congress of the Communist Party of China, which emphasizes the imperative to "integrate the essence of Marxism with the best of fine traditional Chinese culture and with the common values that our people intuitively apply in their everyday lives. We should keep endowing Marxist theory with distinctive Chinese features." The approach of directly redistributing wealth from the affluent to the impoverished evidently does not align with the deeply ingrained values of the populace.

Thirdly, it is imperative to establish China's own innovation system, also known as a new system for mobilizing resources nationwide. What prompts this necessity? Firstly, it arises from shifts in the external landscape, a crucial consideration. Secondly, looking toward the future, the global order is fraught with uncertainties, compounded by variables in cross-strait relations. In extreme cases, should China face a comprehensive blockade without its own innovation system, industries may flounder without self-sustaining industrial chains and risk descent into a state of passivity.

The evolution of Chinese path to modernization has transitioned from "standing up" to "becoming stronger." Today, our focus is directed toward achieving the second centenary goal, during which we may encounter new variables and challenges. Therefore, it is crucial to possess a comprehensive understanding of China's modernization journey, particularly the connotation of Chinese path to modernization.

Interpreting Chinese Path to Modernization

Shouying Liu

Keywords of the Report to the 20th National Congress of the Communist Party of China (CPC)

The report to the 20th CPC National Congress highlights several key points that deserve close attention.

The first is the central task of the CPC. The report clearly laid out the second centenary goal, emphasizing the need to building China into a great modern socialist country in all respects.

In the first centenary, the CPC has already finished building a moderately prosperous society in all respects. Currently, the modernization process of countries generally unfolds in two phases. The first phase involves breaking free from the poverty trap. For any country aspiring to integrate into the modern global community, the most challenging aspect is to transition from rural society. This transition crucially hinges on escaping the so-called poverty trap, which essentially involves a shift

This article is derived from a speech delivered by the author at the 23rd session of *The Economic Observer*'s annual training program "Jingguan Jingtang (Economic Observer Classroom)."

S. Liu (✉)
School of Economics, Renmin University of China, Beijing, China

W. Xianqing (ed.), *Understanding China's Path to Modernization*,
https://doi.org/10.1007/978-981-96-7051-2_3

from agrarian to industrial structures and thus achieve modern economic growth.

Throughout its first centenary, the CPC accomplished one of humanity's greatest feats by leading a country with a large population, pronounced regional disparities and strong rural ties from an agricultural society into modernity.

I believe that the second centenary goal marks the second phase of modernization, aimed at building a strong modern country. To date, only a select few countries have achieved true modernization. What defines a modern country? It includes not only achieving economic development reaching the levels of a prosperous country, but also broader indicators such as adherence to the rule of law, civilization, political systems, and social and economic modernization.

Central to the second centenary goal is to become a strong modern country.

Our foremost challenges lie in the pursuit of building a strong modern country under a socialist framework. After World War II, global pathways to modernization diverged significantly. One involved latecomer countries and regions emulating developed counterparts to achieve modernization by adopting capitalist models. However, very few of these countries or regions have succeeded, with notable exceptions include several East Asian economies like Japan, South Korea, and Taiwan of China. Alternatively, the Soviet Union, devoid of capitalist foundations, pursued a distinct path, striving to navigate the so-called Caudine Forks within a socialist framework. But what were the final results of this approach? In the 1980s and 1990s, Eastern Europe transitioned, the Soviet Union dissolved, and China thus emerged as the foremost beacon of hope. Therefore, building a strong modern socialist country is an arduous journey in itself. Using a socialist framework as the vehicle for building such a country constitutes China's second centenary goal.

The second keyword is Chinese path to modernization, which has been hotly discussed in the world. It is a term initially proposed by Deng Xiaoping in the 1980s.[1]

First, the Chinese path to modernization outlined in the report to the 20th CPC National Congress is the trajectory we will pursue in constructing a strong modern country in the next century. In other

[1] Editor's note: "Deng Xiaoping and Chinese Path to Modernization" (Reference: http://cpc.people.com.cn/n1/2019/0228/c69113-30906462.html).

words, the second centenary goal is to build a great modern socialist country in all respects, pursued through the Chinese path to modernization.

Second, the building of a modern country unfolds in two phases. The first phase aims to basically realize socialist modernization by 2035, while the subsequent phase aims to establish a strong modern socialist country by 2050. It is noteworthy that this statement departs from previous central governmental documents by advancing the timeline for basically realizing socialist modernization from 2050 to 2035.

Third, Chinese path to modernization emphatically emphasizes two key points. Firstly, it underscores the paramount leadership role of the CPC. Moving toward modernization marks the beginning of a nation-state, where the hallmark of such a nation-state is its party system. Parties play a significant role in leading the modernization journey of a nation-state. While party systems are ubiquitous in modernization endeavors across all countries, what sets China apart is the distinctiveness of its party system. China's modernization epitomizes socialist modernization, characterized by both universal attributes of modernization observed globally and distinctive Chinese characteristics rooted in our national conditions. Therefore, understanding Chinese path to modernization solely through its distinctive features, without due consideration of its commonalities, may lead to misconceptions.

To Understand Modernization

To understand modernization, it is imperative to comprehend Chinese path to modernization and the common attributes of modernization outlined in central governmental documents. I categorize modernization into five fundamental aspects:

First of all, modernization stands as the most intense, profound, and extensive social transformation in human history. Pre-modern societies were characterized by stable agricultural communities, where the primary focus lay in the relationship between humans and nature, with relatively stable fundamental forces driving societal changes. However, the advent of modernity marked a pivotal shift in the fundamental forces driving such changes. As for technological advancements and institutional reforms, the evolving social contradictions within these two forces and relationships led to dramatic social changes.

Second, modernization is also a comprehensive revolution across various facets of human society. Unlike societal changes before modern times, modernization entails multifaceted changes spanning political, economic, social, and psychological dimensions, which is not evolutionary but revolutionary, marking a shift from one societal paradigm to another.

Third, modernization signifies the transition of human civilization from agrarian to industrial societies.

Fourth, modernization is a global phenomenon, originating in Western Europe and subsequently spreading to North America, Latin America, Africa, and Asia. The process of modernization is intrinsic to the global landscape.

Lastly, modernization exhibits significant variations among countries and regions. With the progression of human modernization, there are always diverse models and pathways.

Common Attributes of Modernization

What are the common attributes of modernization worldwide?

The first common attribute is transformative development. Modernization is driven by advancements in science and technology, leading to structural changes and developmental transformations. Continuous technological progress fuels the ongoing modernization process of human society, precipitating successive industrial revolutions.

During the same period, the regions within China's Jiangnan area[2] achieved a level of industrialization surpassing that of Britain, so why didn't the Industrial Revolution occur in Jiangnan? This was because technological change revolves around power. Britain possessed abundant coal resources, whereas Jiangnan relied heavily on the use of elements within rural communities, posing challenges for significant technological advancements centered around power. Consequently, as Britain transitioned into an industrialized society, its market struggled to absorb the sudden surge in supply, resulting in overflow. Subsequently, British expertise, technologies, and capital flooded Western Europe and the United States, driving them into the waves of modernization collectively.

[2] The Jiangnan area, literally refers to the south of the Yangtze River, is renowned for its fertility, abundant water sources, flourishing silk and handicraft industries, and high population density as well as advanced industrialization.

The Second Industrial Revolution, also fueled by technological advancements, shifted the world from the age of steam to the age of electricity. Subsequently, the Third Industrial Revolution in the late twentieth century propelled human civilization into the information age, also known as the digital age.

Therefore, if a society experiences stagnation in technological progress, its Industrial Revolution will stall, halting the country's modernization process. Successive industrial revolutions have facilitated continuous upgrades in economic, technological, and industrial structures, leading to the increased complexity and sophistication of socioeconomic systems.

Economic complexity plays a crucial role, serving as a primary indicator of a country's industrial, economic, and technological advancement. In traditional societies where there is a lack of division of labor, the economy remains notably simple. Conversely, modern societies are distinguished by their economic complexity. Economists from the Massachusetts Institute of Technology (MIT) and Harvard University established the Observatory of Economic Complexity (OEC), employing a methodology wherein globally exported products are categorized into a basket. Their findings revealed a pattern akin to a forest, with products from wealthier countries located closer to the center, while those from poorer countries positioned at the periphery. Products of higher complexity tend to cluster toward the center, with countries producing them typically enjoying greater wealth. The difference between complex and simple products lies in the variance of knowledge. As knowledge density increases, product complexity becomes higher, fostering the development of more competitive products and enhancing the economic competitiveness of countries.

Since the introduction of reform and opening-up policies, China's most significant progress lies in the increase in product complexity. Initially, the country's export portfolio predominantly comprised agricultural products, followed by furniture and textiles. However, in the 1990s, it transitioned toward exporting appliances and daily necessities, and now, it exports more sophisticated electronic products and machinery. This higher economic complexity stems from an increase in knowledge content and the expansion of products with comparative advantages. China's engagement in globalization has further fueled its economic complexity, heralding the initial outcomes of the Industrial Revolution.

Meanwhile, the term "sophistication" refers to industries, products, and enterprises operating at the higher end of international competitiveness, transitioning from lower level competitive states to advanced ones. The economic complexity and sophistication brought about by the Industrial Revolution have facilitated the enhancement of comparative advantage capabilities, ultimately propelling China toward an elevated level of economic development.

The second common attribute is institutional innovation, which, along with reform, essentially constitute the modernization process. The progression of humanity into the modern era necessitates technological advancements. Similarly, the absence of continual institutional innovation and changes inhibits societal advancement into modernity. This premise finds its foundation in the dialectical framework proposed by Karl Marx, which highlights the contradiction between productive forces and the relations of production. As productive forces advance, they inevitably disrupt prevailing the relations of production, leading to changes in these relations, which translates to institutional reform.

Let us consider the first major historical instance of institutional reform. Medieval Western Europe operated under the manorial system, wherein serfs were bound to the land, constraining their autonomy and impeding societal structural changes. It was only when the Black Death struck that significant institutional reforms were triggered, reshaping societal dynamics. The catastrophic impact of the Black Death, resulting in widespread mortality, precipitated shifts in the relationship between individuals and land ownership. Consequently, the original manorial system became infeasible, prompting a shift from the ambiguous feudal land ownership system to a modernized land ownership structure, accompanied by the emergence of private property rights. This transformation naturally led to the dissolution of serfdom. Concurrently, changes in land and labor market institutions facilitated the expansion of rural markets, fostering the development of capitalism and initiating the trajectory toward modernization.

The second wave of institutional reform centers on the establishment of nation-states, marking a significant shift in governance dynamics from fragmented institutions to a unified form of governance. This transition from decentralized feudal political structures to nation-states led to the rise of authoritarian monarchies. Nation-states, established by autocratic monarchy, operated within a restrictive framework of concentrated power.

These monarchies had established and consistent objectives, such as national unity. To achieve these goals, they formed alliances between political and economic entities to prevent violence, thereby fostering conditions conducive to economic development. Therefore, the autocratic regimes instituted by many Western European countries during this period provided a conducive environment for economic growth under delineated boundaries, propelling these countries toward the starting line of modernization.

However, autocratic regimes themselves could give rise to what is known as the North Paradox, which revolves around the notion that for a country to achieve modern economic growth, there must be a national framework defining property rights, maintaining order, and upholding fairness. However, the order established within autocratic monarchies typically embodies a restrictive power structure, often prioritizing arrangements that serve the interests of the monarchy in safeguarding property rights, maintaining order, and upholding fairness. Without transitioning from such a restrictive power structure to a more open one, these countries cannot achieve true modernization.

The third wave of institutional reform involves transitioning from the restrictive power structures of absolute monarchies toward more open systems. This inclusivity meant embracing diverse organizations and sharing political and economic authority. The United Kingdom spearheaded this transformation by overcoming absolute monarchy, set the stage for political modernization and became one of the most liberal countries globally, thereby allowing the British to pursue intellectual freedom, technological advancements, and wealth accumulation. The Glorious Revolution in England and the subsequent Atlantic Revolutions in the Atlantic world paved the way for capitalist production methods in Britain and other Western European countries.

The fourth wave emerged through the institutional reform undertaken by the Americans. Despite establishing an inclusive power structure, the British system encountered challenges within its political and economic institutions, notably corruption, impeding its true modernization. A group of British immigrants migrated to the United States and developed institutions that addressed these shortcomings while retaining the strengths of the British model. This catalyzed further evolution in the capitalist system, fostering economic prosperity in the United States and propelling U.S. modernization to a preeminent global position.

The third common attribute lies in value orientation. Human modernization has consistently entailed a rebellion against traditional worldviews. For instance, the Renaissance and Religious Revolutions offered new perspectives on the modern world, shaping fresh outlook on development. Such outlook emerged from the rationalization and secularization of values, marking a major value change as human beings move toward modernization.

During the Renaissance, asceticism fell out of favor as proponents began advocating for individual liberation, promoting scientific and cultural advancements, and rejecting traditional authorities and doctrines in favor of rationalism. The Religious Reform sought to break free from the constraints imposed by the Catholic Church. Max Weber's idea of Protestant ethics highlighted initiative and the pursuit of material wealth, fueling sparking entrepreneurial endeavors and contributing to the drive for modernizing capitalism. The establishment of new trade routes facilitated a commercial revolution, transforming commercial activities toward market transactions as the primary mode of trade. This restructuring reshaped commercial structures and organizational methods, instilling a commercial mindset early on in Western Europe and setting the stage for industrialization.

The fourth common attribute is the conscious exchange between humans and natural resources. Before entering modern economic growth, humanity had been held back by the Malthusian trap.

Throughout my academic journey, Thomas Robert Malthus, the bourgeois economist, was often depicted by teachers as somewhat villainous, emphasizing his belief that if population growth exceeded available resources, extreme measures such as warfare and disease were necessary for population control. However, my time at the University of Cambridge revealed a different perspective, where Thomas Robert Malthus and Alfred Marshall were revered as the most esteemed economists. The latter, in particular, offered a theoretical analysis of the struggles faced by humanity during the era of traditional growth before modern economic expansion.

In the pre-modernization era, production methods and lifestyles were largely determined by the availability of resources. As populations continued to grow, it created a strained relationship between humans and the natural environment. In the absence of technological advancements, this relationship eventually led to the so-called Malthusian trap, wherein population growth outpaced the limited supply of natural resources.

The Industrial Revolution introduced a new paradigm shift in both production methods and lifestyles. In modern times, humanity transitioned from a resource-dependent development model to one focused on human capital, knowledge, and technological progress. Innovation began to emerge as the driving force behind progress, marking a transition from the low-level pre-modern growth to the high-level modern economic growth, and advancements in productivity began to outstrip population growth rates.

The fifth common attribute is global openness. No country can achieve modernization in isolation.

During the Middle Ages, Western Europe largely trailed behind other major contemporaneous civilizations. However, around 1500, a series of events within the region catalyzed a regional civilization transformation, paving the way for the emergence of a new civilization. The Age of Discovery played a pivotal role in fostering global interconnectivity, facilitating exchanges between countries and propelling Western Europe to the forefront of human development.

As for industrialization, the core of modernization, it swept across the globe in three waves. The first wave spread from the Industrial Revolution in England to Western Europe, marking the early stages of industrialization. The second wave saw industrialization spreading to Europe and North America, exerting significant influence on non-Western regions. The third wave involved advanced industrialized countries progressing to higher levels of industrialization, with underdeveloped countries also participating in the process. Henceforth, industrialization unfolded as a global phenomenon.

Modernization became a global phenomenon, originating in Western Europe before expanding to Central and Eastern Europe, North America, subsequently penetrating West Asia and North Africa, and culminating in its spread to South Asia, East Asia, and South America. By the twentieth century, modernization had evolved into an unstoppable trend.

China's Quest for Modernization

Now let's turn to China's modernization journey. China's path is distinct from Western modernization and divergent from the socialist modernization pursued by the Soviet Union. In the half-century from the late nineteenth century to the early twentieth century, China was on a journey in search of its own path.

As internal turmoil and external threats surfaced, China's traditional structures that had lasted for thousands of years began to shift. Initially seeking change, the imperial court aimed to preserve its established system through reform, while regional elites pursued progress within this reformed framework. Collaboratively, they established state-controlled military industries and introduced both state-supervised capitalist enterprises and privately owned ventures—a trajectory similar to that of early-stage modernization observed worldwide. However, what remained lacking in China was a driving force for modernization, particularly in terms of institutional reform. The country's first Self-Strengthening Movement emphasized a strategy of "Chinese learning for fundamental structure, Western learning for practical use," steering clear of reforms to the political structure, which, regrettably, hindered the initiation of modernization.

The defeat in the First Sino-Japanese War awakened the Chinese, prompting a period of introspection and contemplation of systemic changes, such as the Hundred Days' Reform in 1898. While China sought to emulate Japan's military successes and studied constitutional movements in Germany and Japan, it did not adopt the capitalist modernization approach pursued by these countries, primarily due to the absence of essential prerequisites at that time. As a result, the Qing government failed to effectuate a transition from autocratic rule to a modern constitutional monarchy during the first and second waves of reforms, impeding the establishment of a modern institutional framework necessary to drive the country's modernization efforts or to facilitate the transformation from a restrictive, authoritarian power structure to a modern, open governance system.

The Revolution of 1911 marked the end of a 2000-year era of dynastic governance in China, signaling the conclusion of top-down modernization efforts within the imperial system. However, this event witnessed the failure of the Chinese bourgeoisie to institute a modern political structure, consequently leading to a decline in central authority within the traditional structure and fostering intensified regional fragmentation and social disorder.

Over the next 40 years after the Revolution of 1911, China had steadfastly attempted to establish a new institutional paradigm within a modern framework, aiming to support the country's modernization journey through the establishment of a cohesive state apparatus and a viable political structure. During this period, the global system began to diverge. One significant consequence was the rise of fascism due to the world economic crisis, leading Germany, Japan, and Italy to choose the fascist capitalism. Another notable development was Russia's introduction of a socialist model for modernization.

Between the Revolutions of 1911 and 1949, China faced a critical choice between two developmental paths. The Kuomintang pursued a German-inspired approach, emphasizing controlled economic measures and centralized military authority. Despite their establishment of a new military regime, they struggled to develop the requisite state capacity for effective nation-building endeavors, hindering the formation of political and economic alliances between central and regional entities, ultimately leading to the Kuomintang's eventual downfall.

Initially, the CPC looked to the Soviet Union for guidance, prioritizing urban worker-led revolutions as the linchpin for modern institutional development. However, they soon realized the limitations of this approach and adopted a dual strategy, combining Marxist principles with Chinese realities and integrating traditional elements, shifting their focus to rural regions as foundational pillars for establishing a socialist institutional framework. This strategic pivot delineated a distinctive trajectory in China's modernization journey.

The War of Liberation emerged as a decisive arena for the clash between these divergent pathways in China. It brought an end to attempts at capitalist development and ushered in a new era wherein the country achieved remarkable political unity. This transition marked a new phase in China's modernization movement, which now aimed to secure national sovereignty and pursue development through a non-capitalist modernization trajectory.

The Essence of Chinese Path to Modernization

The modernization trajectory of the CPC can be observed from two dimensions: It consistently drives national modernization through institutional reforms and steadfastly advocates for the transformation of China from an agrarian economy to an industrial powerhouse. This pivotal shift constitutes a cornerstone of China's modernization and continues to expand in scope and significance.

At the 7th CPC National Congress in 1945 and the second plenary session of the 7th CPC Central Committee in 1949, the CPC delineated a modernization goal aimed at methodically transitioning the country from an agrarian society to an industrialized powerhouse. This marked a definitive departure from the paradigms of previous dynastic systems.

Traditional Chinese governance structures relied on centralized authority and the stability afforded by small-scale agriculture for long-term national stability, lacking the impetus for industrialization-driven progress.

However, the CPC remained committed to industrialization as its paramount modernization objective, never losing sight of it even during the most challenging times. Despite encountering adversities in 1954, the CPC explicitly aimed to build a great country endowed with advanced industrial capabilities and a vibrant cultural landscape. "Former Premier Zhou Enlai later called for striving to build our country into a socialist country with modern agriculture, industry, national defense, and science and technology within a not-too-distant historical period."[3] Even amid the tumultuous Cultural Revolution, during which the system grappled with myriad difficulties, China persisted steadfastly in its pursuit of the Four Modernizations.[4] This unwavering commitment necessitated that all leaders attached paramount importance to modernization as a core goal.

Following the introduction of reform and opening-up policies, Deng Xiaoping introduced the concept of Chinese path to modernization, characterized by three fundamental attributes: It necessitated alignment with socialist principles; entailed comprehensive advancements across economic, political, and cultural domains, transcending mere material prosperity to build a prosperous, democratic, and culturally enriched modern socialist country, a vision underscored during the 13th CPC National Congress; and introduced the concept of *xiaokang* (moderate prosperity), accentuating the importance of raising economic standards and enhancing people's well-being through modernization efforts.

Furthermore, the interpretation of modernization continues to evolve with changes in economic development paradigms. China's reform and opening-up initiatives have sustained for over 40 years, primarily due to the establishment of a foundational trajectory within the primary stage of socialism. This foundation hinges on two key points: Firstly, addressing the inherent contradiction between the ever-growing material and cultural

[3] Editor's note: "Premier Zhou Enlai's Governmental Work Report" (Reference: http://www.gov.cn/test/2008-03/10/content_915173.htm).

[4] The term "Four Modernizations" refers to four areas of development—agriculture, industry, science and technology, and defense. It emerged in the late 1970s as China's focal point, with the goal of achieving full modernization across these sectors by the end of the twentieth century.

needs of the people and backward social production, a theme that permeates the entire primary stage of socialism, aiming to reconcile society's fundamental contradictions. Secondly, it underscores the need to develop productive forces, recognizing development as an essential imperative. Within this foundational trajectory, as economic development advances, the essence of modernization continually shifts. By the time of the 16th CPC National Congress, China introduced the concept of comprehensive coordination and scientific development as cornerstones of modernization, expanding the modernization goals to be more holistic in goals. Why the emphasis on comprehensive coordination? It was necessary due to emerging disparities in areas such as urban and rural divides, regional discrepancies, and socioeconomic class distinctions. Simultaneously, there was a push for higher levels of moderate prosperity and the implementation of the Three-Step Approach.[5] By the 17th CPC National Congress, the focus shifted to a people-centered, comprehensive, coordinated, and sustainable development perspective, known as the scientific outlook on development. The main challenge at this point was coordinating various aspects, leading to the proposal of the Five Balanced Aspects.[6] Additionally, new requirements emerged to achieve the goal of building a moderately prosperous society in all respects. Following the 18th CPC National Congress, this emphasis turned toward building a great modern socialist country in all respects, outlining a two-step strategic plan: basically realizing socialist modernization from 2020 to 2035, and building China into a great modern socialist country from 2035 through the middle of this century.

The process of Chinese path to modernization is dynamic. The term denotes that, from the initiation of modernization to its advancement, the selection and transformation of institutions are integrated with China's

[5] Following the introduction of the reform and opening-up era, the CPC formulated a strategic plan for China's socialist modernization. Unveiled at the 13th CPC National Congress in October 1987, this strategy envisaged three steps for economic development, drawing inspiration from Deng Xiaoping's strategic conclusions. The underlying premise rested on addressing the major challenge in the primary stage of socialism, that is, rectifying the inadequate level of development and meeting the people's growing material and cultural needs. Aimed at enhancing people's well-being by raising the level of development, the strategy outlined specific targets for each of the three steps.

[6] The term refers to the pursuit of balanced urban and rural development, balanced development across regions, balanced development between man and nature, and balanced domestic development with increased engagement with the global community.

unique national conditions and developmental phases, rather than being arbitrary decisions.

Common Attributes Between Chinese Path to Modernization and Global Modernization

When comparing Chinese path to modernization with global modernization, it is pertinent to explore their common attributes.

Firstly, both share a common thread of developmental essence. In China, modernization unfolds as an ongoing developmental journey where development is crucial for achieving modernity. Over thousands of years, China remained rooted in its local environment due to a lack of progress. However, a concerted focus on development, particularly emphasizing economic growth since the introduction of reform and opening-up policies, has propelled the country forward. Looking ahead, the 20th CPC National Congress unequivocally emphasizes the prioritization of high-quality development as the core mission in building a great and modern country over the next century. China's modernization journey, transitioning from standing up and becoming prosperous to becoming strong, fundamentally hinges on development. The country's shift from a backward agrarian society to a modern industrialized country can also be credited to development initiatives and structural reforms implemented by the country.

Secondly, both Chinese path to modernization and global modernization exemplify the pivotal role of institutional reform in driving progress. The essence of Chinese path to modernization fundamentally rests on institutional transformations. In contrast to Western models, the prominence of institutional reform in propelling China's modernization trajectory is not only pronounced but also consistently applied. This augmented emphasis on institution-driven reforms stems from China's position as a developing country striving for rapid advancement in the modernization process, where mere technological advancements fall short. To expedite modernization effectively, China embarked on a steadfast course of comprehensive institutional reforms.

The new democratic system marked a significant institutional shift that set the stage for China's transition from an agrarian society to an industrialized country. Following the completion of socialist transformation, the subsequent phase involved the establishment of socialist systems and planned economies to further propel China's industrial growth. With the introduction of reform and opening-up policies, China delineated its unique socialist system, laying a solid foundation for building China into a great modern country.

Thirdly, both Chinese path to modernization and global modernization share a commonality in being guided by core values. The victory of the CPC over the Kuomintang in the battle of institutional and ideological choices can be attributed to the CPC's cultural advancement and foresight. Early Chinese revolutionary movements were not solely rural uprisings but were steered by visionary intellectuals envisioning a progressive future. Throughout China's modernization drive, the CPC has been consistently seeking to uphold a socialist value system, focusing on improving people's livelihoods while remaining dedicated to its original aspiration of building China into a great modern country.

Fourthly, both Chinese path to modernization and global modernization acknowledge the significance of material change. China's modernization efforts, involving a vast population and compressed timelines for rapid industrialization and urbanization, theoretically pose more significant risks to resources and the environment compared to any other country. However, China's environmental Kuznets curve has rapidly narrowed owing to proactive shifts away from resource-intensive development models, such as embracing innovation-driven strategies, and transitioned toward more environmentally friendly practices.

Fifthly, both Chinese path to modernization and global modernization highlighted a commitment to openness and globalization. China's reform and opening-up is an approach where openness drives reform. Without this openness, the impetus for reform would have been constrained, as broadening horizons are crucial for identifying shortcomings. Following the waning momentum from systemic reforms post-reform and opening-up era, China's accession to the World Trade Organization (WTO) and integration into the global division of labor system enabled the utilization of global rules to capitalize on opportunities presented by economic globalization. The advocacy for open structures, trade mechanisms, financial systems, and the restructuring of state-owned enterprises during that era exemplified a reform agenda driven by openness. Amid unprecedented changes today, China continues to refine its approach to global engagement and advocates for building a community with a shared future for mankind. Throughout its modernization journey, China has consistently intertwined openness and globalization into its developmental paradigm.

The Uniqueness of the Chinese Path to Modernization

The uniqueness of Chinese path to modernization is evident in the distinctive characteristics and role of the CPC, which facilitates catch-up modernization for latecomers through institutional development and continuous institutional reforms.

Firstly, the CPC's distinctiveness is noteworthy. In any country's modernization journey, the political party framework assumes pivotal importance. Within the framework of Chinese path to modernization led by the CPC, the Party's distinct qualities come to the fore.

To begin with, this distinctiveness is rooted in its values and ideologies. The CPC's ability to steer China a mission-driven entity, with original aspirations and mission established at its inception. Throughout generations, CPC members have tenaciously pursued these aspirations, as evidenced by the CPC's resilience in overcoming setbacks and its unwavering commitment to modernization in the pursuit of progress.

Furthermore, it is distinguished by its remarkable organizational strength. The CPC's organizational prowess includes a robust mechanism for selecting individuals, attracting exceptional talents from society, and a distinctive training system that enables selected individuals to undergo diverse forms of development and experiences. This process equips them to effectively fulfill their leadership roles in advancing societal progress.

Lastly, self-revolution serves as a defining feature that sets the CPC apart from other political parties.

The second point is to achieve catch-up modernization for latecomers through institutional development and continuous institutional reforms. The new democratic system facilitated the transformation of an agrarian country, while the socialist system and planned economy fostered industrialization, and the reform of the socialist market economy system further propelled Chinese path to modernization. Currently, the building of a great modern socialist country under the system of socialism with Chinese characteristics relies on ongoing institutional reforms to drive forward the modernization process.

Chinese Path to Modernization Also Addresses Global Modernization

The concept of "Five Modernizations," proposed for constructing a great modern socialist country in the ensuing 100 years, aims not only to address issues related to modernization in China but primarily to tackle fundamental questions that persist in the global modernization process.

Firstly, Chinese path to modernization is the modernization of a huge population. The key issue at hand is ensuring the equitable distribution of modernization benefits among the majority of the populace. While modernization has global implications, it does not inherently guarantee an even distribution of its advantages. With a population of 1.4 billion, achieving modernization by 2050 would entail integrating approximately 18% of the world's population into the modernization fold, fundamentally altering the global modernization landscape and echoing the significance of solving poverty-related issues. By resolving China's poverty challenges, we concurrently confront global poverty concerns. Additionally, the vast population size indicates a larger consumer market, facilitating the realization of modernization on a grand scale. Modernization also should not be confined to specific regions but must instead encompass the entire population comprehensively. Finally, addressing urban–rural disparities is crucial for achieving modernization within a population of such magnitude.

Secondly, Chinese path to modernization is the modernization of common prosperity for all. This addresses a pervasive modernization challenge, as despite strides in alleviating poverty, the issue of wealth inequality persists throughout human history. Without mitigating wealth disparities, it remains impossible to overcome the middle-income trap in high-income stages. Failure to address mechanisms for wealth distribution could disrupt societal cohesion, impacting not only the affluent and impoverished but also destabilizing the middle class.

The CPC's vision of Chinese path to modernization seeks to realize a modernization paradigm that ensures common prosperity, with the socialist system and leadership by the CPC serving as foundational pillars.

To achieve common prosperity, it is essential to elevate the quality of life for all citizens, ensuring that economic development benefits everyone, while reducing inequality and narrowing the gap between the rich and the poor. These goals hinge on fostering high-quality development and leveraging the uniqueness of the system and the CPC.

Thirdly, Chinese path to modernization is the modernization of material and cultural-ethical advancement. While rationality and secularization have driven humanity toward material progress and modernization, it has also been paralleled by a diminishment of sensibility, as reflected in Western modernization trajectory, ultimately leading to what Herbert Marcuse described as "one-dimensional man," thereby instigating a struggle within cultural-ethical advancement.

In response to this dichotomy, the paradigm of Chinese path to modernization seeks to build a great modern country through economic advancement while concurrently nurturing a sophisticated socialist civilization. This requires a shift in the approach to modernization, placing emphasis on the synchronized development of industrialization, urbanization, information-based development, and agricultural reform. Furthermore, it entails assimilating lessons from past environmental mismanagement and charting a new course for industrialization. In essence, the emphasis should not be exclusively on material modernization during economic modernization. Conversely, it involves exploring methods to pursue cultural-ethical development alongside material modernization, thereby actualizing the creative revitalization and innovative development of traditional Chinese culture.

Fourthly, Chinese path to modernization is the modernization of harmony between humanity and nature. Historically, human modernization has inadequately addressed sustainable development, failing to strike a balance between economic growth and environmental preservation. Achieving symbiosis between humans and nature necessitates integrating environmental considerations into economic development. Concepts such as "clear waters and green mountains," resource conservation, and low-carbon development are proposed to confront the sustainability challenge in human modernization.

Fifthly, Chinese path to modernization is the modernization of peaceful development. Unlike Western modernization trajectory that has often resulted in zero-sum outcomes, China's approach aims to circumvent this pitfall by promoting cooperation, equality, dialogue, and reconciliation to foster collective global development. The proposition to establish a community with a shared future for mankind endeavors to steer clear of zero-sum games in modernization.

To build a great modern socialist country, the Chinese nation must harness these Five Modernizations to tackle the common challenges encountered globally during modernization, charting a distinctive path of Chinese path to modernization.

Chinese Path to Modernization and High-Quality Development

Sustaining Economic Growth and Achieving High-Quality Development Are Crucial for Tackling Challenges and Navigating the Bigger Picture

Justin Yifu Lin

Amid unprecedented global changes and the ongoing pandemic, the world has entered a period of turbulent transformation, presenting significant new challenges to China's economy. Sustaining economic growth and achieving high-quality development are crucial not only for realizing the great rejuvenation of the Chinese nation but also for navigating through these unprecedented challenges, unseen in a century.

Currently, China faces notable challenges within its international development landscape. U.S. then President Joe Biden has perpetuated the trade and tech wars initiated against China during the Trump administration, seeking to politically isolate China and facilitate the economic

This article was published on page 3 of *CPPCC Daily* on June 7, 2022.

J. Y. Lin (✉)
Institute of New Structural Economics, Peking University, Beijing, China

Institute of South-South Cooperation and Development, Peking University, Beijing, China

National School of Development, Peking University, Beijing, China

W. Xianqing (ed.), *Understanding China's Path to Modernization*,
https://doi.org/10.1007/978-981-96-7051-2_4

decoupling of more nations from it, while encouraging some other countries to relocate their supply chains away from China. In addition to containment and isolation actions taken by the United States against China, the Russia–Ukraine conflict, which erupted in late February 2022, has led to triggered significant spikes in global oil, natural gas, and food prices. As a major importer of oil and, to some extent, reliant on imported food, China is impacted by the rising costs not only of oil and food but also of specific mineral resources. Consequently, the Russia–Ukraine conflict is expected to increase China's import costs and affect economic growth in the short term. Looking ahead to the medium to long term, the distrust between Russia and the European Union, coupled with the tense dynamics stemming from the conflict, may prove challenging to be resolved immediately. Certain factions attempt to muddy the waters, leveraging this conflict to sow discord in China–Europe political relations and advocate for economic and trade decoupling between Europe and China under the guise of security concerns.

Starting from the third quarter of 2021, China's economy experienced a downturn, primarily attributed to the triple pressures of shrinking demand, disrupted supply and weakening expectations. Moving into March 2022, the domestic economy faced exacerbated challenges stemming from the impact of the highly transmissible Omicron variant outbreak. Major first-tier cities such as Shenzhen, Guangzhou, Shanghai, and Beijing have all witnessed substantial outbreaks, somewhat impeding various facets including production, investment, and consumption, consequently leading to an overall slowdown in economic growth. Achieving the targeted growth rate of 5.5% has become notably more arduous.

In light of the persistent domestic and international challenges, more efforts should be made, especially in the following two aspects, to maintain China's rapid economic development and achieve high-quality development:

Sustaining Growth and Embracing Openness to Tackle International Challenges

When it comes to overseas challenges, the United States is actively pursuing a strategy to encourage countries to disengage from China in an attempt to coerce China into reverting to a closed economy. However, in response to this strategy, we also see conditions favorable for ourselves: China currently stands as the world's largest trading nation and, in terms of purchasing power parity, already ranks as the world's largest economy with the most extensive market. Trade is inherently mutually beneficial, particularly for smaller economies, which stand to gain more from trade than their larger counterparts. While the United States may be inclined to sacrifice economic interests to maintain its political dominance and advantages, a scenario where the European Union, the Association of Southeast Asian Nations (ASEAN), and other economies sever ties with both the United States and China would necessitate them to forfeit their own economic gains, essentially aiding the United States in maintaining its position of power at their own expense.

Since 2008, China has consistently contributed between 25 and 30% annually to global economic growth. If China maintains this level of contribution, no country aside from the United States can afford to overlook the Chinese market, considering its significance for employment, social stability, and development. This makes it challenging for the United States to successfully enforce its plan to decouple other countries from China, providing China with an opportunity to pursue an international environment conducive to its own development.

In summary, while the United States may prioritize maintaining its political hegemony at the expense of economic interests, China's growth, openness, and development present crucial opportunities for the progress of other countries. Therefore, sustaining rapid growth, fostering openness, and advancing globalization are not only imperative for achieving the second centenary goal and national rejuvenation but also serve as the most efficacious means to counter U.S. strategies and external challenges.

Rebuilding Confidence, Maintaining Focus, and Addressing Domestic Economic Challenges

Examining the domestic economic challenges, since 2021, we have faced triple pressures—shrinking demand, disrupted supply and weakening expectations. I believe the most critical concern lies in the weakening expectations: when expectations falter, they engender a lack of confidence in investments, diminished supply, disruptions in the supply chain, and a loss of impetus to surmount obstacles. This downward spiral culminates in dwindling employment opportunities, stagnant income growth, and ultimately, a contraction in consumer demand.

The underlying causes of weakening expectations largely trace back to challenges in policy implementation. The Central Economic Work

Conference of 2021 pinpointed several fallacies of composition in policy execution. Key initiatives such as platform governance, the pursuit of the dual carbon goals, reforms within the real estate sector, and the pursuit of common prosperity are all crucial and indispensable reforms, policy adjustments, and developmental trajectories. However, in practice, certain long-term, holistic policies have been disjointed, localized, and short-sighted, resulting in fallacies of composition that have corroded confidence in economic development, particularly among entrepreneurs and investors. It is widely acknowledged that confidence holds greater value than gold. To illustrate, following the introduction of the goal of common prosperity, it is imperative for relevant authorities to provide comprehensive explanations to preclude misinterpretations that could impact entrepreneurs' investment decisions and long-term confidence in development. Achieving common prosperity necessitates initially expanding the economic pie, with early beneficiaries aiding those who are trailing behind, alongside the formulation of sensible tax policies aimed at incentivizing charitable contributions from affluent members of society.

As imperative as rebuilding confidence is, it is equally essential to prioritize economic development as the core. Recognizing that development serves as the bedrock and key to addressing all problems is of significance, and it must be fully integrated into our approach to tackle various developmental challenges.

Presently, it is imperative to effectively coordinate pandemic prevention and control measures with socioeconomic development. All local governments should expedite efforts to revive production and daily activities. Proactive fiscal and monetary policies should be implemented to underpin new infrastructure initiatives, thus facilitating structural transformation and upgrades. Through collaborative efforts, we must mitigate the adverse impacts of the COVID-19 pandemic and strive to achieve the targeted economic growth of approximately 5.5% in 2022. Sustaining economic growth and achieving high-quality development not only fosters confidence in our self-advancement but also upholds international confidence in China—a pivotal factor in achieving the great rejuvenation of the Chinese nation amid unprecedented changes unseen in a century.

New Development Stage and New Development Philosophy of the Chinese Economy

Miaojie Yu

The current challenges facing the Chinese economy revolve around two hot phrases: "triple pressure" and "three-period overlapping."

"Triple pressure" primarily refers to the "shrinking demand, disrupted supply and weakening expectations affecting China's economic development," as highlighted during the Central Economic Work Conference held at the end of 2021. As for "three-period overlapping," it means that China's economy had reached a new normal of development and was transitioning from a stage of high-speed growth to a stage of high-quality development. Our traditional growth model could no longer be sustained in the face of a complex situation in which we must simultaneously deal with the slowdown in economic growth, make difficult structural adjustments, and absorb the effects of previous economic stimulus policies.

This article is derived from a lecture delivered by the author during an online seminar held on April 7, 2022.

M. Yu (✉)
Liaoning University, Shenyang, China

National School of Development, Peking University, Beijing, China

W. Xianqing (ed.), *Understanding China's Path to Modernization*,
https://doi.org/10.1007/978-981-96-7051-2_5

Why Is China's Economy at a New Development Stage?

The Chinese economy is currently in a new development phase, with the key *new* aspect being high-quality economic growth. This is notably observed across six main domains.

Firstly, there is a sustained increase in the added value of Chinese products, particularly evident in the elevation of added value within manufacturing goods. Trade is conventionally categorized into general trade and processing trade. The latter involves substantial imports and exports, where China imports raw materials and intermediate products from abroad, processes and packages them domestically, and then exports the finished goods globally. Compared to general trade, processing trade typically exhibits lower productivity and added value. From 1995 to 2006, processing trade held a dominant position in China's trade landscape. However, this trend has shifted in recent years, with the proportion of processing trade steadily declining to around one-third currently. Furthermore, its industrial focus has transitioned from primarily producing labor-intensive items such as clothing and footwear to predominantly manufacturing high-value-added products like machinery and transportation equipment.

In addition, the quality of Chinese export products is continually on the rise. How do we measure the quality of export products? One such method is to consider their unit price. For instance, when comparing two bottles of mineral water, priced at RMB 3 and RMB 1, respectively, the higher-priced option may suggest superior quality. Another criterion for evaluation is their market share. If two mineral water brands with the same prices are exported to the United States, and one brand, say mineral water A, secures a larger market share than mineral water B, this indirectly reflects the superior quality of mineral water A. Enterprise productivity can also serves as an indicator, offering insights into product quality from the supply side. According to the theory of competitive suppression, robust enterprises tend to exhibit higher productivity, thereby enhancing their influence in the market and potentially enabling them to reduce prices. This price reduction strategy may involve driving competitors out of the market, where the price may not necessarily align with the product quality. Therefore, when evaluating product quality, it is imperative to consider both demand and supply factors.

There have been studies examining data related to the quality of Chinese export products following the country's accession to the World Trade Organization (WTO). By taking data from 2001 as the quality benchmark at a value of 1, it was observed that by 2012, this figure had risen to around 1.3, reflecting an approximate 30% improvement. Subsequently, by 2020, the quality standard had further advanced by roughly 25% relative to 2012. While China still lags behind manufacturing powerhouses like Germany and Japan, the notable enhancement in the quality of Chinese export products in recent years underscores China's stride toward high-quality development in its economy.

Furthermore, the total factor productivity among Chinese enterprises is continuously improving. Total factor productivity encompasses a company's technology and performance. As Paul Krugman, a winner of Nobel Prize for Economics, famously stated, "Productivity isn't everything, but in the long run, it is almost everything." Therefore, when evaluating the strength of a company or a country's production capabilities, the focus lies on whether total factor productivity is on an upward trajectory. He also extensively analyzed the economic development of East Asian countries, arguing that the decline of the East Asian miracle largely resulted from these countries' stagnant total factor productivity over several years. Rather than focusing on accumulation, they had pursued an extensive development model, which is evidently unsustainable. How does China fare in this regard? An esteemed American scholar highlighted in an article that China's total factor productivity in 2001 stood at around 30% of that of the United States, a figure that ascended to 45% by 2015. This data unequivocally demonstrates China's continuous improvement in total factor productivity, marking close to a 50% growth from 2001 to 2015.

Moreover, China possesses unique and palpable advantages across its entire industrial chain. Initially, it stands out as the sole country globally equipped with a complete industrial chain. Official classifications identify 41 major industrial categories and 666 minor industrial categories in China, indicating comprehensive coverage across various sectors. Subsequently, based on estimations using the eight-digit customs code, China exports approximately 10,851 products. Further segmentation according to U.S. standards reveals that China exports up to 15,000 different types of merchandise. The capacity to export such a diverse array of products directly reflects the ability to produce a wide range of goods. Therefore, it is evident that China's prowess in producing varied goods is extensive, showing a clear advantage across its entire industry chain.

Additionally, China's industries exhibit striking characteristics of industrial clustering. Each industrial city in China boasts its own prominent industrial sector, such as Shenzhen's electronics industry, Suzhou's IT sector, and Hebei's cashmere industry and furniture sector in Xingtai and Langfang, respectively. Through such industrial agglomeration, companies can benefit from clustering, reducing transportation costs, and facilitating economies of scale.

Last but not least, let's move on to the distribution of China's three major industries. The proportion of the country's primary industry (agriculture) in GDP is on par with that of developed countries, ranging from 7 to 8%. However, a significant disparity emerges in the secondary and tertiary sectors: developed countries have a more advanced tertiary industry, while China's secondary industry takes the lead. I view this positively because a lower proportion of the secondary industry, encompassing manufacturing and construction industries, would indicate an underdeveloped real economy, impeding China's assumption of the role as the world's factory and limiting employment opportunities. As the saying goes, "with the skin gone, to what can the hair attach itself," implying that without a robust real economy, even the virtual economy, such as finance, cannot thrive. To put it simply, only a robust real economy can prevent excessive bubbles in the virtual economy. Therefore, China's reality, with the secondary industry accounting for 37% of GDP, serves as the cornerstone of its status as a manufacturing powerhouse.

Can China's economic aggregate surpass that of the United States? Consensus among many experts and institutions suggests that such a shift is inevitable. This holds substantial implications given the continued significance of GDP as a measure of a country's strength. However, there remains a considerable disparity in per capita GDP between the two countries due to China's huge population.

When will China's economic aggregate catch up with that of the United States? Such economic overtaking hinges on two key factors: the respective growth rates of their economies and the exchange rate dynamics between the Chinese yuan and the U.S. dollar, as GDP predominantly relies on the latter currency for calculation. Under an optimistic scenario, it is estimated that China could surpass the United States in terms of economic aggregate by approximately 2026. This estimation is founded on underlying economic growth trends in both countries, assuming a relatively consistent annual growth rate of 2.5% for the United States and 5.5% for China. It is also predicted that the exchange rate between the Chinese yuan and the U.S. dollar will stabilize around 6 Chinese yuan to the U.S. dollar, further bolstering the expectation of China's economic overtaking by 2026.

Throughout the analytical process, the fluctuating exchange rate of the Chinese yuan remains an important variable. Following the conclusion of the trade agreement between China and the United States in December 2019, I have publicly made a bold prediction during a speech, stating that the exchange rate of the Chinese yuan against the U.S. dollar would appreciate to 6.8 within three months, and subsequently to 6.2 within three years. Remarkably, both prognostications have since been proven true.

The rationale underpinning this prediction is quite straightforward. While the exchange rate of the Chinese Yuan indeed impacts exports, external demand emerges as the ultimate determinant. The trade agreement inked between China and the United States on December 15, 2019, heralded auspicious developments for both nations. However, the exchange rate mainly decides which party benefits more. Specifically, the country whose currency strengthens as a result of the trade agreement will gain more. Despite China boasting a substantial economy at the time, its scale remained relatively modest compared to the United States. This can be likened to eating mooncake during the Mid-Autumn Festival. A child can be content with just one mooncake, whereas an adult, due to their larger size, requires more than one to feel full. Therefore, China, with a relatively smaller economy, will undoubtedly gain greater benefits from the same good news.

Undoubtedly, exchange rates are subject to a variety of factors, and in recent years, prognostications of the Chinese yuan's devaluation have persisted. Nevertheless, contrary to these forecasts, the Chinese yuan has not only maintained stability but demonstrated a consistent trend of appreciation. Practice is the sole criterion for testing truth. With conviction, I maintain that in the forthcoming years, the exchange rate of the Chinese yuan against the U.S. dollar will remain around 6.

How to Implement the Five Major Development Concepts?

The new phase of development is aligned with the Five Major Development Concepts, which advocate for innovative, coordinated, green, open, and shared development. But how are these concepts put into practice?

Innovation

Innovation is the cornerstone of progress. In the narrow sense, innovation primarily pertains to technological advancements, which can be categorized into process improvements and the creation of new products from scratch. The current national push for a culture of "mass entrepreneurship and innovation initiative" predominantly targets refining process efficiencies. Conversely, the development of entirely new products typically requires concerted efforts from prominent research institutions and scientists.

Across the countries worldwide, there is a pronounced emphasis on bolstering research and development intensity (R&D intensity), which measures the proportion of R&D investment relative to GDP. In China's 14th Five-Year Plan, there is a call to increase R&D funding, with a clear target of achieving around 3% of GDP. This earmarked level signifies a notably elevated commitment, particularly when compared to the average R&D intensity observed among OECD member states, currently standing at 2.6%. In advanced regions like Shenzhen, the R&D intensity has already surpassed 4.1%.

Speaking of which, research and development are not entirely synonymous. While China has made significant strides in development, it still lags in pure research endeavors. As a result, there is a concerted effort to elevate the importance of fundamental research by setting a goal for fundamental research to make up over 7% of total R&D expenditure. Although this may seem ambitious, developed countries have already achieved a ratio ranging between 15 and 20%.

In identifying industries and companies poised for heightened innovation, a general trend emerges wherein companies at the lower echelons of an industry face challenges in innovation. Innovation demands substantial financial resources, and for struggling enterprises, mere survival is already a challenge, let alone allocating resources for significant R&D endeavors. While leading companies may demonstrate innovation to some degree, the breadth and pace of innovation often pale in comparison with Huawei. In practice, it is often the mid-level companies that are the most innovative, compelled to differentiate themselves through inventive solutions amid fierce market competition.

In my opinion, it is imperative to foster innovation in the broader sense. Innovation, in the broader sense, starts with the transformation of social norms. For instance, the seamless amalgamation of production, education, research, and application stands as a requisite for flourishing within free trade zones. Currently, China's R&D efforts predominantly concentrate on domains aligned with the Technology Innovation 2030 Project, emphasizing the importance of integrating production, education, research, and application, especially between universities and local communities, across all regions.

Since 2013, we have established 21 free trade zones, primarily targeting four key dimensions: formulating national treatment and negative lists before foreign investment access, guided by the principle of "what is not prohibited by law is permitted"; promoting trade liberalization and investment facilitation through initiatives such as opening up frontier zones while efficaciously regulating secondary zones areas (regulatory protocols within free trade zones), and implementing zero tariffs; enhancing the business milieu and implementing the policy of "streamlining administration, delegating power, and improving regulation services"; and reforming capital projects or expanding access to capital projects.

Currently, these 21 free trade zones predominantly cluster eastward of the Hu line. This line, also known as the Heihe–Tengchong line, is a demographic partition proposed by geographer Hu Huanyong, demarcating China's population density from north to south and dividing China into eastern and western regions. Among the provinces situated east of this demarcation, only Jilin, Shanxi, Jiangxi, and Guizhou do not have free trade zones, but anticipations suggest breakthroughs within these four provinces within the coming one to two years.

In terms of the functional positioning of free trade zones, I believe that beyond the exploration of replicable and scalable best practices, it is essential to uncover the distinctive attributes of various regions. For example, Beijing specializes in service trade, while other free trade zones pursue distinctive developmental paths.

The conceptualization of free trade ports is a more pioneering approach compared to free trade zones.

In June 2020, *the Overall Plan for the Construction of Hainan Free Trade Port* was officially unveiled. The plan is essentially a dual-phased endeavor: achieving initial milestones by 2025 and full operational readiness by 2035. The initial milestones revolve around the opening up of basic elements such as land, capital, and data, as well as measures such as relaxing controls in certain domains while upholding stringent regulations in others to foster trade liberalization, facilitate investment, and enable the free flow of factors.

One of the key aspects of free trade ports is regulatory innovation, especially in terms of tax structures. Within the Chinese mainland, individuals earning over RMB 960,000 annually face a personal income tax rate of up to 45%, whereas in Hainan, individuals who stay for at least 183 days per year are eligible for a reduced tax rate of merely 15%, akin to tax rates observed in Hong Kong and Singapore. Concerted efforts will also be directed toward bolstering financial fraud prevention and health risk management in Hainan.

Furthermore, the idea of free trade ports extends beyond notions tied solely to river or sea ports, potentially including inland airports. Cities like Chengdu, Zhengzhou, and Beijing, each boasting two airports, can explore high-value-added service trade as part of their reform strategies.

Green

"Green," an analogy to environmental friendliness, has emerged as a buzzword in today's discussion. In September 2020, Chinese President Xi Jinping delivered a seminal address at the 75th session of the United Nations General Assembly, unveiling China's commitment to implementing more stringent policies and measures aimed at peaking carbon dioxide emissions by 2030 and striving for carbon neutrality by 2060.[1]

To realize these objectives, the proportion of non-fossil energy sources, such as nuclear and hydropower, needs to reach around 25% by 2030. Non-fossil energy presently accounts for 15%, highlighting a significant gap from the targeted 25%, underscoring the urgency of the situation. Consequently, there is now a proposal to shift focus from "dual control of energy consumption" to "dual control of carbon emissions." At the

[1] Editor's note: Xi Jinping's speech at the general debate of the 75th session of the United Nations General Assembly, see: https://www.ccps.gov.cn/xxsxk/zyls/202009/t20200922_143558.shtml.

same time, China faces considerable pressure to meet the demanding dual carbon goals. In the 2022 Report on the Work of the Government, Chinese Premier Li Keqiang emphasized the need to coordinate these objectives while allowing for appropriate flexibility. The journey ahead in the realm of green initiatives indeed presents formidable challenges.

Coordination

The term "coordination" also encompasses three primary dimensions: regional coordination, urban–rural coordination, and industrial coordination. While industrial coordination often arises spontaneously within the economy, our discussions tend to concentrate on regional and urban–rural coordination.

At this developmental juncture, we are pursuing a path of urbanization and the development of large cities to realize the convergence of the "new four modernizations": industrialization, urbanization, new IT application, and agricultural modernization. The pivotal determinant lies in the harmonious integration of new industrialization and urbanization.

Primarily, the close interconnection between new industrialization and urbanization is not always readily apparent, as evidenced by certain countries lagging behind due to the absence of effective synergy in these domains. For example, in South Africa, urbanization is prevalent, with many citizens seeking migration to urban centers for employment opportunities. However, since industrialization has not been achieved in full, many struggle to find employment in cities, leading to the emergence of shantytowns and subsequent social unrest. Conversely, a country achieving industrialization without concurrent urbanization may experience rapid industrial and corporate progress, yet contends with issues like soaring labor costs and dwindling profits due to labor shortages, thereby impeding sustainability. Therefore, the harmonious alignment of urbanization and industrialization is of paramount importance.

Secondly, IT-driven industrialization predominantly aims to empower industrialization leveraging technologies such as 5G and artificial intelligence. The primary objective of urbanization is to establish five major urban clusters, that is, the Yangtze River Delta, the Guangdong–Hong Kong–Macao Greater Bay Area, the Beijing–Tianjin–Hebei urban cluster, the Chengdu–Chongqing economic circle, and the Central Yangtze River Region urban clusters. Among these, the Yangtze River Delta and the Greater Bay Area notably stand out, as they have effectively synchronized urban development with industrial progress, resulting in comparatively robust growth.

In the Beijing–Tianjin–Hebei urban cluster, Beijing and Tianjin exhibit flourishing dynamics, whereas the three counties in northern Hebei (Langfang, situated near Beijing) show relatively subdued performance. At the same time, the Chengdu–Chongqing economic circle, anchored by Chongqing and Chengdu, holds substantial growth potential, particularly with Chengdu delineating one-hour and two-hour urban catchment areas. Meanwhile, cities like Wuhan, Changsha, and Nanchang in the central Yangtze River region appear somewhat isolated, suggesting significant opportunities for development within these first-tier urban clusters.

Beyond the first-tier urban clusters, there exist four second-tier urban clusters: the Shandong Peninsula, Central Plains (featuring Zhengzhou in Henan and Bozhou in Anhui), the Harbin–Changchun city cluster, and the Taiwan Strait west coast urban agglomeration (encompassing Quanzhou, Fuzhou, and Xiamen).

In the current era marked by fierce competition, the pace of development in second-tier city clusters may not necessarily lag behind that of first-tier counterparts. The 2022 Report on the Work of the Government emphasizes the imperative of urban cluster and metropolitan area construction, alongside a concentrated effort on urbanization development, with a strict prohibition on county withdrawal. From my perspective, the central government is committed to fostering urban clusters while acknowledging the significance of both urban agglomerations and urban clusters, facilitating a dual-track approach.

Sharing

Coordinating between urban and rural areas and narrowing the urban–rural gap are closely related to the concept of sharing.

The key elements of the poverty alleviation campaign include lifting 55.75 million rural impoverished individuals out of poverty, delisting 832 counties from the country's poverty index, and successfully achieving the goal of granting urban residency to 100 million individuals from rural areas and other permanent residents without local household registration. This campaign has unequivocally succeeded. However, China's poverty line remains within the spectrum delineated by the United Nations' absolute poverty line and relative poverty line. Therefore, following the triumph in poverty alleviation, the arduous task of rural revitalization still looms large.

How can we efficiently advance rural revitalization in the ensuing phase? One proposal is to achieve rural revitalization through a graduated transition in processing trade. As the saying goes, "Give a man a fish, and you feed him for a day. Teach a man to fish, and you feed him for a lifetime." With rising labor costs, certain processing trade industries can be relocated from coastal regions to western inland provinces to foster job opportunities and invigorate rural areas in those regions. Taking this opportunity, Guangdong's coastal areas can introduce new industries and upgrade their industrial landscape.

Different regions adopt varied approaches to industrial upgrading. Labor-intensive industries should be relocated overseas to countries such as Bangladesh, Cambodia, and Vietnam, primarily leveraging comparative advantages. Just as labor-intensive industries historically migrated from the United States to Europe, then to Japan, the Four Asian Tigers, and subsequently to the Chinese mainland, there is now a discernible trend of relocating them out of the Chinese mainland, driven by comparative advantages. Conversely, capital-intensive industries should move in the opposite direction, shifting toward the central and western inland regions of China, thereby stimulating local economic development.

In recent times, "common prosperity" has become a focal point of concern for many entrepreneurs. After several rounds of deliberations across various sectors, I believe that a consensus must have been established to some extent: Firstly, common prosperity undoubtedly involves striking a balance between efficiency and fairness, where efficiency entails expanding the economic pie and fairness pertains to equitable distribution. Secondly, achieving common prosperity is a gradual process and not an immediate outcome, yet it is certainly feasible. Thirdly, currently, the notion of common prosperity is in the phase of "continuously expanding the economic pie," prioritizing efficiency while ensuring fairness.

The central government's rhetoric on common prosperity echoes similar sentiments. For instance, policies aimed at curbing unbridled capital expansion and reckless growth. I understand unbridled expansion as encompassing horizontal breadth, such as encroaching from one's own market territory into others'. Reckless growth, on the other hand, alludes to vertical depth, akin to monopolizing market shares. Therefore, at this stage, it is important to persist in expanding the economic pie, prioritize efficiency, ensure fairness, encourage diligence and wealth generation, further reduce the Gini coefficient, and foster a bell-curve society characterized by reduced extremes and a larger middle class.

Openness

In 2021, China demonstrated remarkable export performance, boasting a trade surplus of USD 4.4 trillion and a total foreign trade volume surpassing USD 6 trillion. This means that out of over 200 global economies, China alone accounted for over 20% of the total export volume, a figure unprecedented. In my opinion, China's exports in 2022 are poised to maintain their momentum from 2021 and are anticipated to reach the target of constituting 15% of the total export volume.

Changes in our main trading partners have been notable. Previously, the United States was our primary trading partner, while the European Union also held significance in our trade relations. However, with the ratification of the Regional Comprehensive Economic Partnership (RCEP) in 2021, ASEAN has emerged as China's primary trading partner. Given the ongoing repercussions of the Russia–Ukraine conflict, trade dynamics with the United States and the European Union may shift for China. Consequently, I anticipate ASEAN retaining its status as our primary trading partner in 2022.

Has globalization as a fundamental trend changed? I believe that it has not, but there have been notable shifts in its manifestations. Assessing globalization primarily involves evaluating two key indicators: the emergence of regionalization and trade multilateralism in production and trade. For instance, the manufacturing of smartphone components across different countries, their assembly in a single location, and subsequent global distribution exemplify production regionalization and trade multilateralism.

The advent of U.S. President Donald Trump's trade protectionism has posed challenges to multilateral economic and trade cooperation under the WTO, leading to a near-paralysis of the WTO's dispute resolution mechanism. Consequently, countries have begun to bypass the WTO, turning their attention instead to various regional trade agreements. Before China's accession to the WTO, the global economic and trade landscape was under a dual leadership by the United States and the European Union. However, it has gradually evolved into a three-pronged structure of regional trade cooperation: the North American Economic and Trade Zone, centered around the United States, the

European Economic and Trade Zone, anchored by Germany, and the Asia–Pacific Economic and Trade Zone, with China at its core.

This three-pronged structure is interconnected, with close ties among them. The United States-Mexico-Canada Agreement (USMCA) is engaged in negotiations for the Transatlantic Trade and Investment Partnership with the European Union; there exists the Comprehensive Agreement on Investment between the European Union and China; and negotiations are ongoing between RCEP countries, the United States, Mexico, Canada, and China for the Comprehensive and Progressive Agreement for Trans-Pacific Partnership (CPTPP).

How to Ensure Dual Circulation Within the Chinese Economy?

The term "dual circulation" was first introduced in official documents during the meeting of the Standing Committee of the Political Bureau of the Communist Party of China Central Committee in May 2020. It emphasized the imperative to deepen supply-side structural reforms, harness China's significant market advantages and domestic demand potential, and establish a new development paradigm wherein domestic and international circulations mutually reinforce each other.

China has long since bid farewell to the era of low-cost labor. The main reason for optimism regarding the Chinese economy lies in its unified domestic market comprising 1.4 billion individuals, including a middle-income group of 400 million. This not only serves as China's competitive advantage but also remains the fundamental source ensuring the country's relatively stable growth potential.

The dual circulation model stresses the importance of prioritizing domestic circulation while recognizing the significance of external circulation. Despite China's economy accounting for 18% of the global total, with the remaining 82% attributed to other countries, we cannot afford to disregard the significance of the 82% market share in favor of the 18% market. From this vantage point, the objective is to pursue a dual circulation strategy, one that does not exclusively rely on domestic circulation.

Is there a quantifiable standard for dual circulation? For external circulation, the proportion of China's foreign trade in global trade serves as a key metric. I believe that surpassing the 18% threshold can be deemed favorable, and in 2021, China's global share of foreign trade exceeded

20%, marking a significant achievement. As for domestic circulation, benchmarks akin to those employed in the United States can be applied. These standards gauge whether domestic trade accounts for over three quarters of GDP or if foreign trade contributes less than one-quarter to GDP.

To enhance domestic circulation, several strategies can be pursued.

Firstly, fostering a market environment that is "fair, just, and transparent" while promoting factor market allocation. It is essential to manage the relationship between state-owned enterprises (SOEs) and private enterprises. It is noteworthy that SOEs are not unique to China; countries like the United States and France also have numerous SOEs. Strengthening and expanding SOEs, particularly ensuring their leadership and dominant role in upstream industries, is essential. However, it is also vital to prevent SOEs from receiving preferential treatment, thus preserving a fair, equitable, and competitive market environment.

For private enterprises, it is essential to establish clearer guidelines and foster a more equitable, transparent environment to support their sustained growth and development. Currently, private enterprises are no longer merely robust supplementary entities within the national economy but rather integral components. The term "56,789" underscores the substantial contributions of the private sector in China: nearly 50% of tax revenue, 60% of GDP, 70% of innovation, 80% of employment, and 90% of business entities originate from this sector. Notably, within large enterprises, 90% are privately owned, reflecting the predominant presence of private enterprises among the 1.5 billion market entities.

Concerning recent developments in the private sector, the notion of "the state advances while the private sector retreats" has emerged. However, I strongly oppose this notion. Before China's accession to the WTO, the state-owned economy accounted for approximately two-thirds, but its share has since decreased to half. Undoubtedly, the significance of the private economy has escalated and warrants vigorous promotion.

In my perspective, the digital economy is a pivotal determinant of China's potential for economic breakthroughs. While China exhibits strength in fostering innovative small businesses, this advantage may not be readily apparent when compared to Germany. However, the digital economy presents a different scenario—mastery of emerging technologies and values will shape the future landscape. Therefore, industries such as the digital economy, characterized by their knowledge intensity, represent an important trajectory for China's developmental pursuits.

Furthermore, advancing trade liberalization through a new pattern of openness and facilitating investment facilitation through a new business environment. The Report On the Work of the Government explicitly underscores the importance of stabilizing the Six Fronts.[2] Stabilizing the Six Fronts emphasize gradual progression rather than simultaneous dispersion. Stabilizing expectations serves as the foundational principle. Presently, the Chinese economy confronts unprecedented changes and challenges, including shrinking demand, disrupted supply and weakening expectations—a triple pressure. Stabilizing employment emerges as the ultimate objective, as instability in employment engenders societal unrest, leading to various associated issues.

How can we stabilize employment? This necessitates the implementation of measures to stabilize foreign capital, investments, and the financial sector. The 15 policy measures proposed by the State Council primarily target four key areas: foreign trade, foreign investment, domestic investment, and finance.

Additionally, augmenting consumer spending through an active fiscal policy and a prudent monetary policy. Offering support to small and medium enterprises (SMEs) through active fiscal and prudent monetary measures remains pivotal. Only by preserving employment opportunities and ensuring the stability of market entities can we drive consumption and stimulate domestic demand.

How do we alleviate the difficulties faced by businesses? Directly providing monetary assistance may not be the most effective approach. For example, distributing RMB 100 to each of the 1.4 billion people may have negligible impact on the wealthy, while the less affluent are more likely to save this amount for future needs rather than spend. Therefore, to bolster consumption, issuing consumption vouchers proves to be a more effective strategy. Rather than solely subsidizing consumers, prioritizing support for producers yields greater efficacy. Safeguarding SMEs prevents job losses. If these enterprises can weather the challenging period, both businesses and the economy will gradually recover vitality. Over the past two years, there has been consistent emphasis on a prudent monetary policy, aimed at providing relief for businesses.

Since 2020, the People's Bank of China has consistently emphasized a strategy of "more flexible, moderate, and targeted prudent monetary

[2] Stabilizing the Six Fronts refer to stabilizing various aspects including employment, finance, foreign trade, foreign investment, domestic investment, and expectations.

policy" in its reports. To sustain a reasonable growth in the money supply chain and the scale of social financing, the central bank may increase certain aspects of the money supply, but overall expansion will remain moderate. The concept of "reasonable scale growth" indicates a measured expansion, implying that the Chinese government will refrain from excessive easing measures. Concurrently, the United States has pursued easing policies, leading to the devaluation of the dollar and consequently, the appreciation of the renminbi.

It is imperative for monetary policy to be precisely targeted, meaning not a deluge of strong stimulus policies. We should strike a balance between overall quantity and structural considerations, focusing on supporting vulnerable sectors and key enterprises, such as those in the hospitality, tourism, and catering industries severely impacted by the pandemic. Previously, large banks primarily extended loans to small and medium-sized banks, which, in turn, provided funding to micro and small enterprises. However, there is now a specific emphasis on large banks directly extending loans to these smaller enterprises.

Furthermore, an active fiscal policy involves tax and fee reductions, with the government assuming responsibility for covering the costs, thereby continually increasing the proportion of disposable income. To stimulate domestic demand, it is essential to progressively enhance the proportion of residents' disposable income relative to total income. For instance, if an individual's pre-tax salary amounts to RMB 10,000 and the post-tax income is RMB 5000, the individual with limited disposable income would lack the capacity to effectively drive domestic demand. To encourage consumer spending, they must first have the means to do so.

Fiscal policy revolves around three key aspects: the revenue sources, the available financial resources, and the allocation thereof. For example, in 2020, China had RMB 30 trillion in available fiscal funds, with a portion earmarked for direct allocation at the local county-level grassroots, a notion holding particular significance. Essentially, funds disbursed from the central government bypass provincial and municipal levels, proceeding directly to the county level. The approach in 2021 has emphasized "local direct allocation," with a predominant focus on "two new and one major" areas, referring to launching new infrastructure and new urbanization initiatives as well as major transportation and water conservancy projects.

The concept of "new" in new infrastructure marks a departure from conventional infrastructure, where supply determines demand, to a paradigm where demand dictates supply. Conventional infrastructure operates under the premise of "building roads before becoming wealthy," implying that goods can only be sold if roads reach villages, thereby generating demand through supply. In contrast, new infrastructure takes an opposite approach by deploying high-voltage lines, charging stations, 5G, and AI technologies in densely populated areas, illustrating how demand influences supply. In 2021, China underscored new energy vehicles as a significant industry, and in 2022, it included another forward-looking sector—charging stations. Presently, the government mandates a 1:1 ratio of electric vehicles to charging stations. Approximately 60 million electric vehicles are currently on the roads in China, highlighting a substantial market for charging infrastructure.

To bolster China's economic external circulation, several strategies can be pursued:

Firstly, we should sustain a focus on exports. Enterprises should not solely concentrate on established markets like Europe and the United States but should also explore diverse export destinations, particularly in Southeast Asian countries.

Secondly, we should expand import volumes. From the Canton Fair to the China International Import Expo, it is evident that expanding imports has become a national strategy. China's imports primarily encompass three categories: consumer goods enhancing well-being, automotive products prompting industry innovation, and service trade products where China lags in development.

What is service trade? For instance, from a national perspective, despite being a small transaction, buying a ticket from United Airlines to fly to the United States constitutes buying a service from the United States. While China maintains a significant surplus in goods trade, it faces a deficit in service trade. Encouraging imports in service trade can facilitate the promotion of diversified reforms within the country.

The service trade develops in the direction of "expanding volume, adjusting structure, and building distinct characteristics." Expanding volume is crucial due to the relatively low total volume of service trade in China. Adjusting the structure is necessary because in sectors such as education, transportation, and tourism, China experiences a reverse flow of output. Each year, many Chinese students pursue studies abroad in English-speaking countries; however, the influx of students to China remains relatively low, calling for structural adjustments. Cultivating distinctive characteristics entails establishing unique attributes within China's service trade. For example, while South Korea boasts a flourishing cosmetics industry, can China similarly develop its traditional Chinese medicine sector and promote its distinctive offerings on a global scale?

Thirdly, there is a need to prioritize the development of digital trade. What exactly is digital trade? It encompasses various activities, from Chinese engineers writing code for overseas enterprises to the establishment of platforms like Alibaba Cloud, Huawei Cloud, and others. Digital trade assumes an increasingly pivotal role in today's economy, characterized by the cross-border provision of digital services.

Fourthly, it is crucial to promote the dual approach of "Going Local" alongside "Going Global" for Chinese enterprises. Currently, Chinese enterprises lead globally in terms of going global. I suggest that Chinese companies not only broaden their global footprint but also invest in local markets. At times, when Chinese companies venture abroad, they encounter vilification fueled by anti-China sentiments. In my opinion, while Chinese companies have done many good deeds, they should also shoulder social responsibilities to counter prevailing biases against China. For example, Yutong Bus invested in Mauritius and contributed to the construction of numerous local bus shelters, garnering a positive reputation.

Fifth, it is necessary to prioritize differentiated development within the Belt and Road Initiative (BRI). It is my belief that China should prioritize the development of the Maritime Silk Road over allocating equal attention to all facets of the BRI. The recent conflict between Russia and Ukraine starkly underscores the geopolitical intricacies, uncertainties, and substantial risks inherent in the land-based Silk Road. China has established robust economic ties with countries along the Maritime Silk Road, which has been further bolstered by the recent signing of the RCEP agreement. Therefore, emphasis should be placed on advancing the Maritime Silk Road.

Finally, we should strengthen regional economic and trade collaboration. The ratification of the RCEP is a significant stride forward and serves as an excellent platform. For China, the subsequent endeavor should involve extending invitations to Japan to participate in the agreement.

Following the signing of the RCEP, China faces the decision of prioritizing either the EU–China Comprehensive Agreement on Investment (CAI) or the CPTPP. I argue that priority should be given to the former. The CAI entails China's commitment to opening up its maritime, medical, and state-owned industries to the European Union, while the European Union reciprocates by facilitating renewable energy investments from China. Initially progressing smoothly, the CAI implementation has encountered setbacks, partly due to political considerations. Realizing that the United States makes promises it cannot keep, strategically, the European Union is inclined toward a policy of "signaling left yet turning right," wherein it aligns politically with the United States while shifting economically toward the Chinese market. Unlike the United States, the Chinese market holds substantial importance for the European Union. The successful signing of the CAI would entail China opening up its manufacturing, maritime, and financial sectors while gaining access to the European Union's new energy market. This arrangement is mutually beneficial for both parties involved.

What is the difference between CPTPP and RCEP? Generally speaking, CPTPP adopts a "one-size-fits-all" approach, imposing high standards uniformly across participating countries, regardless of their developmental stage. In contrast, RCEP offers more flexibility, allowing for exceptions tailored to each country's level of development. While China has signaled its intent to seek membership in the CPTPP, I believe that the current situation presents significant challenges for accession. Joining the CPTPP requires unanimous approval from all 11 member states. At present, Australia's opposition is evident, while Japan's stance remains somewhat neutral. Furthermore, China diverges greatly from CPTPP member states on issues pertaining to the environment, labor standards, and the role of SOEs. Given Japan's pivotal role within the CPTPP, it may prove advantageous for China to first pursue a bilateral free trade agreement with Japan and South Korea, as such an arrangement could serve as a precursor to potential agreements with other countries.

Despite grappling with unprecedented changes unseen within a century and enduring the profound impacts of a once-in-a-century pandemic, China has transitioned into a new phase of economic development. I firmly hold that by steadfastly adhering to the Five Major Development Concepts of innovation, green development, coordination, sharing, and openness, and harnessing the dual circulation model as a driver to construct our new development paradigm, we can assuredly attain a brighter tomorrow.

The Three Circulations Within the Chinese Economy

Gao Xu

Apart from the ongoing discourse surrounding internal and external circulations, I believe there exists a third circulation within the Chinese economy. I would like to offer a unique perspective on this matter, diverging slightly from the mainstream market viewpoint.

There is a notable disparity between many economic theories found in textbooks and real-world scenarios, akin to a plug failing to fit into a socket. This disparity between theory and reality predominantly stems from inherent deficiencies within the theories themselves. Consequently, I have progressively examined the Chinese economy through a dual-perspective approach, taking into account both theoretical frameworks and practical realities.

This article is derived from a speech delivered by the author at the inauguration ceremony of the Chengze Garden at the National School of Development at Peking University and the Institute of South-South Cooperation and Development on September 19, 2021. The speech took place within the framework of the sub-forum titled "Macroeconomics and Financial Markets in the New Development Landscape."

G. Xu (✉)
BOC International (China) Co., LTD, Shanghai, China

National School of Development, Peking University, Beijing, China

W. Xianqing (ed.), *Understanding China's Path to Modernization*,
https://doi.org/10.1007/978-981-96-7051-2_6

Understanding China's Economy from Two Perspectives: "Water" and "Rocks"

The dual perspective can be characterized using the metaphors of "water" and "rocks." "Water" represents the fluidity of the market economy, capable of adapting to changing conditions. However, the operation of a market economy is heavily influenced by the constraints and boundary conditions it faces, analogous to "rocks," which are often imposed by non-market factors. Especially in a transitional economy like China, many "rocks" from planned economy still impede the free flow of the market economy.

In this context, it would be insufficient to understand China's economy by solely relying on the principles of a market economy. Western countries have had extensive experience with market economies; they have gradually overcome obstacles, allowing them to understand economic dynamics through concepts such as "fluid dynamics," essentially constituting Western economic theories. However, in the Chinese market economy, numerous "rocks" persist, hindering the smooth progression of the economic river. An understanding based solely on Western economic theories is, thus, inadequate. To gain a comprehensive understanding of the Chinese economy, it is imperative to incorporate both the "water" and "rocks" perspectives.

In the discourse surrounding internal and external circulation, the crux of the matter lies predominantly within the former. The Chinese economy is fundamentally structured around the internal cycle of the market economy, encompassing production, income generation, and demand. Currently, the smooth functioning of internal circulation is impeded by insufficient demand. While the Chinese economy heavily relies on external circulation to propel growth, a weakened external circulation could result in economic challenges. Over the past 20 years, external circulation has dictated the major cycles of the Chinese economy. Following the outbreak of the COVID-19 pandemic, China's external circulation experienced improvement owing to stimuli from European and American demand. However, domestic demand faced excessive cooling due to the effects of poorly managed macroeconomic policies.

Disparity Between Western Economic Theories and China's Realities

Macroeconomic principles are typically described using three equations.

The first equation, $Y = F(K, L)$, delineates the production function. This equation illustrates how output is generated by combining capital and labor, thereby indicating the distribution of output between capital and labor.

The second equation is the capital accumulation equation, underscoring the process by which capital is accumulated through investment, accounting for capital depreciation.

The third equation, $Y = C + I + G + NX$, encapsulates output utilization. For example, GDP is equivalent to the sum of consumption, investment, and government expenditure.

It is worth noting that while the first two equations pertain to the production side (supply side), the first addresses a natural science issue, and the second is a simple dynamic equation, both of which have limited economic implications. Conversely, the third equation pertains to the demand side and encompasses primary economic theories, making it the most significant among the three equations.

The equal sign in the third equation summarizes a wealth of understanding, serving as both an accounting identity and a reflection of market equilibrium. On the left of the equation, we find output (Y), while on the right, we have the various uses of output, which are the total demand (domestic demand + international demand). As output (Y) converts into income for individuals, businesses, and the government (driven by factors of production, particularly capital), the shift from the left side to the right side of the equation represents an income distribution process involving primary and secondary distribution. Once individuals receive their income, they are confronted with decisions regarding the allocation of funds between consumption and savings. Therefore, the equal sign in the third equation hides the intricate processes of income distribution and the decision-making involved in consumption and savings allocation.

Furthermore, upon deeper examination of the third equation, it reveals two underlying assumptions rooted in Western economic theory. Firstly, it presupposes that the total output in the economy represents the initial income of individuals, implying individual ownership of capital. Secondly, it assumes that investment is sensitive to the rate of return on capital since all output is acquired by individuals. Investment carries an opportunity cost for individuals, increasing when interest rates are high and decreasing when they are low.

However, these two assumptions do not hold true in the current reality of China's economy.

In the context of the Chinese economy, only a portion of the total social income is allocated to household earnings. A substantial share of this income flows toward the broader governmental sector, encompassing SOEs and remains largely disconnected from the daily lives of citizens. Moreover, within the funds directed to the expansive government sector, a significant portion—post deduction for government consumption—transforms into investments in a relatively inflexible manner. With government investments exhibiting a lack of opportunity costs, there exists a rigidity in terms of returns or interest rates, facilitating sustained investment even in scenarios with low-return rates.

The disparity between Western macroeconomic theories and China's realities poses challenges in applying conclusions derived from these theories to the intricacies of China's economic framework.

As per China's third economic census, SOEs hold a majority stake of 54% in the corporate asset domain, while foreign-owned enterprises and enterprises from China's Hong Kong, Macao, and Taiwan regions hold 10%, and other domestic firms make up the remaining 36%. This statistic indicates that the average citizens possess just over one-third of corporate assets. Furthermore, the distribution of these corporate assets among residents reflects notable inequality; prominent business figures hold a significant number of corporate shares, whereas the average citizen's holdings are comparatively meager. Consequently, the connection between the corporate sector and individual wealth in China appears significantly fragmented.

Looking at international comparative data, it is commonly observed that there is a negative correlation between the savings of residents and businesses, a phenomenon often termed "piercing the corporate veil" in macroeconomics. This implies that businesses are regarded as a separate layer from the residential sector, with minimal influence on residents' decisions on spending or saving. In countries with privately owned enterprises, the income generated by these businesses ultimately contributes to residents' wealth through their shareholdings. Therefore, the direction of income flows between residents and businesses becomes less crucial; when business profits and savings increase, residents tend to see growth in their wealth, which leads to heightened spending and reduced savings. Hence, there is generally an inverse correlation between the savings of residents and businesses worldwide.

In China, both business and resident savings are substantial, yet the negative correlation between them is less evident. This phenomenon arises from the ownership structure of SOEs, which severs the wealth connection between the corporate and residential sectors. This means that people do not necessarily increase consumption or reduce savings based on the profits generated by SOEs in a given year, a distinctive feature characterizing the Chinese economy.

China's investments exhibit limited responsiveness to interest rates while being substantial in scale. Looking back at the first two equations, increased investments result in accelerated capital accumulation, increased capital stock, and increased output. However, this disparity between output and demand engenders a long-term challenge of insufficient demand.

Aligned with prevailing tenets of Western mainstream neoclassical economics, economies are expected to operate in the vicinity of their potential output levels (production capacities) over the long haul. While economic activities may temporarily deviate from this level due to various shocks, such discrepancies are considered transitory. In cases where the economy operates below its potential output level, short-term macroeconomic policies can be deployed to stimulate growth. Conversely, measures can be implemented to temper the economy when it exceeds its potential output level. Nonetheless, the sustained application of stimulative macroeconomic policies is deemed unsustainable, as it is assumed that economies cannot persistently function below their potential output levels. This forms a fundamental premise in Western economic theory.

China's economic landscape is characterized by an overabundance of savings and insufficient consumption, leading to surplus production and excess capacity. Therefore, China's economy operates below its potential output level over the long term. Even during fluctuations, the economy predominantly remains below its potential output level.

I concur with the notion that China has the potential to achieve long-term GDP growth of 8%; however, the realization of this potential hinges on the presence of adequate market demand. In instances where the Chinese economy operates long term with insufficient demand, the operational dynamics deviates from those outlined by mainstream Western economics. In such scenarios, I find Keynes' argument more plausible:

when demand falls short, bolstering it can improve economic conditions. At such times, both external demand and domestic macroeconomic stimulus policies demonstrate a multiplier effect.

In reality, the dynamics of the Chinese economy indeed show a multiplier effect. Domestic savings in China serve two primary purposes: investment and current account surplus by lending to foreigners. A distinct negative correlation exists between the current account surplus and investment in ASEAN and EU countries, suggesting that these economies operate under constraints where increased investments lead to reduced current account surpluses, potentially leading to deficits. In contrast to ASEAN and the European Union, China exhibits a positive correlation between its current account surplus and investment, showing a positive feedback loop in its economic operation. In China, heightened investments lead to increased savings and a larger current account surplus, implying that investments in China primarily contribute to increasing savings, highlighting the insufficiency of demand in the Chinese economy.

For the Chinese economy, external demand transcends the simple exchange of an item worth 1 dollar for another item of equal value; it involves generating additional domestic demand through that 1 dollar. This, in turn, improves the economy, stimulates savings, and spurs investments. It is evident that the overall operational dynamics of the Chinese economy diverge significantly from the principles advocated by mainstream Western economics.

To Overcome Its Challenges, the Chinese Economy Needs a Third Circulation

Following the COVID-19 pandemic, I proposed the concept of "re-circulation." The pandemic spurred a phenomenon of "complementary recovery" between China and the United States, wherein China saw a swift output rebound, paralleled by a swift recovery in the U.S. demand.

In response to the pandemic's repercussions, the United States initiated substantial fiscal and monetary stimulus measures. After the pandemic, China exhibited a more robust recovery in industrial output compared to the United States, attributed to its effective containment efforts. However, the United States witnessed a stronger resurgence in retail sales due to its proactive stimulus policies. Ultimately, through consumption incentives, the United States generated significant external demand for Chinese goods. Leveraging its surplus production capacity from pre-pandemic times, China notably increased exports to the United States, resulting in a simultaneous expansion of China's trade surplus and the United States' trade deficit, reminiscent of the situation prior to the subprime crisis.

From early 2021 onward, Chinese exports have transitioned into a growth phase. Despite challenges posed by soaring container shipping rates, China's post-pandemic economy finds itself in a more favorable position, buoyed by external demand.

Then, why is the economy once again experiencing significant downward pressure? In the first half of 2021, although there was not an urgent need for domestic monetary policy changes, fiscal austerity measures were remarkably stringent, reaching an intensity unseen since the turn of the twenty-first century—surpassing even the intensity observed since the RMB 4 trillion market bailout in 2008. Furthermore, deficits in land finance, government fund budgets, informal local government financing, and local government special bonds have all markedly contracted. The fiscal contraction during this period accounted for 7% to 8% of the GDP during the same period.

As a result of the impact of tight domestic macroeconomic policies, the three major investments within China are currently operating at subdued levels. Manufacturing investment, infrastructure spending, and real estate development had all experienced a significant decline by July 2021. Coupled with several consecutive months of declining total retail sales for consumer goods, China's economy is facing notable downward risks.

When analyzing the rationales behind the tightened domestic macroeconomic policies, most Chinese analysts, including policymakers, continue to rely on Western theories, believing that China's economic growth model led by infrastructure investment is unsustainable. However, I maintain that this interpretation of the Chinese economy is flawed.

Looking ahead, I hold an optimistic outlook on the future trends of the economy. The meeting convened by the Political Bureau of the Communist Party of China Central Committee on July 30, 2021, has clearly signaled a policy shift. Statements such as "reasonably manage the progress of budgeted investments and local government bond issuance to drive the completion of tangible work by the end of this year or early next year" and "correct the rush for 'carbon reduction,' establishing the new before abolishing the old." However, we must remain vigilant in monitoring the intensity of forthcoming policies.

Both internal circulation and external circulation are crucial for the Chinese economy. When the internal flow from income to demand encounters obstacles, China's reliance on external circulation will persist for a considerable period. In short, taking a long-term economic perspective, the performance of the Chinese economy is influenced by both external demand and domestic macroeconomic policies.

To overcome the current challenges, the key lies in expanding domestic demand through enhancing the third circulation. Specifically, through reforms in income distribution and the cultivation of an income cycle between enterprises and residents, particularly between SOEs and individuals, we can elevate household income and consumption.

Only when a greater portion of income flows into the household sector, translating into increased consumer income and spending, can the internal circulation of the Chinese economy attain robustness. This shift would diminish reliance on external demand and domestic stimulus policies, allowing the Chinese economy to transition toward a more internally driven and sustainable growth trajectory. Therefore, optimizing all three circulation is imperative to achieve progress.

Chinese Path to Modernization and Common Prosperity

The Essence and Focus of Common Prosperity

Yang Yao

How To Define Common Prosperity

Since the introduction of the concept of "common prosperity" in 2021, there have been various interpretations. Some radical perspectives circulating online even suggest a return to the nationalization policies from 1956. Such opinions have engendered significant societal confusion, particularly among entrepreneurs. It is evident that such statements clearly do not align with the principles espoused by our Party and government.

Alternatively, another perspective suggests that common prosperity should prioritize the expansion of the economic pie, as we have done over the past 40 years of reform and opening-up, to benefit everyone.

This article is derived from the keynote speech at the Economic Cooperation Symposium for the Celebration of the 25th Anniversary of the Establishment of the Government of Hong Kong Special Administrative Region on May 25, 2022.

Y. Yao (✉)
National School of Development, Peking University, Beijing, China

Beijing International MBA, Peking University, Beijing, China

Institute of South-South Cooperation and Development, Peking University, Beijing, China

W. Xianqing (ed.), *Understanding China's Path to Modernization*, https://doi.org/10.1007/978-981-96-7051-2_7

However, with the introduction of the concept of common prosperity, I believe the focus extends beyond mere pie expansion to include equitable distribution.

One other perspective posits that common prosperity means strengthening the middle-class cohort, a viewpoint that appears rather rational and resonates well with the middle class. However, the crux of the matter lies in the persistent challenge wherein despite the expansion of the middle class, a significant number of people invariably experiences income growth that lags behind economic expansion.

In my view, the true essence of common prosperity should be to ensure that all citizens enjoy the benefits of economic growth equitably.

Now, what does "equitably" mean? Different political ideologies offer varying interpretations. Personally, I believe that the goal should be to minimize income disparities and enhance equal opportunities across the populace to the greatest extent possible. This is closely aligned with the ethos of our socialist country and is inherent in the communist ideals put forth by Marx and Engels. By ensuring that all citizens enjoy the benefits of economic growth in a fundamentally equitable manner, the outcome would be that people can increase their incomes at a relatively similar pace. It is important to note that immediate attainment of income equality, however, would likely dampen people's motivation.

Income and Wealth Distribution Pattern in China

As seen from foundational aspects, attention should be directed toward the low-income stratum, given their income growth trails behind the societal average.

On the left side of Fig. 1 is the income and wealth distribution pattern in China in 2016, drawn from the Peking University China Family Panel Studies (CFPS), of which I am a co-founder. The survey is conducted every two years. Although figures for 2018 and 2020 exhibited slight changes, the distribution pattern remains largely the same. The data reveals that the annual income of the lowest 10% of households amounts to merely RMB 2,217, with nearly half of households earning less than RMB 34,000 annually. Correspondingly, the bottom 50% of the population holds only 17% of aggregate income, whereas the lowest 10% accounts for a meager 0.5% of aggregate income.

It is also from Fig. 1 that there is a substantial disparity in wealth distribution. The average wealth of the top 10% of households is approximately

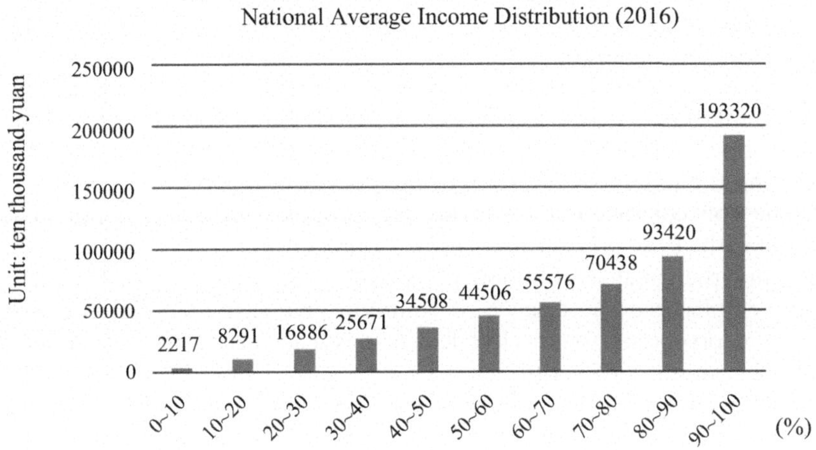

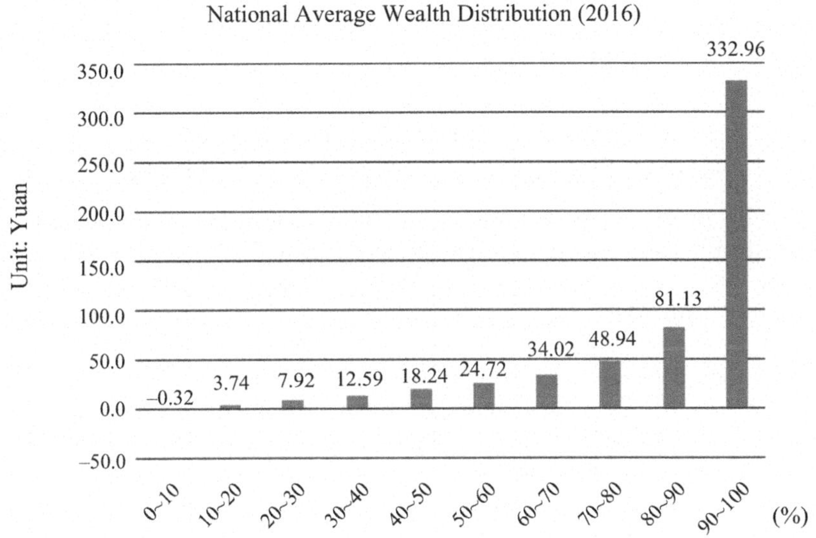

Fig. 1 Income and wealth distribution pattern in China (*Data source* 2016 China family panel studies [CFPS])

RMB 3.33 million, while the lowest 10% of households are in debt and have negative net assets.

Therefore, China's income and wealth distribution patterns exhibit significant disparity, primarily due to the starkly low incomes of 50% of the population. This is why I stress the significance of directing efforts toward uplifting the low-income groups in the pursuit of common prosperity.

The concept of common prosperity, proposed in 2021, is not new. In the early 1980s, Deng Xiaoping encouraged some people to get rich first and then realize common prosperity. The latter part of his statement emphasized the essence of common prosperity, highlighting that allowing prosperity for a select few first is a means to the overarching goal of common prosperity.

The GDP per capita in China was USD 12,684 in 2023. Barring unforeseen circumstances, we should be able to achieve the World Bank's threshold for high-income countries, set at USD 12,600, within the forthcoming two to three years. Against this backdrop, we cannot afford to further widen our income gap.

Common Prosperity: The Enduring Ideal Pursued by the Chinese People

Common prosperity is not only a goal of socialism but also one of the ideals deeply rooted in traditional Chinese culture.

The definition of common prosperity, as a goal of socialism, can be glimpsed from Marx and Engels' vision for a classless society, as articulated in the *Manifesto of the Communist Party*, in which "the free development of each is the condition for the free development of all." In other words, the free and comprehensive development of every member of society should be the most fundamental goal pursued by socialism.

The concept of "freedom" is philosophical, encompassing two essential dimensions, both of which are indispensable. In addition to freedom from poverty and fear, as proposed by former U.S. President Franklin Roosevelt, freedom is also the notion of being "able to" take specific actions. One of the core differences between socialism and capitalism lies in socialism's emphasis not only on individual's freedom from constraints but also on their capability to pursue particular endeavors.

Meanwhile, "comprehensive development" is to realize one's full potential. As Marx and Engels envisioned in the *Manifesto of the Communist Party*, in such a societal construct, everyone could seamlessly switch between various roles—working as a fisherman in the morning, a farmer in the forenoon, a worker in the afternoon, and becoming a philosopher in the evening—affording every individual the opportunity to achieve comprehensive development.

I believe that such a conviction—such an aspiration for the society in the future, is something no one would refuse.

The goals of socialism are consistent with the bedrock principles of Confucianism and Chinese culture. While many believe that Confucianism undermines innate human nature, I strongly disagree. Confucianism, particularly in its Pre-Qin era, highly values the intrinsic worth of each individual. Mencius believed that "all humans have four innate seeds of virtues,[1]" asserting that everyone is born with equal potential and possesses the capacity to achieve saintliness and wisdom. The Confucian school of thought further emphasizes the crucial role of personal cultivation and societal milieu in determining the extent of individual attainment. One important difference between our cultural perspective and that of other religious countries lies in our recognition of the awards accorded to personal cultivation, according to which, those who exhibit virtuous conduct and make significant contributions merit commensurate recognition and rewards. In this regard, early Confucian principles align with Marx and Engels' idea of fostering the freedom and comprehensive development of every individual.

There are two seemingly contradictory yet reconcilable aspects within traditional Chinese cultural values.

At the micro level, Chinese society upholds the principles of meritocracy, asserting that intellectually adept and capable individuals who contribute significantly to society merit material rewards. This social recognition and wealth correspond directly to their societal contributions, aligning with Aristotle's principle of proportionality. Therefore, Chinese society holds an affirmative view toward the wealth acquired through individual efforts, with prominent entrepreneurs serving as heroes and role models for the younger generation. This contrasts with Europe, the birthplace of marketization, where entrepreneurial figures may not necessarily be idolized by youth. However, following the proposed pursuit

[1] Mencius posited that all humans have four innate seeds of virtues: the heart of commiseration, the heart of shame and dislike, the heart of deference and compliance, and the heart of right and wrong.

of common prosperity in 2021, concerns and opposition have arisen surrounding the prospect of "re-nationalization" as a result of such a goal.

At the macro level, Chinese society, like many other cultures, faces the issue of inequality. Amartya Sen, esteemed Indian economist and philosopher, Nobel laureate in Economics, states that all cultures aspire for equality, albeit with varying emphases on different aspects thereof.

This creates a tension: while the micro level advocates for merit-based rewards, the macro level demands greater societal equality. Resolving this tension requires investment in the potential of each individual and ensuring equitable access to opportunities for all, through which people can leverage their strengths, ultimately achieving equality and realizing the ideal of common prosperity.

Improving Individual Abilities

How, then, can we enhance individual abilities?

Historically, rural entrepreneurs could thrive without much formal education; but this paradigm has shifted, and education has emerged as the utmost priority in today's society. China now finds itself in the era of "intellectual entrepreneur," where educational attainment holds paramount importance.

Currently, higher education in China has achieved widespread accessibility, boasting a gross enrollment ratio of 55% for higher education. Individuals aged 18 to 22 enrolled in educational institutions account for 55% of the corresponding population. Our calculation indicates an annual enrollment rate exceeding 70% among high school graduates in recent years, meaning that 70% of youth have been admitted by universities.

However, we have observed that a significant portion of non-college-bound youth hails from rural regions. Many of them may not even complete high school, opting instead for vocational or technical education. Our research indicates that the predominant outcome for youth attending such institutions is perpetuation within low-income occupations and sectors. Alarmingly, vocational education in reality often acts as a mechanism reinforcing social stratification, with an overwhelming 90% of attendees originating from rural backgrounds.

Figure 2 shows the distribution of educational attainment among individuals born between 1930 and 1985. Encouragingly, the percentage of individuals holding university degrees has increased from nearly negligible levels in 1930 to 20% among those born in 1985. Regrettably, within the cohort born in 1985, not even reaching 40 years old, 8% did not complete primary education, while 70% only finished their education at the junior high school level. Although recent years have witnessed some improvement, the extent of progress remains modest.

In the face of such a pronounced educational gap, it becomes markedly challenging to achieve common prosperity. Many studies have found that the phase wherein the return on educational investment increases most steeply is at the high school and college levels. Completing junior high school education satisfies the demands of low-skilled employment, a sector undergoing diminution due to technological advancements and expected to be replaced by automation and artificial intelligence. Therefore, to establish oneself in Chinese society's future landscape, having at least a high school or college-level education becomes imperative.

Against this backdrop, equalizing educational resources emerges as a paramount objective. On May 1, 2022, China enacted the new Vocational Education Law, featuring a provision stipulating that "Vocational education is a type of education as important as general education." This means that junior high school graduates are no longer forced to choose

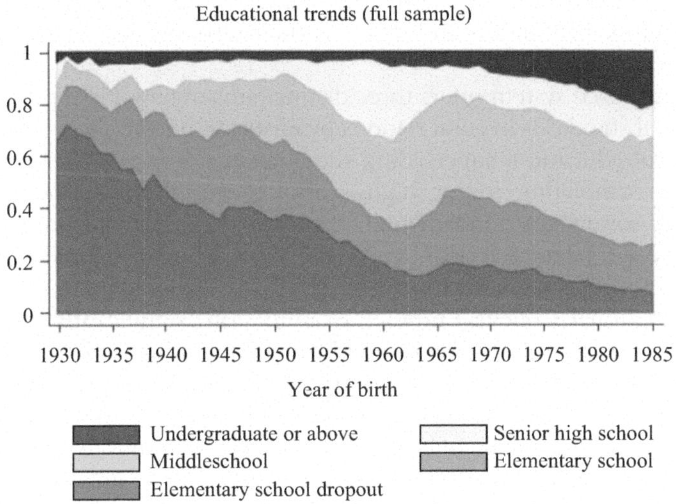

Fig. 2 Evolution of educational level composition in China (Population born between 1930 and 1985) (*Data source* 2016 China family panel studies [CFPS])

between regular high schools and secondary vocational schools, a crucial step in line with scholars' advocacy, including mine, over the past year.

However, this measure remains insufficient; I believe an optimal solution would be the establishment of a continuous compulsory education system spanning ten years. Transitioning the current nine-year compulsory education model into a ten-year model encompassing elementary through high school levels would eliminate the need for stress-inducing transitional examinations, such as *zhongkao* (Senior High School Entrance Examination), ensuring access to ten years of education for all. Students start primary school at age 7, with the option of one year of preschool before, and graduate high school at 17, with the option of another year of university preparatory courses depending on their chosen university majors. Upon graduation, these soon-to-be young adults can further their education based on individual preferences, including pursuit of bachelor's or associate degrees, vocational training (including technical schools), or entry into the workforce.

The prevailing practice of streamlining youth following junior high school graduation, at an age when they are not yet mature enough, causes distress among both youth and their parents. However, by 17, when they complete high school, the youth would likely become more mature and better equipped to understand that it is their responsibility to shape their own futures.

This proposed system offers three distinct advantages. Firstly, it elevates educational standards in rural regions by ensuring universal completion of high school education, superseding the current norm of entering society after just completing junior high school. Secondly, it reorients basic education toward its fundamental purpose of talent cultivation rather than exclusive talent selection, a pivotal shift. Thirdly, it holds promise in partially mitigating educational anxieties. At present, the stress of the *gaokao* (National College Entrance Examination) significantly influences the anxiety surrounding *zhongkao*. Given that graduation from general high school essentially secures university admission, parents often push their children toward attending general high schools over vocational alternatives. The implementation of a ten-year continuous compulsory education system could substantially ease this anxiety and would prove profoundly beneficial for China's future as it fosters holistic learning experiences that extend beyond mere rote memorization and question–answer paradigms. Economic research requires a broad skill set, yet I have observed that many students lack this kind of versatility, proficient in problem-solving but deficient in theoretical innovation. A nurturing educational environment from an early age could greatly improve overall competencies.

The government currently encourages collaboration between enterprises and vocational-technical colleges, although the practical outcomes have not been ideal. From my investigation of technical universities in Germany, I have noticed that each institution typically receives support from two or three major companies. These companies establish laboratories directly within the universities, creating a synergy where companies save on certain research and development costs, while educators and students can engage in part-time work or internships within these corporate environments. In turn, universities gain valuable technical expertise, faculty, and equipment resources. Therefore, governmental support in the form of tax incentives and other benefits is essential for encouraging large companies to engage in partnerships with vocational colleges and technical universities.

Optimizing the Basic Economic System

Expanding upon this premise, China's basic economic system should prioritize building a society that harmonizes efficiency with equity.

The primary distribution should adhere to the market principle of factor allocation, one of the key lessons gleaned from the past four decades of reform and opening-up. This approach has been instrumental in facilitating our current achievements by effectively incentivizing individual productivity. The previous idea of pitting factor allocation against labor distribution was misguided; in reality, labor distribution is included within factor allocation. Reflecting Marx's labor theory of value, capital is fundamentally a product of labor accumulation, even though this connection may seem inconspicuous due to the extended periods for accumulation. Therefore, the returns gained by capital ultimately derive from labor. Upholding this principle is paramount, serving as the fundamental guarantee for enhancing efficiency and fostering economic expansion.

Meanwhile, secondary distribution involves redistribution, aligning with socialist goals by investing in the development of each individual's capacities, including education, training, basic welfare, and other essential aspects.

The concept of "tertiary distribution," proposed in 2021, with a primary focus on fostering common prosperity, has garnered significant attention. However, this concept is unsound; the notion of tertiary distribution fundamentally lacks clarity as distribution inherently involves a subject. In this context, the subject of the primary distribution is enterprises, while the government serves as the subject of the secondary distribution. Who, then, is the subject of the tertiary distribution? Clearly, this concept is flawed. The so-called tertiary distribution, which involves enterprise donations, does not align with the essence of distribution. Entrepreneurs' donations serve to assist the underprivileged, foster cultural and artistic endeavors, and fulfill individual aspirations while voluntarily giving back to society. This voluntary act should not be categorized as distribution.

Chinese entrepreneurs have already demonstrated a significant commitment to charitable donations. In the United States, individual contributions make up 60%, whereas corporate donations constitute 40%. Conversely, in China, this proportion is reversed, indicating a notable emphasis on social responsibility among Chinese entrepreneurs. To address this, there should be concerted efforts to incentivize entrepreneur donations through mechanisms such as tax incentives and reputation-building strategies. However, it is imperative to ensure that public welfare and charitable contributions maintain their original intent of being voluntary for all individuals, rather than compulsory distributions. This distinction holds significant importance; otherwise, it risks dampening entrepreneurs' enthusiasm for wealth creation, thereby impacting the attainment of common prosperity.

Developing Private Economy Is the Foundation of Common Prosperity

Weiying Zhang

The regional disparity in China is more pronounced among rural regions rather than urban regions. The income gap within urban regions remains relatively small, suggesting that the development of private enterprises and market-driven urbanization can narrow the income gap between regions. The reduction in the per capita GDP gap we have seen is largely attributed to the increasing proportion of the urban population. A higher urban population share tends to correlate with a smaller regional gap, owing in part to the contributions of private enterprises.

The development of private enterprises is the foundation of common prosperity. These enterprises not only contribute to expanding the economic pie but also foster a more equitable distribution.

This article is based on a speech delivered by the author and Wang Bo, chief editor of *CAIJING* magazine, at the 2021 Sanya International Forum held on December 18, 2021, focusing on the theme "Private Economy and Common Prosperity."

W. Zhang (✉)
National School of Development, Peking University, Beijing, China

Center for Market and Network Economy, Peking University, Beijing, China

W. Xianqing (ed.), *Understanding China's Path to Modernization*,
https://doi.org/10.1007/978-981-96-7051-2_8

Fig. 1 China's marketization index (1997–2019) (*Data Source* National Economic Research Institute)

To illustrate, let's look at the marketization index. The National Economic Research Institute has been tracking the marketization index since 1997, with data available up to 2019. It is evident from Fig. 1 that China's degree of marketization has steadily risen over time, experiencing only three declines in 1999, 2010, and 2019. We can see that the marketization index is highly correlated with the development index of private enterprises. In fact, one sub-index of marketization directly reflects the growth of private enterprises or the non-public sector economy.

While marketization is experiencing a nationwide upsurge, there exist notable variations among regions. Generally, eastern regions exhibit the highest degree of marketization, followed by central regions, with western regions registering the lowest levels. This provides us with an opportunity to understand other issues through regional comparisons: How will the evolution of the private economy or the degree of marketization impact the income dynamics of Chinese people?

In Fig. 2, the horizontal axis represents the marketization index, while the vertical axis represents the per capita disposable income of each province, with each data point representing a specific province. It is quite evident from this figure that regions with higher levels of marketization

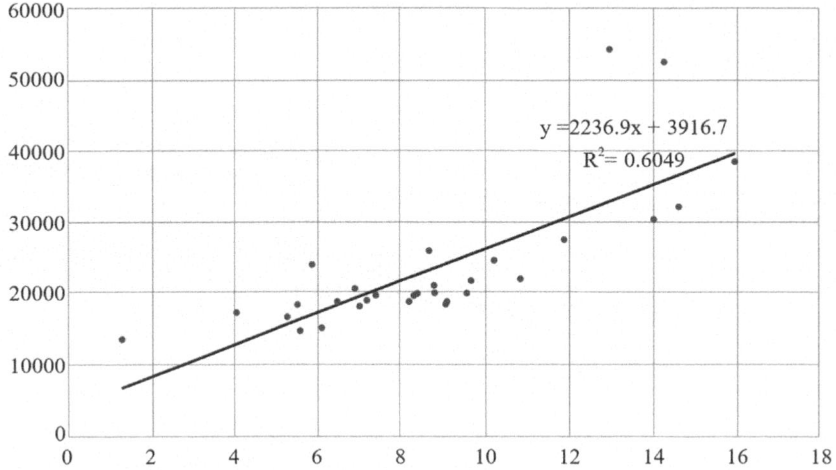

Fig. 2 Marketization and per capita disposable income (2016)

and well-established private enterprises tend to enjoy higher per capita disposable incomes. For instance, in 2016, with every one-point increase in marketization, the per capita disposable income could see an increase of RMB 2237.

Next, let us delve into an analysis of income distribution, including the correlation between profits and wages, urban–rural income gaps, inter-regional income disparities, as well as the Gini coefficient, examining the vertical flow of income.

Let's start by observing the relationship between wages and profits. In regions with more advanced private enterprise sectors and heightened levels of marketization, there tends to be a corresponding elevation in the average wages of employees within private enterprises. Using 2016 data as an example again, with every one-point increase in marketization, the average wage of private enterprise employees could see an approximate increase of RMB 1826 (Fig. 3).

We also see that in regions with higher levels of marketization, the net profit margin of assets within private enterprises is on the rise. However, these two are only moderately correlated. As a result, within regions with high marketization levels and well-established private enterprise landscapes, the proportion of wages to total revenue in private enterprises is ascending, alongside the ratio of wages to total costs, indicating that the

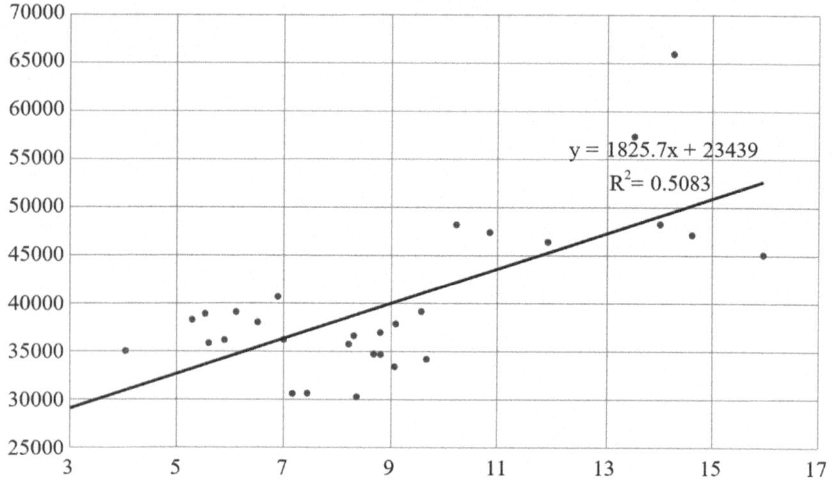

Fig. 3 Marketization index and average wage of employees in urban private enterprises (2016)

enhanced development of private enterprises is conducive to a shift in income distribution favoring the general workforce.

When examining urban–rural disparities at the national level, we can observe through the ratio of per capita disposable income between urban and rural regions, offering insights into the extent of divergence. The most pronounced urban–rural income gap was recorded in 1957, where urban per capita disposable income stood at 2.6 times that of rural regions. While this gap marginally decreased in 1978, it experienced subsequent fluctuations before gradually narrowing from 2003 onward. By 2020, the ratio of urban to rural per capita disposable income was roughly equivalent to that of 1978.

Analyzing this phenomenon at the provincial level yields significant insights. It is evident that regions with higher levels of marketization and well-established private enterprise landscapes tend to exhibit narrower urban–rural income gaps, and the development of the private economy and market-oriented reforms have helped reduce urban–rural disparities over the course of two decades.

Rural impoverishment stands as a significant concern for many. As seen in Fig. 4, regions with a more mature private economy and higher levels of marketization typically exhibit a lower proportion of rural poverty, a

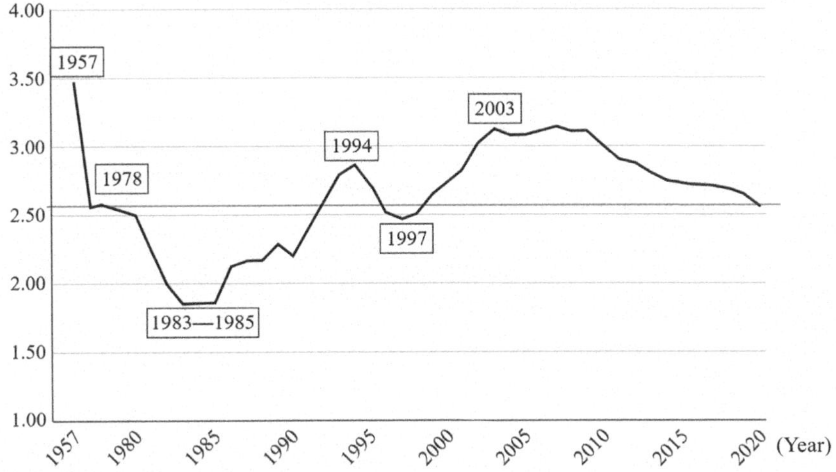

Fig. 4 Per capita disposable income (Urban/Rural)

trend observed in both 2010 and 2016. Furthermore, it is apparent that the development of the private economy and the increase in marketization levels contribute to a faster decline in poverty rates, suggesting the role of private sector development in mitigating urban–rural disparities.

Meanwhile, inter-regional income disparities refer to variations among China's 31 provinces, municipalities, and autonomous regions. Figure 5 illustrates the per capita GDP of each provincial-level administrative region from 1952 to 2019. It is clearly illustrated in Fig. 5 that, when assessing per capita GDP, regional disparities were more pronounced before the reform and opening-up era in comparison with the subsequent period.

In this analysis, I compare the per capita GDP of the province or region with the highest income to that of the lowest income province or region. Typically, Shanghai or occasionally Beijing represents the highest income regions, while Gansu Province and more commonly Guizhou Province are the lowest income regions. In 1978, Shanghai's per capita GDP was 14.2 times that of Guizhou Province; however, by 2019, this ratio had decreased to 5 times, even dipping below previous levels. Therefore, it is evident that since the beginning of the reform and opening-up era, regional disparities in terms of per capita GDP have not been widening, but rather contracting.

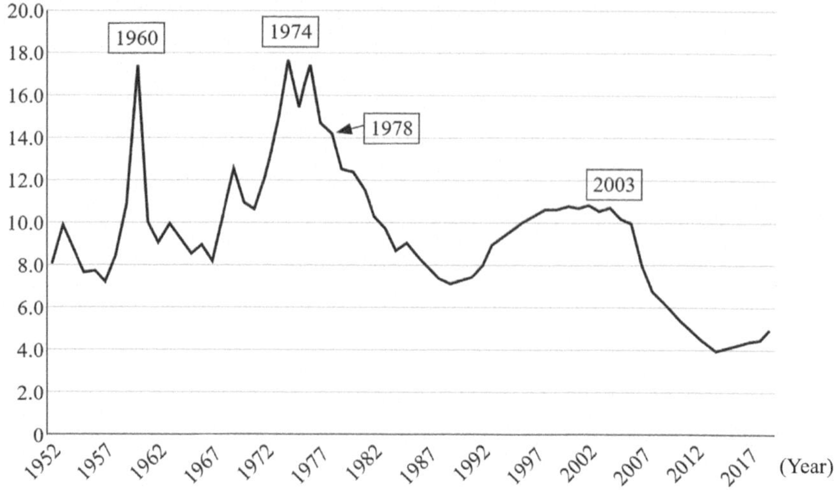

Fig. 5 Maximum/minimum GDP per capita in china's provincial-level administrative region

I have also used another metric, the coefficient of variation (Fig. 6), derived from the standard deviation of per capita GDP divided by the mean per capita GDP. A coefficient of variation at zero means uniformity across regions, while higher values indicate greater disparity. The insights gleaned from Fig. 6 aligns with our above-mentioned discussion. In 1978, the coefficient of variation for regional per capita GDP peaked, gradually declining until 1989, followed by an ascent, and subsequent descent starting from 2002, with a slight uptick evident in the past two to three years. Broadly, when measured by per capita GDP, regional disparities were more pronounced before the reform and opening-up era compared to those afterward.

There are also disparities between rural and urban regions. We observe fluctuations in the disparities of per capita disposable income among rural regions, yet a downward trend becomes evident after 1993. Similarly, urban regions show a declining trend after 1994.

The key point here lies in the regional disparity within China, primarily manifesting among rural regions rather than among urban regions. The income gap among urban regions is relatively narrow (see Fig. 7), suggesting that urbanization driven by the growth of private enterprises

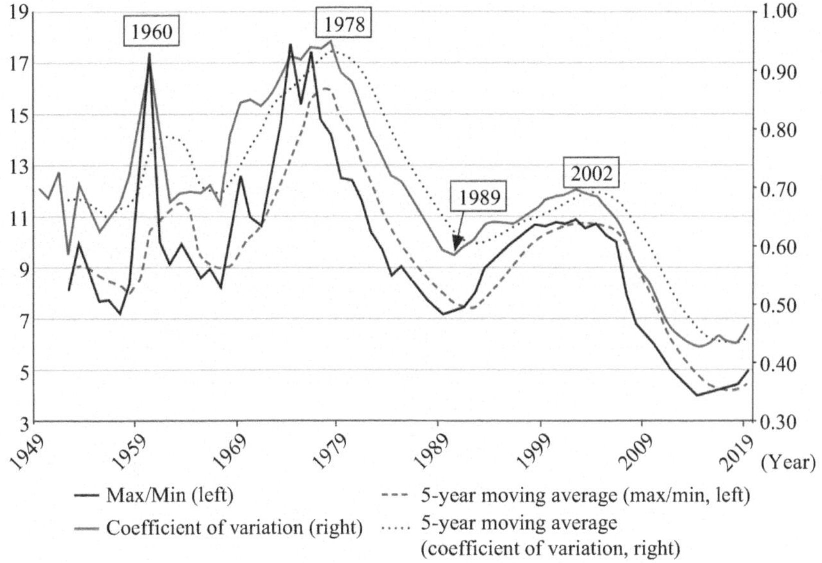

Fig. 6 Inter-regional disparities in per capita GDP: Maximum/minimum and coefficient of variation (1949–2019)

and marketization itself inherently diminishes the income gap between regions. The substantial reduction in the gap of per capita GDP we observed previously is largely tied to increase in the urban population. The higher the proportion of the urban population, the smaller the gap between regions, which, of course, is also attributed to private enterprises' contributions.

Now, shifting our focus to the Gini coefficient, utilized to measure general income inequality. The overall income inequality after the reform and opening-up, as measured by the Gini coefficient, had been widened nationwide. However, it began to decline around 2010, with a slight rebound in recent years.

Interestingly, a nuanced examination of different regions yields significant insights. Take the year 2001 for example. In Fig. 8, each data point represents a province, indicating that regions with more developed private enterprises and higher levels of marketization have narrower disparities in income distribution.

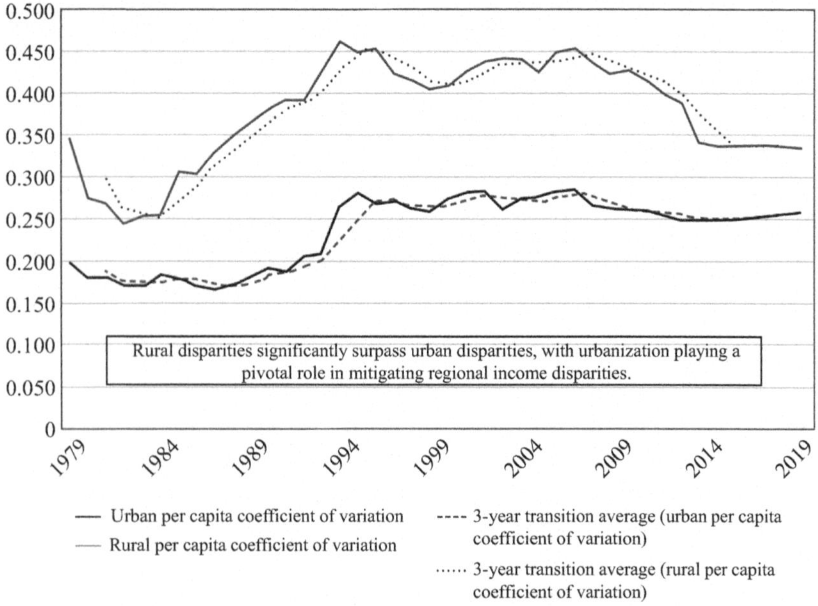

Fig. 7 Comparison of coefficients of variation between urban and rural regions

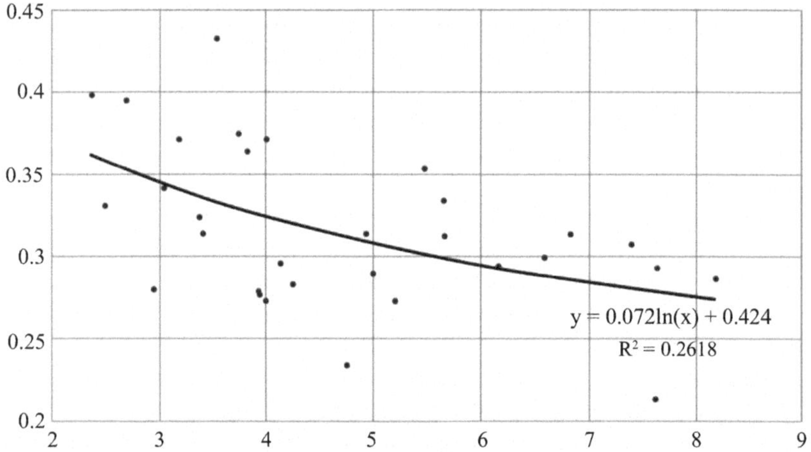

Fig. 8 Marketization and the Gini coefficient (2001)

The situation in 2013 echoes similarities with 2000, albeit with a lower correlation, evidenced by a negative coefficient, a trend further reflected in the 2017 data. Therefore, on the whole, the increase in marketization and the development of the private economy play pivotal roles in mitigating the income gap within these regions.

We also utilized another indicator, sourced from the National Bureau of Statistics, which divides per capita income into five categories, comparing the disposable income of the top 20% earners with that of the bottom 20%. It can be observed that in regions with higher marketization and a more mature private economy, the income gap, as measured by this indicator, also tends to decrease.

At the same time, there exists an intriguing phenomenon. Fiscal expenditure is, typically, presumed to facilitate redistribution, thereby decreasing income disparity. However, the situation in China has not been promising thus far. In 2001, regions with a higher proportion of fiscal expenditure to GDP tended to have a greater income gap. This trend persisted in 2013, with a notable shift occurring only by 2017, where the correlation between the proportion of government fiscal expenditure to GDP and the Gini coefficient became statistically insignificant on average within those regions. It is hoped that future endeavors will yield further improvements, ideally manifesting as regions with a higher proportion of fiscal expenditure exhibiting lower Gini coefficients.

Lastly, let's discuss income vertical mobility. In a market economy, social mobility, such as transitioning from a low-income class to a high-income class or vice versa, is of paramount importance.

China has demonstrated advancements in this domain as well. A study conducted by two Stanford University professors in 2006 reveals that only 44% of the top 20% income earners in 1990 remained in the highest income bracket after five years, while the remaining 56% dropped to other income brackets, with 5% entering the lowest income bracket. On the other hand, less than half of the bottom 20% income earners in 1990 remained in the lowest income bracket by 1995, with over half of this cohort transitioning to other income brackets, including 2.1% ascending to the highest income group.

As far as I am concerned, many of the affluent individuals featured in wealth rankings were once low-income earners, some only a decade or two ago. Analyzing the changes in rankings on the Hurun Global Rich List, it becomes evident that in 2010, only 30 out of the top 100 richest individuals remained on the list by 2020, with the other 70 no longer on it. This suggests that a considerable portion of those currently the wealthiest will likely exit this cohort in the future, a trend I hope to persist.

As Joseph Alois Schumpeter famously stated, "the upper strata of society are like hotels which are indeed always full of people, but people who are forever changing."

In summary, to achieve common prosperity, China must vigorously cultivate the private economy and persist in market-oriented reforms. Only then can we not only expand the economic pie but also foster a more rational and equitable distribution thereof. Of course, there remain many other measures to initiate, but the paramount priority lies in establishing fair competition regulations that foster wealth expansion and ensure improved and more equitable distribution throughout the growth trajectory.

Fostering China's Economic Growth Through a More Equitable Income Distribution System

Fang Cai

With China's Demographic Trends Hard to Reverse, Reforms Must Place Greater Emphasis on Income Distribution

When studying China's inequality, international scholars and entrepreneurs show particular interest in two key issues: Is the policy orientation aimed at realizing common prosperity appropriate for China? And how can China's economy sustain rational growth over the forthcoming 15 years?

China's developmental trajectory since the late 1970s can be categorized into three distinct stages, each characterized by unique features in income distribution.

In this first stage, the vestiges of the centrally planned economy system engendered widespread poverty. By 1978, the rural population living below the poverty line, defined then by an annual income of RMB 100,

This article is the keynote speech delivered by the author at the 6th CF40-PIIE China–US Young Scholars Forum on the theme "How to Divide the Cake: Wealth Disparities and Policy Choices."

F. Cai (✉)
Chinese Academy of Social Sciences, Beijing, China

W. Xianqing (ed.), *Understanding China's Path to Modernization*,
https://doi.org/10.1007/978-981-96-7051-2_9

reached 250 million, reflecting dire conditions of extreme poverty. One of the inherent limitations of the planned economy system was its pursuit of egalitarianism, which lacked incentive mechanisms and perpetuated the issue of the "iron rice bowl."[1]The introduction of incentive measures during this stage inevitably exacerbated income disparities. However, income inequality was not the foremost concern at this juncture; rather, improving worker motivation and living standards were the most pressing imperatives.

In the second stage, China experienced rapid economic growth characterized by dual economic development. A considerable influx of surplus rural laborers migrated to urban regions, furnishing a continuous labor pool that propelled economic growth via demographic dividend. Despite the rise in the Gini coefficient and the widening urban–rural income gap, the Chinese economy exhibited inclusive features during this phase, as the income of both urban and rural demographics increased. The expansion of employment opportunities and rural-to-urban migration became the primary driving forces behind economic growth during this period.

In the third stage, China's demographic landscape is experiencing population aging, as seen in the deceleration of rural-to-urban migration, urbanization, and consequently, economic growth. During this period, it is no longer feasible to achieve income equality solely through labor market mechanisms or initial distribution channels. To address the emerging challenges faced in this new era, a diverse array of policy tools must be deployed, augmented by intensified efforts in redistribution.

China currently faces two main challenges. Firstly, with the implementation of the *14th Five-Year Plan for Economic and Social Development (2021–2025) and Long-Range Objectives through the Year 2035 of the People's Republic of China*, there arises the question of whether the gradually declining potential economic growth rate in China is deemed acceptable. The answer is yes. Projections from a decade ago anticipated a continued slowdown in China's potential GDP growth rate, and the outcomes of the past decade have validated that the country's actual economic growth is, indeed, decelerating, corresponding to the potential GDP growth rate. Provided China's actual economic growth rate

[1] The term "iron rice bowl" is a Chinese idiom referring to employment within an industry that offers exceptional job security, attractive remuneration, benefits, and occasionally supplementary perks.

remains consistent with its potential growth rate, and the latter significantly exceeds the global average, the aforementioned planning goals are attainable. Looking ahead, China's economic growth rate is expected to eventually converge with the global average, albeit not foreseen until 2050.

Secondly, whether the demand side can continue to support China's economic growth. This rests on several factors. In terms of demand composition, three primary factors have underpinned China's economic growth since 2012—net exports, capital formation, and final consumption. But what lies ahead? Recent developments reveal that, firstly, findings from China's seventh national population census in 2020 showed a total fertility rate of only 1.3, indicating an irreversible shift in China's population dynamics. In 2021, the natural population growth rate stood at a mere 0.34%, suggesting that the population has peaked in size. Meanwhile, the proportion of individuals aged 65 and above is 14.2%. As per definition, a country is considered to have entered an aging society if the proportion of elderly population exceeds 7%, and an aged society if it surpasses 14%. It is evident that China has officially transitioned into an aged society.

The changes in the three aforementioned indicators pertaining to population are poised to weaken demand, particularly in consumption. Firstly, the effect of total population dictates that a positive population growth rate correlates with consumption growth, while a negative growth rate presents challenges to consumption expansion under similar conditions. Secondly, the effect of age structure distinguishes China from developed countries. The elderly population in China exhibits relatively lower consumption capacity and willingness, as well as consumption levels. Therefore, shifts in population age structure will weaken consumption. Thirdly, the effect of income distribution, which manifests in two ways: affluent individuals may not significantly increase consumption levels despite income growth, while low-income groups face consumption constraints due to inadequate earnings.

This demonstrates the difficulty in reversing China's demographic transition trend, emphasizing the viability of improving income distribution to tackle the challenge of declining consumption. Notably, in the 1930s, Gunnar Myrdal, Maynard Keynes, and Alvin Hansen made seminal contributions to understanding the interplay between population dynamics, economic growth, and income distribution, leading to a common policy recommendation: addressing stagnant population necessitates the introduction of new policies, with a strong emphasis on income redistribution. Subsequently, welfare states were established in Sweden, the United States, and the United Kingdom as a response to these insights.

China Surpassing the Middle-Income Trap: Demand to Become a Key Constraint on Economic Growth

According to World Bank standards, China is projected to surpass the threshold of high-income countries by 2025 and transition to a moderately developed country by 2035. Therefore, it is safe to say that the country has already evaded the so-called middle-income trap. However, despite these achievements, new challenges persist, with demand factors poised to play a crucial role in China's economic growth.

In 2021, China's GDP per capita exceeded USD 12,551, approaching the threshold of high-income countries. Even if China statistically enters the ranks of high-income countries, its economy will continue to face numerous challenges. Foremost among these challenges is the imperative to overcome consumption constraints. The fundamental approach lies in increasing household income, improving income distribution, and fortifying social welfare provisions.

Wagner's law, named after the German economist Adolph Wagner, posits that as residents' per capita income rises, government spending, particularly on social welfare, tends to increase to meet the growing demand for public goods, an observation confirmed by many economists. Analyzing international data reveals that during the phase wherein GDP per capita escalates from USD 10,000 to USD 23,000, government expenditure as a percentage of GDP experiences its most rapid growth. Therefore, this period can be referred to as "Wagner's acceleration period."

Aligned with the objectives of economic development, China has entered the Wagner's acceleration period as it transitions from its current GDP per capita exceeding USD 10,000 to USD 23,000, a phase expected to extend until 2035. While GDP and per capita GDP growth exhibit decelerating trajectories, China will grapple with challenges such as inadequate basic public services and unequal income distribution. Against this backdrop, the establishment of a welfare system with Chinese characteristics emerges as an imperative and inevitable undertaking.

The establishment of a welfare system with Chinese characteristics hinges crucially on both initial distribution and redistribution. Various reforms in these domains, such as human-centered urbanization reforms, can bring benefits to China while tackling income distribution issues. Currently, China confronts challenges on both the supply and demand sides. Supply-side constraints primarily revolve around labor shortages, contributing to a prevailing pessimistic outlook on the Chinese economy, partly driven by projections of negative labor force growth. On the demand side, constraints mainly arise from expectations of continued weak consumption. Both of these issues can be addressed by narrowing, or even closing, the gap in urbanization levels with regard to higher income countries.

The aforementioned gap has two main aspects: the disparity in urbanization rates among permanent residents and the difference between the urbanization rates of permanent residents and those holding urban *hukou* (household registration) status. The latter suggests that migrant workers who have moved to cities have yet to acquire urban *hukou*, with this gap currently standing at a significant 18 percentage points. Eliminating these gaps would provide China with a significant labor pool and boost its potential economic growth by reallocating this workforce to non-agricultural sectors. Moreover, transitioning 260 million migrant workers into urban residents with local *hukou* would markedly enhance consumption. As per OECD projections, this shift would result in a 30% increase in migrant worker consumption, representing a significant reform dividend.

China's working-age population peaked in 2010, followed by a significant labor shortage that is not just about numerical deficits but also concerns regarding human capital. As the influx of new labor into the workforce slows down, the rate of human capital accumulation also decreases. Additionally, there is an increase in the capital-labor ratio, leading to a persistent decline in investment returns. This presents two implications: firstly, a continual reduction in the economy's potential growth rate, and secondly, China's erosion of its competitive advantage in labor-intensive products, culminating in a sustained decline in the manufacturing sector's share. This explains why, after China's economic growth rate slowed, export growth rates also dwindled—it is losing its competitive and demographic strengths.

Meanwhile, China boasts a sizable middle-income group and a substantial populace lifted out of poverty. Enhancing the purchasing power of these people will unleash significant consumer demand, underpinning China's rationale behind the dual circulation strategy. From this perspective, China is not severing its ties with other global regions but rather unlocking its domestic consumption potential. While China may presently be relinquishing former competitive advantages, it is poised to cultivate fresh dynamic competitive edges in the future. Consequently, the country may increasingly pivot toward the domestic market.

In essence, an equitable income distribution stands as a prerequisite for sustaining economic growth. Only through equitable income distribution can economic efficiency be upheld. Put differently, addressing the current economic challenges hinges on equitably dividing the economic pie as a fundamental step toward expanding it.

The Most Urgent Need for Reform: Enhancing Labor Mobility and Accelerating Urbanization

To advance substantial reforms, we must first identify the areas where the dividends of reform can be realized. If we break down China's income inequality index, it can be divided into three components: income inequality within urban regions, income inequality within rural regions, and income inequality between urban and rural regions. Previous studies have shown that roughly 50% of income inequality arises from discrepancies between urban and rural regions. Assuming this remains valid today, recent studies suggest a surge in income inequality within rural regions. This means that within the remaining 50% of factors contributing to the income gap, a notable portion comes from within rural regions, while the impact of urban residents on income inequality is comparatively minor.

This highlights inequality in the urban–rural dichotomy, primarily attributable to the divergent opportunities between these settings. A key determinant of this inequity is the contrast in employment opportunities, and the solution lies in fostering migration and mobility. Facilitating the relocation of rural inhabitants to urban labor markets enables them to naturally access employment opportunities on par with those available in urban regions. Another crucial aspect is the accessibility of public services, particularly educational opportunities, as facilitating labor mobility empowers individuals to pursue better educational prospects. Therefore, while many reforms are imperative, eliminating *hukou* barriers and promoting unrestricted movement may be the most pressing requisites at present.

If urban and rural residents remain segregated by *hukou*, the stability of the labor supply will be compromised, hindering effective resolution of labor shortages. In China, the proportion of the labor force engaged in agricultural production significantly surpasses the average of upper-middle-income countries. Various institutional barriers concerning land, *hukou*, and social welfare prevent farmers from relocating outside rural regions due to their *hukou* status. If rural residents are allowed to move into urban regions and acquire local *hukou*, they would be granted the access to basic public services, enabling more secure settlement, which, in turn, would ensure a steady supply of labor for non-agricultural sectors, curb abrupt increases in labor costs, and slow down the pace of labor substitution by capital. Such a transition would undeniably enhance the potential growth rate. Certainly, disparities persist among different industries and groups within cities, with monopolistic sectors or companies enjoying preferential conditions such as advanced technology, resulting in income disparities among workers. China is actively working toward resolving these issues through strategies aimed at lowering, broadening, and raising standards to promote greater equality.

When considering the reform of the *hukou* system in China, the selection of cities to prioritize is of paramount importance. With nearly 700 cities across the country, the resettlement of migrant workers could be more effectively initiated in large and mid-sized cities, rather than solely focusing on first-tier cities such as Beijing, Shanghai, Guangzhou, or Shenzhen. Here, large cities refer not only to these major metropolises but also include 68 other cities with populations exceeding two million. Smaller county-level cities currently lack sufficient job opportunities and may not be as appealing to migrants. It is thus more feasible to target multiple moderately productive large cities and medium-sized cities without overwhelming population pressures. Over time, populations from these cities will naturally redistribute toward mega-cities and smaller towns, ensuring that the benefits of urbanization outweigh social costs.

The issue of the economic implications of land for families in rural China is paramount. I support the notion of enabling farmers to generate property income from the land they cultivate. Various types of land in Chinese rural regions present distinct challenges: Collective construction land necessitates decisions on usage to be made by local villagers' autonomous organizations and farmers, as a whole, particularly for activities such as joint venture investments. As for arable land, its ownership, contracted operation rights, and usage rights are vastly distinct. The land is collectively owned by villagers, with each household entrusted with specific fields under contract. This arrangement empowers farmers to derive income from the land by leasing or subleasing it to neighbors or external investors, provided the agricultural purpose for crop cultivation and agricultural production is maintained. Meanwhile, residential land reforms are currently undergoing pilot initiatives in China, holding the promise of enabling farmers to earn property income from such land in the future.

In terms of the digital economy sector, precise statistics on informal employment are lacking. Many individuals are not directly engaged in digital work but occupy roles within the informal sector facilitated by online platforms and technology—think food delivery riders and drivers. Despite exceeding what previous generations earned in factories, and growing fast in numbers, these workers cannot fully represent all migrant workers. Moreover, these food delivery jobs tend to be short-lived, with individuals likely moving on as they age. While flexible gig jobs do not always mean informal work, in China, flexible employees often find themselves in informal settings, grappling with unstable employment, income, and a lack of essential social insurance coverage. To tackle this issue, it is imperative to advocate for the regularization of such work and continuously expand social insurance coverage.

Furthermore, the pandemic has, without a doubt, exacerbated inequality. By December 2022, office workers could opt for remote working, yet workers in the essential industries were required to report to their workplaces. At the same time, many service industry employees lost their jobs due to business closures. Talking about pandemic response strategies, it is crucial to conduct counterfactual experiments. Without control groups, it becomes challenging to make comparisons or evaluations of these strategies. Nonetheless, I remain optimistic about the resilience of China's economy, albeit anticipating some fluctuations. Alongside this, there are concerns about the effectiveness of implementing any strategy. Therefore, it is important to constantly enhance governance capabilities and policy effectiveness.

Chinese Path to Modernization and High-Level Market Economic System

Chinese-Style Modern Industrial and Market Systems

Qifan Huang

Prioritizing the Real Economy and Accelerating the Development of a Modern Industrial System

The 20th National Congress of the Communist Party of China (CPC) emphasized the need to concentrate efforts on developing the real economy, fostering new industrialization, and expediting endeavors to enhance China's prowess in manufacturing, product quality, aerospace, transportation, cyberspace, and digital development. Given that manufacturing is the backbone of industry, the foundation of the economy, and the safeguard of people's livelihoods, the pursuit of high-quality development of manufacturing is key to building China's modern industrial system.

When comparing with developed countries, China's manufacturing industry faces two key challenges in its development. On the one hand, there has been a significant drop in the contribution of manufacturing

This article is compiled from two speeches delivered by the author at the end of 2022, titled "Accelerating the Construction of a Modern Industrial System With the Economy as the Core" and "Building a Sound and Mature High-level Socialist Market Economic System."

Q. Huang (✉)
China Finance 40 Forum, Beijing, China

W. Xianqing (ed.), *Understanding China's Path to Modernization*,
https://doi.org/10.1007/978-981-96-7051-2_10

value added to gross domestic product (GDP) since 2011. According to World Bank statistics, China's manufacturing value added peaked at 32.5% of GDP in 2006, steadily decreasing since 2011 to 26.3% in 2020—an aggregate decline of 5.8 percentage points over nine years. Major industrialized countries such as the United States, Germany, Japan, France, Italy, the United Kingdom, and South Korea all witnessed a contraction in their manufacturing sectors after achieving developed or high-income status. Compared to these developed counterparts, China's decline in manufacturing share from its peak has been more pronounced and rapid. On the other hand, relative to global benchmarks, China's manufacturing sector continues to grapple with the following four major shortcomings concerning product diversity and quality:

Firstly, Chinese manufacturing often lacks high-end, top-quality products, with many items being perceived as low-end and subpar, exhibiting noticeable gaps in performance, reliability, durability, and output when compared to international standards, and typically occupying the lower end of the value chain. Furthermore, the industry faces intense competition marked by a lack of diversity and specialization in segmented markets. Despite many companies operating within the same manufacturing domain, they often neglect specialized collaboration based on the division of labor. This situation fosters homogeneous competition, where there is an influx of manufacturing enterprises into a thriving sector, resulting in redundant production, fierce rivalry, and surplus capacity. Additionally, key technologies are being constrained, with a lack of control over many vital technologies in various manufacturing sectors. This dependency on external sources leaves China's industrial chains vulnerable to external pressures. The country is also facing a struggle for global leadership through its top-tier brands, or the lack thereof, given the fact that China's manufacturing industry heavily relies on low-end processing, which hinders the establishment of high-end brand presence and the associated market advantages. Building a brand requires years of focused dedication to gain market acceptance and establish effective marketing channels. However, with millions of new businesses launched annually in China, a significant number cease operations or change paths within five years. Data reveals that small and medium-sized enterprises in the United States typically last an average of 8 years, and in Japan, 12 years. In contrast, Chinese counterparts have an average lifespan of just 3 years, presenting challenges in creating a lasting brand impact.

The outline of the 14th Five-Year Plan makes it clear that China will intensify efforts toward realizing the strategy of becoming a manufacturing powerhouse, aiming to maintain a stable share of manufacturing in the economy and drive high-quality development within this sector. Looking at the guiding principle of economic development, four key observations emerge: Historically, as economies progress toward developed status, the share of manufacturing typically diminishes over time. However, it is important that this decline occurs gradually and not too rapidly or prematurely. Ideally, it should commence only after the country's per capita GDP surpasses USD 15,000. Although China is experiencing a decline in manufacturing's share before reaching this income threshold, we need to take measures to slow down this trend. Moreover, given China's unique circumstances, it is crucial to ensure that the contribution of the manufacturing sector does not decline excessively. By 2035, manufacturing should still constitute no less than 25% of the economy, and by 2050, it should remain above 20%. When taking into consideration sectors such as mining, electricity, heat, gas, and water production and supply, it is imperative that the collective secondary industry maintains a level exceeding 35% by 2035 and surpassing 30% by 2050. This approach serves to avert the extreme scenario seen in countries like the United States, where the secondary industry contributes less than 18% to GDP. As the manufacturing sector's contribution to GDP peaks and gradually declines thereafter, it becomes essential to sustain the impetus of industrial development through substantial increases in research and development investment, thereby positioning innovation as the primary catalyst for industrial manufacturing. For any country or region, keeping research and development investment within 3 to 4% of manufacturing output, with basic research innovation constituting over 20% of total research and development investment, and ensuring that leading innovative unicorn enterprises in manufacturing make up over 30% of the capital market's aggregate value, all serve as clear benchmarks of a manufacturing powerhouse. Furthermore, the advancement of high-quality manufacturing goes hand in hand with a specific ratio of productive service industries. As the manufacturing sector's contribution to GDP gradually decreases, the added value of services related to manufacturing should increase to between 50 and 60%. Upon meeting these four criteria, the proportion of value-added in the real economy—primarily manufacturing, mining, construction, and productive service industries—within GDP will reach around 65%. At this stage, China will have established a robust foundation for transitioning from a manufacturing giant to a manufacturing powerhouse, concurrently propelling its economic scale toward the world's largest throughout the high-quality manufacturing development.

To liberate itself from existing dependencies within certain sectors, the modern industrial framework must do more than just stabilize the share of manufacturing value added in GDP; it must also be proactive and enterprising. This necessitates new iterations and enhancements at the organizational level of industries and supply chains. Only through a higher quality industrial system can we seize the initiative amid the new wave of technological revolution and industrial transformation, capitalizing on China's position as the largest single market and harnessing the synergies of both domestic and international circulation. Therefore, we must endeavor to achieve new advancements and breakthroughs across the following five key areas.

First and foremost, it is crucial to leverage industrial chain investment attraction to foster the growth of industrial cluster chains. We need to transition from the previous strategy of soliciting investments on a project-by-project basis toward a holistic approach that targets investments across the entire industrial chain. This shift aims to establish strategically vital industrial cluster chains characterized by spatial concentration, seamless integration upstream and downstream, efficient supply chain management, and the potential for reaching trillion-dollar scales. Looking at China's response to the COVID-19 pandemic, regions with well-established industrial chains and self-sufficient industrial clusters tend to recover more swiftly and effectively than those heavily dependent on international supply chains. This model of clustered production not only mitigates the risks associated with global component procurement but also demonstrates its competitive advantage during times of crisis. Therefore, we should encourage the formation of three types of clusters, especially in regions with conducive conditions. The first is clusters encompassing the entire spectrum of the manufacturing industry, from upstream to downstream. Take the automotive industry, for example, where a single car comprises thousands of components. To establish it into a robust industrial base, it is imperative to achieve localization in 70% to 80% of raw materials, component industries, and various module productions along the supply chain. The second is clusters encompassing similar products and enterprises. When multiple similar large enterprises are established in close proximity, the supporting industries for upstream raw materials and components can serve both the leading enterprise and others, facilitating the clustering of similar products and enterprises. The third is clusters integrating productive service industries with manufacturing. Throughout the development of new products, various productive service enterprises engaged in research and development, design, technology transfer services, and intellectual property applications play crucial roles, extending the innovation chain.

Secondly, it is imperative to further expand openness and accelerate efforts to reinforce, broaden, and fortify the industrial chain. With a focus on strategic emerging sectors, we must implement action plans aimed at strengthening, broadening, and enhancing the chain through heightened levels of openness, thereby achieving a more sophisticated division of labor and vertical integration. In relatively weaker areas such as logistics, insurance, industrial design, financial technology, and the digital economy, we should intensify efforts to attract advantageous foreign investment to address supply chain gaps, a process commonly referred to as "strengthening the chain." This involves either attracting foreign investment to fill supply chain deficiencies or integrating upstream and downstream enterprises into the industrial chain through existing trade relationships, termed "broadening the chain." Furthermore, there is a need to incentivize existing successful enterprises to extend their presence along the smile curve, bolstering China's standing in the global value chain, termed as "enhancing the chain." Fostering the strengthening, broadening, and enhancing of the chain is of great significance to the formation of industrial chain clusters at advanced levels. During phases of subdued international demand, sustaining these clusters by stimulating domestic and internal demand-driven loops becomes necessary for their healthy development. As international markets regain strength, fostering enhanced international collaboration, scaling up industrial clusters, and improving development standards will propel the global circulation of the industrial chain through strengthened regional industrial chain collaboration. Such an approach not only fortifies our resilience against risks such as global chain breaks triggered by natural disasters like the COVID-19 pandemic but also effectively mitigates the vulnerability of critical sectors to future sanctions, given the substantial market shares held by industrial chain clusters.

Thirdly, it is imperative to cultivate and establish a cadre of manufacturing industry leaders capable of organizing horizontal division of labor and vertical integration across the upstream, midstream, and downstream segments of the industrial chain. China's manufacturing sector encompasses a diverse range of industries, culminating in a globally significant industrial prowess—specifically, the proficiency in assembling complex products. While the assembly plants for such high-tech, complex products typically occupy the midsection of the smile curve, and China's value added in this intermediary segment may not rival that of multinational corporations skilled in the "three links," we must not underestimate this capability. These assembly plants epitomize the primary entities within an industrial chain comprising hundreds or thousands of enterprises. The development of this capability is intricately linked to our proficiency in enterprise management and supply chain organization, offering a substantial competitive advantage. Its evolution is also closely intertwined with both the production-to-sale and sale-to-production paradigms, as well as China's infrastructure level, industrial support capabilities, highly skilled workforce, and progressively advanced research and development capabilities. Historically, many multinational corporations have established joint venture automobile assembly factories, mobile phone assembly factories, and consumer electronics assembly factories in China. Following decades of reform and opening-up endeavors, numerous domestic enterprises have acquired expertise in large-scale manufacturing and management, laying the groundwork for cultivating China's own Foxconn and a new generation of manufacturing industry leaders.

Fourthly, it is crucial to cultivate China's own ecosystem-leading "chain-leading" enterprises akin to Microsoft, Google, and Apple in the United States. Apple, in particular, serves as a prominent example; it does not manufacture its own components, a unique business model orchestrating the global value chain leveraging its intellectual property. Despite not directly engaging in the manufacturing of Apple smartphones, the company adeptly manages and oversees the standards of the global industrial chain, functioning as the nucleus of the supply chain and the nexus of the value chain through its patents, trademarks, copyrights, brand, product design, software, databases, and more, leading the entire ecosystem of Apple products. At present, China is witnessing the emergence of similar enterprises in specific sectors, such as Huawei, which we must attach great importance to. It is important to offer robust support by leveraging the expansive Chinese market to promote the application and advancement of these enterprises' technologies. Moreover, we should encourage these enterprises to embrace a global perspective, instilling principles of globalization, and assisting them in expanding their intellectual property and industry standards worldwide through the establishment of international exchange, project collaboration, and market expansion platforms. Furthermore, China should also strengthen intellectual property protection. A common trait among ecosystem-oriented "chain-leading" enterprises is the establishment of independent intellectual property at the foundational technological level. Supporting the growth of such enterprises and enhancing the protection of their intellectual property rights effectively safeguards their competitiveness at its core, necessitating continual reinforcement.

Fifthly, it is crucial to strategically plan and design a series of complete machine products that align with the trajectory of future industrial transformations. This marks the apex of the forthcoming wave of Industrial Revolution. The true battleground for industrial clustering lies in specific globally significant, trillion-dollar durable consumer goods. Every 20 to 30 years, the world witnesses the emergence of four to five emblematic durable consumer goods that permeate households, influencing consumption patterns, whether in China, other parts of Asia, Europe, or the United States. For instance, from 1950 to 1970, it was watches, bicycles, sewing machines, radios, and the like; from 1980 to 1990, it was air conditioners, televisions, refrigerators, washing machines, and so forth; and in the twenty-first century, it has been smartphones, laptops, LCD TVs, automobiles, and more. The market scale of these products often surpasses the trillion-dollar threshold, and the country or city that can cultivate these industries will lead the international competition. Currently, there is a pressing need to direct our attention toward the future "big four" or "big five" sectors. The 14th Five-Year Plan outlines the strategy of "creating an industrial chain of overall strategic importance starting from complete machines that are in line with the direction of future industrial transformation." This means assuming a proactive stance. Over the next two to three decades, the "big five" sectors poised to yield trillion-dollar market capacities broadly include the following five categories: autonomous new energy vehicles (NEVs), household robots, head-mounted augmented reality or virtual reality (AR/VR) glasses or helmets, flexible display screens, and 3D printing devices. Therefore, we should meticulously strategize and undertake preemptive actions and develop a cluster of competitive industrial chains that focus around these key industries.

In essence, building a modern industrial system rooted in the real economy hinges on the dual pursuit of advancement and stability. This strategy aims not only to establish a more robust and competitive domestic industrial chain system in China but also to foster leading enterprises capable of expanding their presence within global industrial and supply chains. Such an integrated approach embodies the fundamental means to balance development and security.

Deepening Reforms Toward a High-Level Socialist Market Economy

The report to the 20th National Congress of the Communist Party of China (CPC) highlights the significance of establishing a top-tier socialist market economic system. What does "high-level" entail? In my opinion, it revolves around adeptly managing two crucial aspects: the relationship between the government and the market, and the dynamics between state-owned and private enterprises. By effectively addressing these issues, we can enhance China's advantage as an extensive single market and capitalize on its dividends.

First and foremost, navigating the government-market relationship is paramount. The third plenary session of the 18th CPC Central Committee clearly articulated the goal of "empowering the market to play a decisive role in resource allocation while optimizing governmental functions," a vision reaffirmed in the 20th CPC National Congress. As the Chinese nation embarks on this new journey, it is imperative to advance reforms that build upon these principles.

In fully unlocking the pivotal role of the market in resource allocation, China's journey from a planned economy to a market-oriented one has been notable. Despite significant strides made through years of reform and opening-up efforts, there remain areas requiring further refinement. The third plenary session of the 18th CPC Central Committee proposed granting the market a decisive role in resource allocation, a stance reiterated and emphasized with the addition of the notion "fully" during the 20th National Congress of the Communist Party of China (CPC). So, how do we embody the notions of "full" and "decisive role"? I believe it is predominantly reflected in two key statements from the report to the 20th CPC National Congress, that is, to "build a unified national market, advance reforms for the market-based allocation of production factors, and put in place a high-standard market system," and to "refine the systems underpinning the market economy, such as those for property rights protection, market access, fair competition, and social credit." In recent years, the CPC Central Committee has issued several significant documents centered around these principles. Concerning the advancement of reforms for the market-based allocation of production factors, the focus is on removing institutional barriers impeding the free flow of factors such as land, labor, capital, technology, and data. This includes expanding the scope of factor market allocation, improving the factor market system, advancing institutional construction in factor markets, and allowing market forces to determine factor prices, thereby facilitating autonomous and orderly factor flows and ensuring efficient and equitable factor allocation. Meanwhile, the emphasis on building a unified national market involves strengthening unified market regulations, enhancing connectivity among market infrastructures, establishing a unified factor and resource market, promoting high-level uniformity in commodity and service markets, ensuring equitable and consistent market supervision, and further regulating inappropriate market competition and intervention. The enhancement of these foundational market systems enables the country to streamline domestic market flows and expansion, establish a stable, equitable, transparent, and predictable business environment, reduce market transaction costs, foster technological innovation and industrial upgrading, cultivate new competitive advantages in international arenas, and ultimately propel economic and broader institutional reforms to higher echelons, aiming for the cultivation of a more systematic, comprehensive, mature, and standardized high-level socialist market economy.

The report to the 20th CPC National Congress places considerable emphasis on the significance of "enhancing government effectiveness." General Secretary Xi Jinping remarked, "Developing a market economy within socialist context is a significant initiative of our Party."[1] I see this initiative not only as the harmonious integration of socialist values with market mechanisms but also as a fundamental redefinition of the government's role. In a socialist market economy, the government's role extends beyond that of a passive observer found in laissez-faire systems. Rather, it actively participates in upholding, complementing, and fostering market development to cultivate an efficient marketplace. Despite significant

[1] Editor'S Note: "From the Perspective of 'Efficiency': A Better Handling of Government–Market Relations - —An Illustrative Review of Xi Jinping's Economic Thoughts in Practice, Part Three" (Reference: https://www.xuexi.cn/lgpage/detail/index.html?id=6234751081844682689).

progress achieved through years of reform, the Chinese government acknowledges the imperative of further efforts in building a modern country. For instance, a key aspect highlighted in the report to the 20th CPC National Congress is the "establishment of a modern central banking system and the reinforcement and refinement of modern financial regulation." This construction of a modern central bank system entails further refinement of mechanisms for issuing the renminbi (RMB) and establishing the RMB's independent anchor. This necessitates clarifying the relationship between fiscal policy and the central bank, instituting a national debt issuance mechanism aligned with major economies, and developing a more seamless and reliable government bond yield curve. Furthermore, the widespread integration of modern technology has precipitated substantial transformations in financial modalities, risk structures, transmission pathways, and security frameworks, underscoring the need to fortify the financial stability assurance system to mitigate systemic financial risks. Ongoing efforts to deepen supply-side structural reforms in finance are also crucial for effectively channeling diverse financial resources toward bolstering the real economy.

Secondly, it is crucial to deal with the relationship between state-owned and private enterprises. The report to the 20th CPC National Congress reiterates two unwavering commitments: steadfastly consolidating and advancing the public sector economy while fostering, supporting, and guiding the non-public sector economy, both of which entails comprehension and practical implementation.

In terms of the proportion of different economic components, from 1980 to 2010, the contribution of the non-public economy to GDP steadily increased from around 18% to approximately 60%, encapsulated as "56,789." However, since 2010, the proportion of value added by the non-public economy to GDP has stagnated at around 60%. Why hasn't it continued to rise? A fundamental logic underpins this concept. The value added within any economy can be segmented into two categories: that which stems from government activities and that which arises from the operational activities of market entities. These market entities can then be subdivided into state-owned and non-state-owned entities, delineating state-owned and non-public economies. Generally, government taxation accounts for around 20% of GDP, with this taxation contributing roughly 15% to the total GDP after government spending. Therefore, the value-added stemming from market entities' activities accounts for approximately 85%. In China, the GDP generated by non-state-owned entities currently represents roughly 60%. Additionally, as China is a socialist country committed to consolidating and developing the state-owned economy, the value added by state-owned enterprises must maintain a certain proportion of GDP. Since the initiation of reform and opening-up, the proportion of GDP generated by state-owned enterprises has consistently decreased, although it is not expected to decline indefinitely. The figure presently stands at approximately 25%, which is considered relatively reasonable, creating a pattern where the economic contributions of government, non-state-owned entities, and state-owned entities are in a ratio of 15:60:25.

In the future, with fluctuations in economic activity, the economic contribution of non-state-owned entities may increase to 65%, but it is unlikely to surpass 70% or higher. However, for provinces such as Guangdong and Zhejiang, a slightly higher proportion of the non-public economy is acceptable, as the economic value added by central state-owned enterprises is not tallied at the provincial level but rather at the central level. For the overall society, "56,789" not only illustrates the contribution of the non-public economy but also aptly summarizes the characteristics of China's socialist market economy. The ratio of "15:25:60" is not only rational but also stable, ensuring that the combined economic contributions of the government and state-owned enterprises, accounting for 40%, can effectively regulate economic operations, while the 60% contribution from non-state-owned enterprises helps sustain economic vitality, employment, and innovation.

Regarding the promotion, facilitation, and guidance of the development of the non-public economy, it is worthy to note that the willingness of entrepreneurs to expand reproduction and engage in innovative and enterprising activities is closely tied to their economic prospects, the fairness of market competition, and the effectiveness of property rights protection. A critical metric for assessing the investment enthusiasm of private enterprises is the net asset growth rate of all private enterprises. Annually, the amount of profit retained as net assets, as well as the infusion of social equity capital into real industries, are crucial factors. If, in a specific region, the total assets of private enterprises increase annually but net assets do not, it signals a rise in liabilities and an escalation in economic leverage, potentially culminating in bubbles. If, across society, businesses are profitable but net assets are decreasing, it indicates that more enterprises are incurring losses or assets are being divested.

Previously, the vast majority of private enterprises experienced significant setbacks due to the COVID-19 pandemic. The key is to implement measures aimed at stabilizing the confidence of private entrepreneurs and fostering a positive long-term outlook for the Chinese economy, the essence of which lies in effectively implementing the six requirements outlined by General Secretary Xi Jinping at a private enterprise symposium in 2018: to substantially reduce the tax burden on enterprises; to address the challenge of difficult and costly financing for private enterprises; to cultivate a fair competition environment, particularly by encouraging private enterprises to participate in state-owned enterprise reforms; to improve policy implementation methods and actualize the strengthening of property rights protection; to forge a new type of government-business relationship; and to safeguard entrepreneurs' personal and property safety.[2] The successful implementation of these six measures will undoubtedly stimulate a substantial influx of private capital.

Concerning the promotion of optimizing and structurally adjusting the state-owned economy, the 20th CPC National Congress reiterated the imperative of strengthening, improving, and expanding state-owned capital investment and operation companies. Notably, the emphasis lies on state-owned capital operation companies, which can effectively mobilize extensive state-owned capital resources while leveraging social capital to foster mixed-ownership economies and empower the overall economic landscape. In 2021, China's total equity of state-owned capital (both at the central and local levels) amounted to RMB 86.9 trillion, with industrial and commercial capital investment companies accounting for 99% of the equity capital. However, the overall capital return rate and total factor productivity remain suboptimal. To address this, it is suggested to reallocate approximately RMB 10 trillion worth of equity assets from existing industrial state-owned capital investment companies to establish several state-owned capital operation companies. These operation companies would, similar to Temasek Holdings in Singapore, Berkshire Hathaway in the United States, or other private equity funds, specialize in alternative investments and equity investments, determining their involvement based on the performance of invested enterprises. By aligning with the capital market, state-owned capital can be revitalized. If this RMB 10 trillion

[2] Editor'S Note: "Creating a Better Development Environment for the Private Economy: General Secretary Proposes 'Six Musts'" (Reference: https://www.xuexi.cn/lgpage/detail/index.html?id=6234751081844682689).

investment can achieve an annualized return of 10%, it would yield trillions of yuan in revenue annually, serving as a sustainable source of funds for areas where state-owned capital needs to intervene, such as national security and public services, without escalating the fiscal burden. The withdrawal of RMB 10 trillion from industrial and commercial sectors can free up over RMB 20 trillion of market space for the private economy, further encouraging and promoting its development. This will establish a financial cycle between state-owned and private economies, conducive to advancing mixed-ownership reforms and activating the overall economic landscape. As the 20th CPC National Congress emphasizes, "We will open up new areas and new arenas in development and steadily foster new growth drivers and new strengths." Against the backdrop of the current green revolution, China's clean energy industry is thriving, witnessing the rise of several eco-leading enterprises and potentially hundreds or even thousands of unicorn enterprises. For these enterprises, we should heed the lessons from Chinese enterprises being subject to foreign investment control during the previous wave of internet booms. With state-owned capital operation companies providing support, we should proactively cultivate these potential unicorns and partake in the dividends of industrial development.

If managed effectively, these two aspects will pave the way for a new dividend in the Chinese economy following the labor force dividend, that is, the market dividend generated by an ultra-large-scale single market. In terms of scale, China's population stands at approximately 1.4 billion, accounting for nearly 20% of the global population. In comparison, the most developed countries in Western Europe, such as Germany, France, and the United Kingdom, have populations ranging from 60 to 80 million, representing only about 1% of the global population. When including Japan's population of 126 million and the United States' population of 330 million, the total population of these high-income countries amounts to 1.215 billion. However, China alone has a population of 1.4 billion, thereby exerting a greater influence on the global supply–demand structure than these high-income countries combined. In terms of market structure, China embodies a unified large market. A single market is characterized by a unified legal system, tax framework, standardized commercial regulations, and linguistic and cultural cohesion. China exemplifies such a single market, governed by a unified legal system. The Han ethnic group predominantly shapes China's ethnic structure, accounting for 91.11% of the total population, fostering harmonious and balanced development among all ethnic groups. Meanwhile, Mandarin Chinese is the official language of China, ensuring consistency in commercial regulations and market environments. This stands in contrast to the fragmented market structure in India and the bulk market model in the European Union.[3] In terms of industrial foundation, China is an integrated economy encompassing all factors, categories, and the entire industry chain. The convergence of these three aspects will yield three types of dividends.

The first dividend is economies of scale. As manufacturing enterprises expand their operations and production volumes in the Chinese market, they can realize significant cost reductions across several key areas. Firstly, research and development costs experience a notable decrease as the per-product research expenditure decreases with increased production volume, enabling enterprises to invest more in original innovation and research and development. Secondly, fixed asset investment costs, including expenses related to factory infrastructure, production lines, and equipment, decrease on a per-unit basis as production scale grows.

[3] India, boasting a population of approximately 1.4 billion people, is often described as a country with a fragmented decentralized market. It is a federal republic, comprising 28 states and 8 union territories. Each state holds substantial autonomy, maintaining its distinct legal framework and commercial regulations beyond the federal constitution, introducing various impediments to the movement of factors of production and goods across state borders. Meanwhile, the country's demographic landscape encompasses over 100 diverse ethnic groups with distinct ways of life, with the largest group, the Indo-Aryans, representing only 46% of the total population. India also embraces a plethora of religions, including Hinduism, Islam, Sikhism, Catholicism, and Buddhism, resulting in intricate dynamics among different religious communities. Furthermore, India is linguistically diverse, recognizing 22 official languages, while over 121 languages are spoken by populations exceeding 10,000 individuals. The country also upholds a rigid caste system, segregating society into five classes, contributing to fragmented markets across different social strata. Therefore, it can be said that India comprises more than 20large and small fragmented markets. In contrast, the European Union, characterized by free movement of people and goods among its member states and governed by a unified legal framework at the EU level, consists of 26 member countries, each operating under its own constitution and corresponding legal systems. Additionally, the European Union recognizes 23 official languages, contributing to its linguistic diversity. For instance, German is the predominant language in the EU, spanning countries like Germany, Austria, Liechtenstein, and Switzerland. When multinational corporations enter individual markets within the EU, they have to undertake new market development initiatives, incurring additional expenses. Conversely, a single market implies that if a company successfully devises an effective business model, it can replicate it across the entire market without significant additional investments. This efficiency gains and cost reductions compared to navigating numerous fragmented markets.

Thirdly, procurement costs witness a decline as larger quantities of materials are purchased, leading to increased discounts. Moreover, labor costs also exhibit a reduction once economies of scale are achieved. Despite the prevailing notion that the core competitiveness of Chinese manufacturing lies in low labor costs, in reality, labor costs typically account for only 10% to 15% of total costs in manufacturing. While labor costs may represent around 40% of total costs in certain labor-intensive product categories, they are not notably elevated in the majority of manufacturing sectors such as equipment manufacturing, durable consumer goods, and heavy industry, in which raw material costs are high and investments in fixed assets like factories and equipment are substantial.[4] Additionally, logistics costs, encompassing expenses related to transportation, warehousing, transshipment, and loading and unloading, decrease per unit as production scale increases. Furthermore, market development costs witness a substantial reduction. Generally, when a company enters a new market, it needs to conduct market research, user analysis, product positioning, and channel expansion. However, in the unified Chinese market, the same strategy and product can be promoted nationwide, significantly reducing market development costs. Economies of scale can typically impact approximately 30% to 40% of total manufacturing expenses. Once a sufficient scale is attained, prices can be lowered by 30% to 40%, furnishing a competitive edge over international counterparts.

The second dividend rests upon "gravitational effect." This effect primarily manifests across various dimensions. Firstly, from a demand standpoint, an ultra-large-scale market implies an equally massive domestic consumption market and an extensive volume of import trade. In terms of domestic consumption, China's total retail sales of consumer goods amounted to USD 6,832.87 billion in 2021, closely approaching the USD 7,417.34 billion figure observed in the United States. China's total retail sales of consumer goods already account for 92.12% of those

[4] There is a prevailing traditional perception that China's manufacturing industry derives its core competitiveness from low labor costs. However, in reality, labor costs typically account for only about 10% to 15% of total manufacturing costs, impacting the overall cost by only a few percentage points. While labor costs may represent around 40% of total costs in certain labor-intensive product categories, they are not notably elevated in the majority of manufacturing sectors such as equipment manufacturing, durable consumer goods, and heavy industry, in which raw material costs are high and investments in fixed assets like factories and equipment are substantial, leading to relatively insignificant proportion of labor costs.

in the United States and are expected to surpass them in the near future. Looking at import trade, China's cumulative goods imports over the next decade are expected to exceed USD 22 trillion, with service imports totaling USD 5 trillion. Collectively, these figures surpass USD 27 trillion, attracting multinational corporations to explore opportunities within the Chinese market. Secondly, from a production standpoint, an ultra-large-scale market implies deeper market specialization, allowing for interconnected and symbiotic industrial clusters across the entire industry value chain and even among various processes. When one or several leading enterprises within a chain establish themselves in a specific area, they catalyze the settlement of upstream and downstream enterprises alongside them. Given the extensive market scale, even commonplace products like buttons and lighters can form substantial supporting capabilities on a large scale. This phenomenon significantly contributes to the prevalence of clustered economies and industrial clusters observed in China. Thirdly, from a temporal viewpoint, an ultra-large-scale market implies a significant symbiotic relationship between supply and demand. Not only does the demand side undergo continuous updates and upgrades, attracting an increasing number of market entities to participate in the supply side, but the production side itself benefits from a learning effect, resulting in the emergence of more innovative products over time. In essence, the process of supply drives the creation of demand, with both sides mutually reinforcing and attracting each other.

The third dividend lies in "ocean effect." During the inaugural ceremony of the China International Import Expo, President Xi Jinping stated that, "The Chinese economy is not a pond, but an ocean. The ocean may have its calm days, but big winds and storms are only to be expected… Big winds and storms may upset a pond, but never an ocean."[5]This metaphor signifies the vast scale of China's economic landscape. In contrast to smaller economies, an ultra-large-scale market fosters enhanced internal circulation and resilience against external risks. It possesses the capacity to weather turbulent storms, as demonstrated by its resilience during crises such as the 1997 Asian financial crisis and the 2008 global economic crisis. Additionally, the vast market scale reduces the impact of industry and regional disparities, mitigating the resonance effect of localized shocks on the national economy. Challenges faced by certain industries or regions

[5] Editor's note: Reference: http://china.nmgnews.com.cn/system/2018/11/05/012595169.shtml.

exert limited influence on the overall stability of the macroeconomy.[6] This resilience was particularly evident during the COVID-19 pandemic. Businesses require a sense of predictability of the fundamentals, which is bolstered by the stability inherent in China's vast economic landscape, akin to the resilience of an ocean against turbulent forces.

These three effects are a direct result of China's super large-scale unified market, which emerges as new dividends organically generated at the current stage of China's development. They are also a natural logic inherent in the Chinese path to modernization, a process occurring on a massive population scale.

[6] Youjia Mao & Changwen Zhao, "Giving Full Play to the Advantages of Super-Large-Scale Markets," *Economic Daily*, August 18, 2021.

What Is the Purpose of a "Unified National Market?"

Bo Zhao and Anji Zhou

On April 10, 2022, the State Council issued the *Opinions of the Central Committee of the Communist Party of China and the State Council on Accelerating the Construction of a Large Unified National Market* ("the *Opinions*"), garnering widespread attention across society. The term "unified national market" was initially introduced in a document endorsed by the Central Commission for Comprehensively Deepening Reform on December 17, 2021, and subsequently referenced in the *Report on the Work of the Government* at the fifth session of the 13th National People's Congress on March 5, 2022.

How to Further Improve Market Efficiency?

The core feature of China's socialist market economic system revolves around the pivotal role of the market in resource allocation. Amid China's recent economic growth slowdown, in order to facilitate a seamless domestic cycle and establish a new development paradigm, we

This article was published on April 18, 2022, by Netease Research Institute (renamed the Netease Financial Think Tank in July of the same year).

B. Zhao (✉) · A. Zhou
National School of Development, Peking University, Beijing, China

W. Xianqing (ed.), *Understanding China's Path to Modernization*,
https://doi.org/10.1007/978-981-96-7051-2_11

fundamentally need to bolster economic growth through heightened market efficiency. In response, the *Opinions* outlines measures aimed at improving market efficiency across seven key domains:

First, we need to strengthen the foundational market system. This involves safeguarding property rights, ensuring equitable competition, fostering equal access, and developing a robust credit system.

Second, we should construct high-quality market infrastructure. This includes enhancing digital advancements in logistics infrastructure, streamlining the dissemination of property rights transaction information, and consolidating public resource trading platforms.

Third, it is necessary to integrate resource and factor markets. This entails accelerating the establishment of unified urban and rural land and labor markets, capital markets, technology and data markets, energy markets, and ecological environment markets.

Fourth, we need to enhance standards for product and service quality. This encompasses refining the product quality system, enhancing standards and measurement systems, and elevating consumer service quality.

Fifth, we should promote fair and unified market supervision. This involves strengthening regulatory frameworks and enforcement mechanisms.

Sixth, it is essential to regulate unfair competition and market interventions. This includes anti-monopoly endeavors, combating unfair competition, eliminating local protectionism and regional barriers, abolishing unequal market access and exit practices, and addressing improper practices in bidding and procurement.

Seventh, efforts should be made to provide organizational support. This entails upholding the leadership of the CPC, refining incentive and constraint mechanisms, prioritizing regional cooperation, and establishing inter-departmental coordination mechanisms.

How the Roles of Market and Government Are Divided?

The *Opinions* points out that we should properly handle the government-market relationship, advocating for a framework known as "an efficient market with an active government," where the market plays a decisive role in resource allocation, complemented by effective governmental intervention. Under this framework, the government acts proactively to rectify imperfections and distortions, thereby achieving market efficiency.

In concrete terms, among the seven measures to improve efficiency, the first two focus on enhancing the development of the market economic system by governmental means. The third measure suggests strategies for improving efficiency within factor markets, while the remaining four outline governmental regulation of market economic activities. These seven measures span various production stages, offering a comprehensive view of the proactive governmental involvement in the market economy.

The Importance of Foundational Institutions for the Market

Institutions serve as the bedrock for the efficient functioning of a market economy and are pivotal drivers of economic growth. Well-functioning institutions help reduce transaction costs and enforcement expenditures, optimizing resource allocation efficiency within the market. Taking property rights protection as an example, the *Civil Code of the People's Republic of China*, enacted in 2021, clarifies civil relationships arising from the ownership and utilization of goods, advocating for the state to state "safeguard the equal legal status and developmental rights of all market entities." However, in practical application, there exists a tendency toward prioritizing public ownership over private ownership in property rights protection. Therefore, the *Opinions* suggests further improving the system to ensure equitable protection of diverse forms of ownership rights under the law. For instance, in addressing the pressing issue of intellectual property rights protection domestically and internationally, China has concentrated efforts on establishing uniform enforcement standards, facilitating cross-regional jurisdiction in intellectual property cases, and resolving conflicts of interests. The establishment of intellectual property courts in Beijing, Shanghai, and other places reflects endeavors to tackle issues related to judicial litigation and arbitration concerning intellectual property rights.

Using market infrastructure construction as an illustration, achieving a unified national market to facilitate the flow of goods across all provinces necessitates reducing the "hidden costs" associated with material transportation from the perspective of external transaction costs, which include direct logistics costs, transportation time, and losses incurred during goods transportation. According to data provided by the China Federation of Logistics and Purchasing, in 2021, China's cumulative logistics costs totaled RMB 16.7 trillion, accounting for 14.6% of the country's annual GDP, still slightly above the targeted 12%. In response, the *Opinions* states that efforts should be made to "promote the construction of national logistics hubs, enhance cost reduction and efficiency improvement across society, and improve the national comprehensive multi-dimensional transportation network." Through improving the supply-side efficiency of logistics enterprises and enhancing national transportation systems and other infrastructure, the objective is to further diminish the costs associated with goods circulation and realize efficient market integration. This approach aligns with the *National Logistics Hub Layout and Construction Plan*, issued by two relevant departments as early as 2018, indicating familiarity with this policy goal among pertinent businesses.

The Importance of Unified Resource and Factor Markets

In a market economic system, factor prices are reflective of their scarcity and their contributions to production, thereby establishing the market as the cornerstone for resource allocation. Guided by the "invisible hand," factors gravitate toward enterprises, industries, and regions where they are most needed. For instance, capital may move from low-return sectors to high-return ones, and populations may relocate from low-income regions to high-income ones. This reallocation of factors driven by price signals inherently enhances production efficiency. However, in reality, if impediments hinder factor mobility in the market, prices become distorted, impeding the free flow of factors and leading to a malfunction of the "invisible hand." To address this issue, it is essential to eliminate barriers to factor mobility and establish unified resource and factor markets. Key factor markets include land, labor, capital, technology, data, energy, and the ecological environment.

Taking the labor factor market as a case study, as of 2022, China's urbanization rate for the resident population has reached 64.7%, but the urbanization rate of the registered population stands at only 46.7%, leaving a gap of nearly 18 percentage points between residents and registered urban populations. This highlights the challenge of rural migrant workers and children living with their migrant worker parents in cities, numbering around 250 million, who have been unable to obtain permanent residency in their work locations. In addition, significant barriers persist in the free movement of rural labor, preventing rural migrant workers from accessing essential social security benefits, including unemployment and medical insurance, at their work locations. Consequently, they face great risks without the safety net provided by welfare systems. Compounded by difficulties in obtaining urban household registration, the children living with their migrant worker parents in cities encounter obstacles in accessing quality education, reducing the returns on educational investment and leading to inadequate investment in education. Rural migrant workers living in cities also face issues such as high education costs, limited healthcare availability, and steep housing costs. These hurdles pose significant challenges to rural migrant populations. According to estimates, even if China were to achieve the 90% urbanization rate typical of developed countries, there would still be a gap of nearly 360 million individuals between rural and urban populations. In the long term, to bridge this disparity, more rural populations will need to be absorbed into urban employment positions. Addressing this imperative necessitates reforming the unified factor market to alleviate barriers and facilitate the assimilation of rural migrant workers as new urban residents.

The Relationship Between the "Unified National Market" and the Goal of Common Prosperity

The implementation of policies and the establishment of new systems often begin with pilot projects before being gradually rolled out.

China's reform unfolds gradually. The implementation of policies and the establishment of new systems often begin with piloting before their implementation, as exemplified by initiatives like special economic zones and free trade zones. The overarching development goal is to prioritize the enrichment of specific individuals and regions, thereby catalyzing prosperity for others and ultimately achieving common prosperity. Over the course of more than four decades of economic development since the introduction of the reform and opening-up policies, distinct income disparities have emerged among regions, urban and rural regions, various forms of ownership, and different factor owners. The establishment of a unified market is envisioned to orchestrate balanced regional and mitigate or even eliminate the factors contributing to these disparities, thereby advancing the goal of common prosperity.

A trend has emerged in recent years, marked by a convergence in economic growth rates among China's provinces and municipalities. Provinces with lower per capita GDP have experienced accelerated economic growth, consequently narrowing income disparities among provinces since the initiation of reform and opening-up. However, disparities in income persist between urban and rural regions, with rural residents typically earning only about half the disposable income of their urban counterparts. To address income distribution disparities among regions, urban and rural regions, various forms of ownership, and different factor owners, and promote equitable distribution of benefits derived from reform achievements, efforts are warranted to tackle the underlying factors contributing to such disparities.

The Challenges of Equitable and Unified Market Regulation

Balancing responsibilities between China's central and local governments has long posed a complex challenge. It has been acknowledged that incentivizing local governments to drive economic development and granting them greater autonomy in formulating economic policies is necessary. However, operating within the framework of a unified national market unavoidably relinquishes some of local governments' policymaking authority in specific domains.

A Unified Market Access System

The *Opinions* emphasizes that the market plays the decisive role in the allocation of resources, highlighting the need to strengthen competitiveness through "liberation" and "relaxation" when necessary, fostering a landscape where diverse ownership economies and numerous market entities can vie. However, in important industries and key sectors critical to national economic and security interests, the state imposes regulatory thresholds to regulate and safeguard them. Nonetheless, the actual implementation of China's economic policies, certain industries find themselves navigating a gray area straddling market competition and regulatory protection. Despite the clear directive from the central government of "if not prohibited, it is granted access," local governments still erect barriers through increased administrative licensing procedures or indirectly levying fees. These actions pose operational challenges for enterprises, dent their investment confidence, and impede the efficient use of resources.

In response to these challenges, the central government has introduced a negative list system for market access, aiming to optimize the business environment through a "single national list," providing consistent market expectations, fostering healthy competition among market entities, and curbing overreach by local governments. On March 28, 2022, the National Development and Reform Commission and the Ministry of Commerce issued the Negative List for Market Access (2022), mandating local governments to diligently fulfill their regulatory obligations. They are required to establish mechanisms for the collection and reporting of violations against the negative list for market access, conduct in-depth evaluations of market access efficiency, and rigorously enforce the list's provisions, aiming to institutionalize, standardize, and precisely implement the market access system, thereby facilitating the formation of a unified national market. The paramount importance attached to this system is comprehensively demonstrated by the reiterated emphasis in the document.

Overcoming Local Protectionism

The historical prevalence of local protectionism in China stems from the intricate interplay between financial and taxation policies such as the fiscal responsibility system and localized tax frameworks, which often directly intertwine the fiscal situation of local governments with the performance of local state-owned enterprises, creating a symbiotic relationship between these entities. However, this dynamic often results in certain local state-owned enterprises trailing behind in reforms, thereby lacking market competitiveness and innovation. In response, local governments often have to implement protectionist measures to support local enterprises and help financially vulnerable businesses to survive in the market, ultimately bolstering local financial stability. The persistence of such policies is primarily attributable to legislative delays concerning local protectionism, insufficient legal constraints on protectionist actions by local governments, and the practical difficulties in delineating and sanctioning such behaviors. Therefore, local protectionism policies continue to pose a significant impediment to the operation of China's market economy.

With the advent of the dual carbon goals, new energy vehicles have emerged as the vanguard of the automotive market. Given the immense market potential and anticipated profitability, both domestic and foreign automotive manufacturers are drawn to compete in this sector. However, across various regions, a trend of imposing "implicit clauses" has emerged, aimed at restricting foreign brands. This is achieved through the provision of targeted high subsidies exclusively for locally manufactured new energy vehicles while neglecting to subsidize foreign enterprises, thereby supporting local enterprises' growth within their respective regions. Additionally, the introduction of a record-filing management system in select regions, which involves approval processes for vehicles entering the market, has indeed provided support for the development of local enterprises to a certain extent. Nevertheless, this regulatory approach has also resulted in efficiency losses and adversely impacted fair competition among enterprises.

At present, the Ministry of Industry and Information Technology is devising strategies to expedite the removal of local protectionist policies. Moving forward, pilot cities are expected, in principle, to refrain from implementing independent lists that restrict enterprise and industry access. A nationwide initiative is also underway to establish a unified market and standardized lists across the country. In addition, the state intends to introduce new policies to foster the entrepreneurial endeavors of new energy vehicle enterprises, promote the adoption of new energy vehicles in public sectors such as bus transportation, and support research and development endeavors in new energy vehicle technologies, all geared toward facilitating the development of new energy vehicle enterprises across various regions.

Understanding and Challenges of China's Industrial Technological Innovation Model

Xiaohong Chen

Technological Knowledge: A Major Source of Innovation

When discussing technological innovation, we are referencing the concept as defined by Joseph Alois Schumpeter. Unlike mere invention, innovation is a new combination derived from the "conditions" of technology. Crucially, innovation must align with market demand; as Schumpeter put it, "demands are the ultimate end of all production." Only by meeting and expanding market demands can innovation successfully stimulate a virtuous cycle of development.

Technological knowledge refers to the knowledge of science, technology, and engineering and serves as an important source and bedrock of innovation. Scientific knowledge reflects natural laws, and technological

This article is derived from the first session of the National Development Series Lecture conducted by the author, held during the spring semester at the National School of Development of Peking University on March 13, 2022.

X. Chen (✉)
Enterprise Research Institute, Development Research Center of the State Council, Beijing, China

W. Xianqing (ed.), *Understanding China's Path to Modernization*,
https://doi.org/10.1007/978-981-96-7051-2_12

knowledge pertains to methods and tools for problem-solving, while engineering knowledge involves functional engineering or product expertise geared toward fulfilling societal needs.

Technological knowledge possesses distinct economic attributes, namely externalities, accumulation, and uncertainty. Externalities refer to the phenomenon wherein once technological knowledge is uncovered, others can access it at minimal or no cost. Meanwhile, scientific knowledge primarily manifests through papers, exhibiting strong externalities, whereas technical and engineering knowledge typically exhibit comparatively weaker externalities. Accumulation implies the progression of technological knowledge building upon existing frameworks. The influence of technological knowledge, particularly fundamental scientific knowledge, is far-reaching and profound. However, it may take a long time for the transition from knowledge discovery to practical application to occur, and the outcomes of technological knowledge exploration and advancement are often uncertain and challenging to predict.

The development of technological knowledge necessitates investment and incentives. The economic characteristics inherent to technological knowledge have prompted the adoption of a developmental model that integrates both public and market inputs. Furthermore, the value derived from basic scientific research predominantly hinges on peer review and third-party application, thus necessitating support from public resources such as government funding. Conversely, the outcomes of technological development and engineering implementation are subject to market validation and are supported by incentives, which are more robust and directly linked to market competition mechanisms. Significantly, there are pronounced disparities, even at a fundamental level, in the knowledge structure, performance outcomes, stakeholders, and incentive frameworks between science, technology, and engineering domains. Therefore, the development of technological knowledge requires the concerted efforts of individuals and organizational support, the latter of which can encompass a spectrum ranging from research institutions and universities to enterprises.

The Relationship Between Science Technology and Innovation

The relationship between scientific and technological knowledge and their development and innovation is intricate and intertwined. The development of technological and engineering knowledge can directly bolster innovation, fostering a close and symbiotic relationship. While the direct relationship between science and innovation may initially appear distant, an increasingly interconnected dynamic is evident: direct interaction support manifests as innovation relying on scientific knowledge, while scientific research leans on new technological means. Human engagement also assumes a crucial role. Experts proficient in both scientific and technological domains actively facilitate the integration of science and innovation, leading to the emergence of industries grounded in scientific principles, including new industry sectors such as pharmaceuticals, digital technology, materials science, among others. The innovative trajectory of enterprises within these fields requires more direct backing from scientific research and knowledge. Therefore, the relationship from basic research to applied research to development becomes intricately interlinked, necessitating scientists' direct involvement in relevant technological innovations.

Science and technology has a close relationship with innovation, yet their objectives, developmental mechanisms, and research methodologies differ significantly. Scientific activities prioritize the resolution of scientific problems, emphasizing the discovery and establishment of reproducible rational knowledge, with research focal points on decomposition and analysis. Conversely, technological and engineering activities center on pragmatic problem-solving, where experiential knowledge plays a pivotal role, and research endeavors emphasize synthesis and balance. Innovation, on the other hand, pivots on achieving commercial success, necessitating a blend of expertise spanning technology, engineering, and business acumen, with research endeavors spotlighting the integration of economic, technological, and business knowledge domains. The subjects and frameworks of these distinct activities also exhibit variance. Understanding the similarities and differences inherent in these activities forms the basis for adept innovation management and the enhancement of innovation policies. Such comprehension then further drives the integration and even fusion of knowledge interactions among different activities, thereby catalyzing innovation.

In economics, technological feasibility, market demand, and the potential for benefit appropriation are pivotal factors influencing the occurrence of technological innovation. The innovation process necessitates investment, which comprises three essential elements. The first element is knowledge information, which directly shapes assessments of technological and business feasibility, serving as the starting point of innovation. The second element is funding, as innovation involves repeated experimentation in technology and business, requiring investment in human resources, materials, and time, making it a costly process where financial support is indispensable. The third element is the presence of entrepreneurs capable of identifying innovative opportunities, mobilizing resources for innovation, and assuming associated risks. Meanwhile, enterprises serve as the organizational carriers of invention and innovation. As commercial entities, enterprises possess both the resources and incentives to foster innovation, as innovative advancements ahead of others can yield temporary or preemptive monopoly profits, thereby fostering a virtuous cycle of development.

Based on input–output dynamics and innovation methodologies, Joseph Alois Schumpeter delineated enterprise innovation modes into five categories: new products, new methods, new materials, new markets, and new organizations. Subsequently, scholars introduced various models of innovation, such as breakthrough innovation, continuous innovation, and disruptive innovation, which offer diverse descriptions and interpretations of innovation structures, mechanisms, and processes from different vantage points. In reality, the implementation of enterprise innovation, driven by decisions and actions of different enterprises and entrepreneurs, is more intricate and tangible than scholarly portrayals. It also evolves in response to shifting internal and external conditions. Therefore, investigating the innovative practices of leading enterprises proves invaluable for understanding the realities of Chinese enterprise and industrial innovation, alongside its influencing factors, and aiding the development of forward-looking insights for the future.

China's Industrial Innovation

Now, let us look at the innovation and development models of 40 leading enterprises within the industry.

In determining leadership among these enterprises, we have two key indicators: the technological sophistication of their products and their market position, including sales volume. For startup enterprises, leadership predominantly hinges on technological prowess. The scales of these enterprises span a wide spectrum, ranging from less than RMB 10 million, constituting two of the aforementioned 40 enterprises, to several hundred billion yuan, with an average net profit margin of 15% and research and development intensity of 18%. In comparison with internationally advanced counterparts, these enterprises typically aligns closely or slightly lags behind in terms of technological competitiveness. However, some enterprises have achieved parity with or even surpassed global standards, while others still exhibit significant gaps.

The characteristics of their innovation and development models, along with their primary influencing factors, are as follows:

First, an innovation strategy coupled with a continuous upgrading process that integrates market-driven technologies with demand.

Second, sustained growth in research and development investment, characterized by long-term high intensity, and a focus on development investment, with an increasing proportion dedicated to basic research investment (e.g., Huawei, iFLYTEK, and Hengrui Pharmaceuticals, all exceeding 5% in this regard).

Third, emphasis on breakthrough innovation, with an increasing emphasis on original breakthroughs alongside the predominant catch-up breakthroughs (e.g., 5G technology). Radical innovation, as defined by scholars, brings about technological transformations and often represents crucial original innovation. In China, radical innovations predominantly manifest as catch-up endeavors, wherein existing technological principles and products serve as the foundation, but the breakthrough lies in overcoming formidable technological barriers, necessitating innovative approaches.

Fourth, various modes such as collaborative innovation, integrated innovation, and iterative innovation play crucial roles.

Fifth, increased emphasis on innovation management, leading to the gradual establishment of research and development innovation management processes that are increasingly scientifically rigorous and integrated with overall strategic objectives.

Sixth, the symbiotic relationship between innovation strategy and development strategy supports the enhancement of research and development capabilities and complementary asset capabilities across manufacturing, sales, and other domains.

Seventh, seizing opportunities for innovation brought about by changes in industry technology trends, evolving demand patterns, and policy changes.

Eighth, national innovation system anchored by industry-academia-research collaboration and capital market support, further bolstered by overarching national development and reform strategies, both general and specialized science and technology, and industrial policies aimed at fostering enterprise innovation development.

The innovation process within leading enterprises is inherently intertwined with innovation across the industry chain. Drawing from insights gleaned from these enterprises, we have made an assessment of China's industrial innovation models and their corresponding capability levels, along with an examination of their current status and future prospects, yielding results as follows:

First, leading enterprises show great progress in their industrial innovation capability. Many industries have already reached international benchmarks, with some demonstrating the capacity to compete on par with or even surpass global advanced standards (e.g., 5G technology and CATL).

Second, China's industrial innovation competitiveness exhibits distinct structural characteristics. While dominance persists in the mid-to-low-end spectrum, strides have been made in achieving international standards for high-end products to varying degrees. Emphasis also predominantly lies on application-oriented and enhancement-driven innovations, resulting in innovations that closely shadow, run in tandem with, or occasionally lead global trends. Although innovative technologies in China predominantly originate from abroad, there has been a profound shift in the knowledge acquisition paradigm, from primarily product imitation to learning technological principles, and an increasing number of innovations are founded on Chinese knowledge bases and indigenous technological research.

Third, China's improvement of industrial competitiveness and innovation capability largely relies on enterprises' independent technological research and development, coupled with their adeptness in bolstering value chain integration. This enhancement is also tied to the abundant innovation learning opportunities brought about by China's expansive market.

Fourth, there are still shortcomings in terms of knowledge, technology, and industrial chains, stemming primarily from gaps in industrial foundations, enterprises' weak research bases, and the historical backdrop of playing catch-up in innovation. The allocation of resources toward basic research within Chinese enterprises remains notably little, with this cost accounting for 0.2% in 2018—significantly lower than the levels observed in the United States (6.2%), Japan (7.8%), and South Korea (10.6%). This disparity is starkly pronounced even when compared against the corresponding figures for the United States in 1980 (3.2%), Japan in 1996 (5.2%), and South Korea in 1996 (8.1%).

Fifth, through strengthening foundational elements and addressing shortcomings via innovative efforts, China stands poised to achieve the level of innovative competitiveness comparable to that of international frontrunners across a broader spectrum of industries. This trajectory is underpinned by the continued rise of Chinese enterprises' investments in research and development and innovation; they possess complementary assets in manufacturing, sales, and value chain integration, coupled with experiential insights, to support this endeavor. Meanwhile, international precedent underscores this potential. The United States, for instance, achieved industrial competitiveness at international forefront despite its basic research lagging significantly behind Europe. Similarly, Japan caught up with the United States and Europe in the early 1980s by assimilating advanced technologies from the United States and Europe, prioritizing applications of basic research and fostering technological innovations.

Trends and Characteristics of China's Industrial Innovation Model

Considering the trajectories of global technological development, industrial transformation, changes in China's domestic and international political and economic landscapes, and insights garnered from an analysis of national development strategies, I believe that the development and changes within China's industrial innovation model exhibit the following trend characteristics across national, industrial, and enterprise dimensions.

At the national level, the foundational advancement of science, technology, and innovation models will transition toward heightened government-backed coordination and integration with market mechanisms. Moving forward, the country will continue to increase investments in research and development, with a focus on strengthening basic research and supporting technology development in four key domains. This will optimize the investment structure and cultivate a robust framework that dynamically combines national strategic scientific and technological capabilities with a market-oriented distributed innovation system, fostering an environment more conducive to innovation. Through a three-year action plan for technological system reforms and ongoing optimization endeavors, a systematic mechanism, policy management framework, as well as stronger technological financing, consulting services, and other supportive infrastructures conducive to innovative development will be established.

At the industry level, China is entering the Fourth Industrial Revolution, marked by the pervasive integration of digital technology as its cornerstone. This transition is characterized by the concurrent upgrading of existing industries, emergence of new industries, and cultivation of cutting-edge industries. The country is transitioning from an era where innovation was predominantly pursued within select industries to a phase wherein a broader spectrum of industries closely follows, aligns, or even spearheads innovation efforts, thereby fostering a landscape conducive to disruptive innovations. Furthermore, the evolution of industrial organization and structure is manifesting through a shift toward a market framework dominated by high-tech industries, accompanied by the coexistence and collaboration of innovative small and medium-sized enterprises. This evolution includes vertical integration, horizontal division of labor, coexistence of platform-based organizations, and competition within pivotal domains in China, all while fostering integration with global counterparts.

At the enterprise level, five characteristics come to the forefront.

First, there is a growing emphasis on various modes of original innovation entering the market first, that is, source innovation. This encompasses original innovations grounded in basic research, applied research, and the development of technological principles, as well as those arising from technological integration and the fusion of technological development with business model innovation.

Secondly, a combination of original innovation-driven initiatives, breakthrough innovations, and catch-up breakthrough innovations aimed at resolving bottlenecks will persist in the foreseeable future. An uptick is also expected in breakthrough innovations driven by important original innovation endeavors.

Third, enterprises will increase their investments in research and development, with a focus on bolstering investment in basic and applied research. Enterprise-level basic research will pivot toward application-oriented basic research, anticipating technological advancement trajectories through basic research to broaden the horizons of technological possibilities and seize new and potentially disruptive innovation opportunities.

Fourth, a refined research and development innovation management model, characterized by heightened scientific rigor, will be implemented alongside an environment conducive to free exploration. Furthermore, there will be an intensified focus on enhancing complementary manufacturing and market service capabilities, aimed at solidifying manufacturing capacity and underpinning industrial technological infrastructure. Collaborative innovation models, emphasizing higher quality and knowledge depth such as synergistic innovation, integrated innovation, iterative innovation, and open innovation, will remain pivotal to enterprise innovation endeavors.

Fifth, various forms of research and development innovation collaboration models, including industry-university-research partnerships and common technology development initiatives, will achieve more pronounced outcomes with deeper understanding and accelerated development processes, facilitated by enhanced governance relationships.

Chinese Path to Modernization and Financial Reform

Target Model for Financial Reform in China

Yiping Huang

The Four Distinctive Characteristics of China's Current Financial Model

Many of China's financial policies during the early phases of the reform and opening-up were originally drawn from and adapted based on Western financial systems. In a way, Western financial systems served as benchmarks for China's financial reform. However, the rapid escalation of the global financial crisis, sparked by U.S. subprime mortgage risks in October 2008, inflicted considerable damage on the global economy. Given the substantial risks associated with previously adopted models, determining the direction and approach for China's next steps in financial reform has become a significant issue demanding attention from policymakers and the broader populace.

This article is derived from the keynote speech delivered by the author during the 28th Pushan Lectures "The Target Model of China's Financial Landscape" & the conclusion ceremony of the 2022 China Finance F40 Forum Road King Scholarship Project, held on July 4, 2022.

Y. Huang (✉)
National School of Development, Peking University, Beijing, China

Institute of Digital Finance, Peking University, Beijing, China

W. Xianqing (ed.), *Understanding China's Path to Modernization*,
https://doi.org/10.1007/978-981-96-7051-2_13

For over a decade thereafter, this matter continued to occupy my thoughts. Since resuming work at Peking University in 2009, I have devoted a significant portion of my research efforts to examining, understanding, and analyzing financial reform policies. How should we evaluate the reform policies implemented over the past few decades? What factors led to challenges within a previously efficient financial system? In what direction should future reforms be directed? The recently released publication, *Understanding China's Financial System: An Economic Analysis of the Reform Policy*, represents a summary of research and reflections undertaken by Dr. Wang Xun and myself over the past decade on these pressing issues.

Let's start by defining a financial model. The term "financial model," in essence, refers to a holistic entity within the financial system that encompasses four levels: financial structure, organizational form, operational mechanism, and regulatory framework. Financial structure primarily includes capital markets or commercial banks, sometimes referred to as direct financing or indirect financing. Meanwhile, organizational form can take on various shapes, ranging from state-owned financial institutions to foreign-funded or private financial institutions. It may also involve specialized or hybrid operational setups. Operational mechanism can be regarded as the interplay between the "visible hand" (market forces) and the "invisible hand" (government policies), determining whether the financial system operates primarily under market dynamics or policy directives. Lastly, the regulatory framework is multifaceted, encompassing aspects such as segregated regulation and integrated regulation in terms of institutional structuring. In practical terms, it can be further broken down into institutional oversight, functional oversight, prudential oversight, among other dimensions.

In the early days of the reform and opening-up era, it could be said that China lacked a definitive financial model. If one were to exist, it was more of a singular financial institution model. The third plenary session of the 11th Central Committee of the Communist Party of China (CPC) in December 1978 set the stage for reform and opening-up initiatives. During this period, the sole financial institution was the People's Bank of China, which acted as the central bank, commercial bank, and regulatory authority, controlling 93% of the country's financial assets. This monopolistic institutional framework existed due to the minimal necessity for financial intermediaries during the planned economy era, where fund distribution was centrally mandated. However, this exclusive institutional model is inadequate to meet the demand for financial services amid the policy imperative of "putting economic development at the core." Consequently, the government gradually began establishing various financial institutions. Looking back now, the adjustment of the financial system entailed two intertwined processes: reconstruction and reform. The former started with a singular institution and culminated in the creation of numerous financial entities, forming a relatively comprehensive financial system, whereas the latter involved the gradual shift from government-led to market-driven financial resource allocation and pricing mechanisms.

After over 40 years of reform and opening-up, China has transitioned from having just one financial institution to establishing a robust financial system. Compared to other countries, especially those with market economies, China's new financial model showcases four key characteristics: large scale, extensive controls, weak regulation, and bank dominance.

The first characteristic is its large scale. Initially, there was only one financial institution with relatively small financial assets. This was due to the era of planned economy, where fund allocation predominantly occurred through central planning, resulting in minimal demand for financial intermediaries. However, following decades of reform and development, China's current financial system has undergone remarkable expansion. With a multitude of financial institutions, including over 4000 banks, the four major state-owned commercial banks hold prominent positions globally. While China's capital markets, including bond and stock markets, are comparatively smaller, they rank second globally. Therefore, both in terms of asset size and institutional proliferation, China's financial system has experienced significant growth.

The second characteristic is extensive control. Previously, we developed a financial repression index (FRI) for evaluating governmental intervention in the financial system, such as influencing interest rates, determining exchange rates, allocating funds, and regulating cross-border capital flows, in financial systems. An FRI value of 0 indicates a fully market-driven economy, while a value of 1 suggests predominant government control over the financial system. Research shows that in 1980, China's FRI was close to 1, indicating minimal marketization. By 2018, this index had decreased to 0.6, signaling a decrease in governmental intervention and an increase in marketization. However, within the global context, China's

2018 FRI of 0.6 ranked 14th out of 130 countries and regions, indicating that despite 40 years of reform and opening-up, China's level of government intervention in its financial system remains comparatively high on a global scale.

The third critical aspect is weak regulation. In China, there exists a fairly robust financial regulatory framework with different commissions and bureaus functioning at both central and local levels. The country has the necessary institutions, skilled personnel, and operational tools in place. However, there are still gaps when it comes to identifying and managing risks effectively. Over the past four decades, China's financial system was largely stable, primarily attributable to two crucial factors: steadfast government support as a safety net and sustained rapid economic growth. These elements ensure that amid uncertainties, the government can shore up investor confidence, preventing situations like bank panics. Such an approach affords the government ample opportunity to address existing risks and put a stop to the build-up of new ones. During the 1997 Asian financial crisis, China witnessed a surge in its banks' non-performing loan ratio, surpassing 30%, without signs of bank runs. In response, the government implemented a series of measures, including separating bad debts, injecting capital, bringing in strategic investors, and facilitating overseas listings, which helped expand the four major state-owned commercial banks, positioning them prominently on the global stage—a remarkable feat. However, the challenge lies in the fact that sustained government support may not be feasible indefinitely, particularly amid China's decelerating economic growth. Many responsibilities that ideally fall within the jurisdiction of regulatory bodies have been assumed by the government, yet effective management of financial risks remains elusive. This has resulted in relatively lax financial regulation in China.

The fourth characteristic is bank dominance. Globally, financial systems typically fall into two primary categories: those driven by capital markets and those by commercial banks, with leadership representing a mere conceptual framework. In China's financial landscape, the dominance of banks is highly pronounced.

Navigating Changes in Traditional Financial Models

This financial model presents numerous challenges. Yet, for the past several decades, it has managed to support economic expansion and financial stability without major disruptions. Nonetheless, recent developments indicate a rise in challenges, with grievances becoming increasingly pronounced. On one front, there is a decline in financial efficiency, while simultaneously, financial risks are escalating.

Why did this system work well for more than 30 years before the reform and opening-up, but now it is problematic? This stem from various factors. Foremost among them is the transition of China's economy into a new phase of development. Back in 1978, at the onset of the reform and opening-up era, China's per capita gross domestic product (GDP) stood at approximately USD 200, placing the country among the world's poorest countries. During that period, China's economy operated with low production costs, facilitating extensive growth reliant on factor inputs. In the initial 30 years after the introduction of reform and opening-up policies, China's annual average GDP growth soared to 9.8%.

However, the dynamics have gradually evolved. By 2021, China's per capita GDP had surpassed USD 12,000, edging closer to the threshold set by the World Bank for high-income economies. This transformation has ushered in a higher standard of living and improved quality of life. Yet, it has also brought forth a challenge: the increase in production costs. This shift indicates that China must move away from its former low-cost advantage and transition its growth model from one reliant on resources to one driven by innovation. Only through innovation, upgrading, and enhanced efficiency can China uphold its competitiveness; otherwise, sustaining continuous economic growth will prove arduous.

The prevailing issues within China's financial system stem from the fact that the previous financial models no longer align with the demands of the new growth model, thus necessitating a transition. In essence, the evolution of China's financial model encompasses various dimensions, predominantly reflected in the following four key aspects.

Bolstering Financial Innovation

Previously, China operated under an extensive growth model reliant on factor inputs, characterized by relatively low uncertainty. This stemmed from the production of goods historically manufactured by others over decades or even centuries, leveraging mature technologies, established marketing channels, and stable markets. So long as production costs remained sufficiently minimized, competitiveness was sustained. Simply put, the level of uncertainty was low, and risks were relatively small. However, this financial system is now inadequate to support an innovation-driven economic growth model.

Historically, governmental emphasis has consistently centered on financing for small and medium-sized enterprises (SMEs). This perennial issue confronts two main challenges: First, there is difficulty in acquiring customers. This involves how financial institutions can identify SMEs, understand their financing needs, and furnish them with appropriate financial services. Given the large number of SMEs and their relatively dispersed geographic distribution, identifying them poses considerable challenges. The traditional approach of establishing branches nationwide to be close to corporate clients is both costly and often yields insufficient returns in many regions. Second, it is difficult to managing risk. For financial institutions, granting financing services to businesses involves not only disbursing funds but also ensuring their timely repayment, which proves to be the more daunting task. This necessitates financial institutions to conduct thorough and rigorous credit risk assessments on SME clients, evaluating both their repayment ability and willingness, a highly complex process, and the conventional method typically involves assessing borrowers based on their financial data and collateral assets. However, SMEs often lack these resources, causing most banks to hesitate in providing financial services to them.

As China's economy transitions into a new phase of development, the challenge of limited financing for SMEs has become more than just a general issue in financial inclusion, elevating it to emerge as a macroeconomic constraint. This shift arises from the fact that private enterprises, particularly SMEs, are the backbone of the current Chinese economy. They play a pivotal role in urban employment, fostering innovation, and driving economic growth. In essence, one of the key hurdles in innovation lies in the capacity to provide improved financial services tailored to SMEs. Viewed from this perspective, there remains substantial room for growth in financial innovation.

The first avenue for innovation is to increase the proportion of direct financing within the financial system. In contrast to bank-dominated financial systems, direct financing via capital markets often provides better support for innovative activities. Numerous factors contribute to this, including the ability of direct financing to better identify innovative projects and the facilitated sharing of risks and rewards with entrepreneurial ventures. In contrast, bank loans require repayment with interest, occasionally imposing significant cash flow strains on businesses. Therefore, capital markets hold a comparative edge in fostering innovation. It is imperative to vigorously develop capital markets and increase the share of direct financing within the financial system.

The second avenue for innovation involves innovating the business models of commercial banks. While China's financial landscape is currently dominated by banks and may not see significant changes in the immediate future, it is crucial for banks to adapt and devise mechanisms to support innovative activities. Internationally, financial systems can generally be categorized into market-led systems, exemplified by countries like the United States and the United Kingdom, and bank-led systems, represented by countries such as Germany and Japan. Despite the United States and the United Kingdom taking the forefront in technological innovation, Germany and Japan also stand as global leaders in economic development and technological advancement. Drawing inspiration from these countries with bank-centric financial systems could prove advantageous, and innovating the operations of commercial banks to bolster their support for innovation holds significant promise for advancement.

The third avenue for innovation lies in the vigorous development of digital finance, particularly in catering to SMEs and fostering innovation. Big tech lending stands out as a particularly noteworthy domain, offering potential for enhancing financial services for SMEs, and can address the challenges associated with customer acquisition and risk management by leveraging digital technology. Traditionally, financial institutions had to establish expansive branch networks nationwide to effectively reach users, incurring high costs and often facing operational inefficiencies. Meanwhile, digital technologies and big tech platforms such as Weixin and Alipay, each boasting over a billion daily active users, have already tapped into a vast customer demographic. These platforms exhibit rapid customer acquisition rates and incur minimal marginal costs, facilitating mass customer acquisition within short time frames, thereby, to some extent, alleviating the challenge associated with customer acquisition. Simultaneously, user engagement across these platforms, including social interactions, e-commerce activities, and financial transactions, generates extensive digital footprints. The aggregation of such data enables platforms to conduct credit risk assessments, thereby determining borrowers' likelihood of default. Research indicates that utilizing big data for credit risk assessment of micro and small enterprises yields reliable results, underscoring the transformative potential of digital technology in addressing challenges that have historically plagued the traditional financial system. Of course, digital finance constitutes merely one dimension of financial innovation; innovations within markets and banking sectors also play crucial roles in driving progress.

Advancing Market-Oriented Reforms

Since the inception of reform and opening-up, China's FRI has dropped from 1 to 0.6 in 2015, although it remains relatively high. In forthcoming endeavors concerning financial resource allocation and credit decisions, it is imperative to ensure equitable treatment for both state-owned enterprises and private enterprises. This stands as a pivotal aspect of market-oriented reforms. Furthermore, there is a pressing need to earnestly pursue genuine market-driven risk pricing. Consider, for instance, the determination of loan interest rates, which epitomizes the fundamental essence of credit market risk pricing. If market risks loom large, loan interest rates ought to reflect this reality, covering the associated risks. Failure to do so may lead to substantial future losses, underscoring the fundamental necessity of market-driven risk pricing. However, in recent years, regulatory bodies have been exerting pressure on banks to reduce financing costs for SMEs through administrative means. While this approach may yield short-term benefits, it is likely to impede both the willingness and capacity of banks to consistently provide loans to SMEs in the long run.

While the challenge of financing remains persistent for SMEs, there have been notable improvements in the financing landscape for these enterprises in China in recent years, as evidenced by two sets of data. Firstly, data from the OECD reveals that the proportion of SME loans in total bank loans in China has reached 65%, placing the country among the top, alongside South Korea and Japan. This statistic underscores the substantial progress China has made in this area after more than a decade of efforts. The second set of data pertains to the asset-liability ratio of private enterprises. Following the global financial crisis, the financing difficulties faced by private enterprises became pronounced, with a noticeable trend toward deleveraging, while state-owned enterprises maintained a relatively stable asset-liability ratio. However, by the end of 2021, the asset-liability ratio of private enterprises in China had surpassed that of state-owned enterprises. The underlying reasons for this shift are multifaceted, given that private enterprises encompass both SMEs and large enterprises. Taken together, these two sets of data at least suggest significant improvements in the financing environment for SMEs in China.

The key matter involves the mechanisms during these improvements. Currently, China still predominantly relies on administrative measures to address issues. Despite the contribution of financial institutions' internal innovations, such as digital financial innovations, the most significant impact still comes from administrative regulatory measures. These typically require each commercial bank to incrementally raise both the total loan volume to SMEs and the percentage of SME loans within their total loan portfolio annually compared to the previous year, otherwise they will face regulatory accountability.

These assertive administrative policies have effectively increased loans to SMEs. However, a significant challenge arises, that is, to ensure both risk manageability and profitability. Without satisfaction of these two criteria, even if short-term policy objectives are achieved, it becomes arduous to sustain them in the long term, potentially engendering further complications. "Profitable" necessitates that costs should remain lower than potential returns, while "risk manageability" requires banks to possess adept customer acquisition and risk mitigation capabilities to maintain risks at a relatively low level.

The approach of employing big data to substitute collateral for credit risk assessment by major tech platforms appears to yield positive results for the time being. For instance, the average credit delinquency rate of loans facilitated by WeBank and MYBank is significantly lower than that of similar loans from traditional commercial banks, indicating the efficacy of this credit risk management approach.

Consequently, while the financing landscape for SMEs has experienced recent improvements, persistently relying on administrative mandates to compel commercial banks to extend loans to SMEs could ultimately lead to significant financial risks and repercussions. Therefore, China must further advance market-oriented reforms, addressing issues within market frameworks, including the realization of market-driven risk pricing and continued reduction of the FRI. Central to this endeavor is fostering financial innovation itself, which serves as the overarching trajectory for future development.

Enforcing Pragmatic Financial Regulations

While China has maintained financial stability without significant issues over the past three decades, this achievement has not solely relied on regulatory policies. Instead, it has largely leaned on government support and sustained economic growth. Nevertheless, this approach may not be sustainable in the long term. As China's financial system continues to expand in size and complexity, it becomes increasingly impractical for the government to consistently provide bailouts during times of crisis. Additionally, China's economic growth rate has been steadily declining. The Bank for International Settlements has highlighted that financial risks have been escalating globally since the financial crisis, encapsulating them as the "risk triangle": rising leverage, declining productivity, and shrinking policy space. Given this context, China can no longer rely on its previous financial model to underpin economic growth.

There exists considerable room for improvement in regulatory practices within China. Despite having frameworks, personnel, tools, and objectives in its regulatory system, the effective implementation of regulatory rules has often been deficient in several areas. Over the past two years, issues have emerged in small and medium-sized banks, with a significant portion of the blame attributed to the ineffective enforcement of regulatory rules. For example, instances of irregular operations by major shareholders, expressly prohibited by regulations, have become relatively prevalent, highlighting the imperative for further enhancement in China's regulatory framework, specifically in three crucial directions as follows:

The first direction lies in objectives. The primary objective of regulation should prioritize ensuring fair competition, preventing monopolies, and safeguarding consumer interests, all while maintaining financial stability as the ultimate goal. Anything beyond this scope should fall outside the regulatory purview. Currently, China's regulatory objectives are overly complex and not entirely consistent with each other—industry regulation and financial regulation inherently clash. The second direction should be in empowerment. Once regulatory objectives are defined, corresponding authorities should be vested with the requisite powers to determine appropriate measures and timing for their implementation.

The third direction is accountability. Historically, the financial regulatory system in China lacked accountability. Even when issues arose, there seemed to be a collective evasion of responsibility. Hence, it is paramount to foster accountability within regulation. After over four decades of financial reform, China has established a regulatory framework, albeit largely formal rather than substantive. In the future, efforts should be directed toward evolving it into a more robust regulatory framework.

Prudently Advancing Financial Opening

Financial opening is, undeniably, crucial, but it warrants a prudent approach. Rushing into capital projects and opening up the financial sector prematurely has led many countries to precipitate major financial crises. Therefore, it is imperative to strike a balance between the improved efficiency of financial opening and financial stability.

In summary, as China transitions into a new stage of development, its current financial system no longer adequately aligns with the growth patterns of the new economy. Therefore, we need to promote corresponding transformation, such as strengthening financial innovation, advancing market-oriented reforms, enforcing tangible financial regulations, and prudently advancing financial opening. Viewed from this perspective, the trajectory of China's targeted financial model becomes evidently clear: following the path of capital markets, pursuing market-oriented reforms, and seeking internationalization.

Fundamental Characteristics of Future Financial Reforms

While the general trajectory of financial reform in China appears relatively clear, there remains considerable room for envisioning its evolution, particularly concerning the future financial model. Will it mirror the bank-dominated financial systems of Germany and Japan, or will it follow the market-led financial model of the United Kingdom and the United States? Can the degree of marketization reach such heights, and how will the regulatory framework be structured? These inquiries are intricately linked with the fundamental characteristics of financial reform in China.

It is worth noting that despite having exemplars to draw lessons from during the financial and economic reforms, even since their beginnings, China has never explicitly outlined a specific reform blueprint or target model. This could be attributed to two primary factors. Firstly, when the decision to implement the reform and opening-up policies was made in 1978, it was challenging to foresee the changes that would unfold over the next few decades. Moreover, the prevailing political climate at that time did not readily allow for the explicit expression of certain radical ideas. For example, the concept of a socialist market economy only emerged after 15 years of reform. Secondly, China's economic reforms, including financial reforms, have been notably pragmatic. The purpose of implementing reform policies has been to address immediate challenges, and sometimes the ultimate goal may not have been as pivotal as the direction, despite being evident.

In light of our analysis, pragmatic financial reforms exhibit the following two characteristics:

First, feasibility is paramount. Any proposed reform policy must satisfy the criterion of feasibility. While certain policies may sound promising in theory, their effective implementation can prove challenging, rendering them impracticable and inconsequential. For instance, the immediate establishment of an extensive capital market overnight is not a feasible endeavor. Additionally, political feasibility holds equal significance, given China's penchant for gradual, dual-track reforms. A key aspect of pragmatism is addressing practical concerns while ensuring feasibility.

Second, the determination and evaluation of reform measures are primarily oriented toward outcomes. Each stage of reform must be substantiated by tangible results—advancing if effective, retreating if ineffective. This approach echoes Deng Xiaoping's philosophy of "crossing the river by feeling the stones" and "it doesn't matter if a cat is black or white; so long as it catches mice, it's a good cat." Despite encountering challenges during the four decades of financial reform in China, the overall outcomes have been satisfactory. However, it is important to acknowledge that this pragmatic approach to reform may sometimes engender new issues. As reforms are incremental rather than radical, they might inadvertently foster new interest groups that could potentially hinder further reform efforts. Therefore, sustained progress in reform is an essential requirement for the success of pragmatic reforms.

China's trajectory of financial reform is becoming increasingly defined. Essentially, the goal is to enhance marketization, internationalization, the role of capital markets, and regulatory effectiveness. Nonetheless, China will persist in implementing pragmatic reform measures over an extended period, advancing steadily one step at a time.

Firstly, while the share of direct financing in China's capital market is expected to gradually increase, it is unlikely to swiftly reach levels seen in countries such as the United Kingdom and the United States. Several factors influence whether a country's financial system leans toward being bank-dominated or oriented, including legal frameworks, cultural contexts, and political structures. Therefore, as the China nation progresses toward a path where direct financing through capital markets takes precedence, banks will remain the predominant source of funding in China for the foreseeable future.

Secondly, China will progressively adopt a mixed-ownership model in the future. However, the ability to transition from segmented operations to mixed ownership hinges on risk management capabilities. While mixed ownership can yield substantial returns and enhance efficiency, the complexities of risk management and identification are heightened. Therefore, the shift from segmented operations to mixed ownership will occur gradually.

Thirdly, market-oriented reforms will not happen all at once. Despite the anticipated decline in China's FRI, the government will still play a significant role in the financial system. So long as administrative intervention proves advantageous, progress will persist.

Fourthly, significant uncertainty surrounds the development of regulatory frameworks. At present, it remains unclear whether China's current sectoral regulatory model will evolve into comprehensive service institutions or transition to a "twin peaks" model, which distinguishes between prudential regulation and conduct regulation.

In summary, back in 1978, China's financial system was not fully developed; what was considered a financial model at the time was actually dominated by a few key institutions. Fast forward over 40 years of market reforms and restructuring, China's financial landscape now reflects four key characteristics: significant scale, stringent regulation, limited supervision, and predominant reliance on banks. However, the effectiveness of this previously successful financial system is now diminishing amid current market dynamics. Looking ahead, China aims to increase direct financing, boost marketization and internationalization, and enhance regulatory efficiency. While the overarching direction is clear, China is likely to move forward in a practical manner. This means that, despite an anticipated increase in direct financing within China's capital markets in the foreseeable future, it will not swiftly match the levels seen in the United Kingdom and the United States. Even as China's financial system embraces greater market orientation, with asset pricing and resource allocation leaning toward market mechanisms, governmental involvement may persist significantly. Furthermore, achieving true property neutrality to ensure fair competition between state-owned and private enterprises is expected to be a slow and gradual process.

However, if we adhere to the principle of pragmatism, with a focus on feasibility conditions and outcome orientation, it is highly probable to achieve a steady and continuous advancement of reform. The envisioned future financial model should be able to better support economic growth in the new developmental stage. Concurrently, we must also remain thoroughly prepared for potential financial risks and turbulence that may arise in the future.

Strengthening Routine Supervision to Direct Healthy Capital Development

Hao Wang

In late April 2022, the Political Bureau of the CPC Central Committee conducted a collective study on conducting law-based regulation and guidance to promote the healthy development of capital within China. Capital was categorized as an important factor of production within the framework of the socialist market economy, emphasizing the importance of regulating and guiding capital development within the context of a socialist market economy, signifying a significant economic, political, practical, and theoretical concern. The session highlighted the necessity to deepen the understanding of various types of capital and their respective roles within the new era, regulate and guide the healthy development of capital, and leverage its constructive role as an important factor of production.

General Secretary Xi Jinping's comments regarding capital are poised to significantly boost confidence across various capital sectors, particularly non-state-owned entities, fostering sustained operations within China. As for conducting law-based regulation and guidance to promote the healthy

---

The article was originally published in the *Beijing News* in May 2022 and was revised by the author before being included in this publication.

H. Wang (✉)
National School of Development, Peking University, Beijing, China

W. Xianqing (ed.), *Understanding China's Path to Modernization*,
https://doi.org/10.1007/978-981-96-7051-2_14

development of capital, it not only epitomize the overarching policy directive to upholding and fulfilling the commitments to the public and non-public sectors, but also underscore the central government's strategy for leveraging various types of capital to propel economic and social development. China presently adheres to a model where public ownership plays the dominant role alongside economic entities under diverse forms of ownership. Irrespective of capital type, adherence to principles that serve the interests of the people and the country warrants developmental opportunities within China's landscape.

The idea of "conducting law-based regulation and guidance to promote the healthy development of capital" is an elaboration on the preceding concept of "preventing the unregulated expansion of capital." It places a stronger emphasis on positive incentives, showing a more proactive approach to capital management. This not only offers more comprehensive directives to governmental regulatory bodies but also signifies a more constructive stance toward capital. Regulation and guidance serve as instrumental means, with the ultimate goal being the "healthy development of capital" that aligns with the broader interests of the country.

Capital Should Be Guided to Serve National Interests

Since the introduction of the reform and opening-up, there has been significant development in the CPC and the Chinese government's understanding of capital dynamics, albeit amid formidable challenges. In the early 1980s, the widespread employment of workers by individual entrepreneurs, represented by figures such as Nian Guangjiu, the founder of Fool's Melon Seeds (*Shazi Guazi*), sparked discussions on the nature of private capital in society. In 1983, Deng Xiaoping made a notable remark, "Certain individual employers have surpassed the regulations established by the State Council; this does not contradict socialism. So long as we stay on the right path and maintain clarity of thought, this issue can be easily resolved—even in eight or ten years, without making any harm."[1] From then on, urban private enterprises have gradually prospered.

[1] This excerpt is sourced from page 252 of *Selected Works of Deng Xiaoping* Vol. 3, published by People's Publishing House in 1993.

Throughout the 1980s and 1990s, township and village enterprises surged in numbers, emerging as a pivotal force driving China's economic development. In addition to enterprises organized by township collectives, there are also many individually owned enterprises that transitioned into township enterprises through a process known as "affiliation."[2] The adoption of the ambiguous property rights model of "affiliation" was partly influenced by the stringent government restrictions on private capital during that period. However, following Deng Xiaoping's Southern Tour Talks, the state gradually eased its policy constraints on the private economy. Private enterprises with clear property rights began to demonstrate competitive advantages over township and village enterprises, eventually supplanting them as the primary force in the non-state economy. Evidence shows that non-state capital has made significant contributions to economic growth and the generation of employment opportunities.

All forms of capital, including state-owned, collective, private, foreign, and mixed, inherently pursue profitability. While state-owned capital primarily serves the broader population, the maintenance and enhancement of value represent vital benchmarks for capital managers' routine assessments. Therefore, even within a socialist framework where public ownership prevails, it remains imperative to thoroughly explore methods to regulate and guide the healthy development of capital.

In a recent collective study session of the Political Bureau of the CPC Central Committee, capital was affirmed for its contributions to the prosperous development of China's socialist market economy during the past 40 years of reform and opening-up. The session also extensively discussed how to regulate and guide the healthy development of capital within the socialist system. This involved addressing issues such as the appropriate management of capital and profit distribution, improving the foundational institutions of the capital market, establishing regulatory mechanisms akin to a traffic light system for capital, enhancing corporate governance efficiency, and cracking down on corruption within the realm of capital, with particular emphasis on investigating corrupt practices associated with unregulated capital expansion and platform monopolies. It was explicitly emphasized that in cases where laws and regulations lack clarity, regulatory responsibilities should be assigned in accordance with

[2] "Affiliation" in its full form is known as "enterprise affiliation operation," an industry-specific term referring to the process by which an institution or organization becomes subordinate or attached to another institution or organization.

the principle of "those who approve and those in charge shall be responsible for regulatory oversight." It is evident that while promoting the sound growth of capital, regulatory oversight over capital should not be relaxed but rather reinforced.

To regulate and guide the healthy development of capital, it is important to incentivize capital to serve the broader interests of the country. "We must foster a culture of integrity that is civilized, healthy, aspirational, and virtuous. We should educate and direct capital entities to uphold core socialist values, emphasizing trustworthiness, social responsibility, and adherence to a righteous path." Given capital's inherent drive for profitability, unregulated capital may veer toward unethical practices in pursuit of gains, resulting in adverse consequences. The regulatory ethos seeks to align the self-interests of market players with national interests through well-defined frameworks and regulations.

Simultaneously, in regulating and guiding the healthy development of capital, we should safeguard against threats to social stability and national security. As a socialist country, China's national framework epitomizes collective welfare and should remain impervious to undue influence or dominance by capital. Furthermore, unregulated capital expansion could exacerbate income disparities, imperiling social equilibrium. Therefore, instituting an equitable secondary distribution mechanism that balances efficiency with equity is of great importance.

The regulation and guidance of capital's healthy development also necessitate the enhancement of government regulatory departments' capabilities. The principle of "those who approve and those in charge shall be responsible for regulatory oversight" reinforces the accountability of regulatory bodies. A failure to adhere to this principle may lead to a scenario wherein officials evade regulatory duties, commonly referred to as "being indolent of duties." Government departments should not only establish a transparent and harmonious relations between political and commercial spheres but also take proactive measures to improve the business environment. This entails fostering robust communication channels with enterprises, offering timely assistance in issue resolution, and fostering complementing dynamics between the market and the government.

Governance of the Platform Economy Should Become a Norm

An essential focal point for regulating and guiding the healthy development of capital lies within the domain of the platform economy. As a new economy, the platform economy boasts innovative models and rapid expansion, presenting substantial challenges to governmental oversight. Within a mere two decades or so, the platform economy has surged from nonexistence to becoming an integral component of China's national economic landscape. This meteoric rise has been accompanied by the emergence of a myriad of dazzling new technologies and products, which not only enrich people's lives and stimulate economic expansion but also generate a multitude of intricate social ramifications.

Given the considerable influence wielded by platforms, the regulation and guidance of capital's healthy development within the platform economy are of paramount importance. Platforms hold the potential for significant societal benefits, yet they also harbor the capacity to inflict considerable negative repercussions. Simply stifling the growth of the platform economy could seriously impede economic progress and technological innovation. On the flip side, allowing platforms to expand without restraint may pose risks to social stability. Therefore, it is imperative to implement well-calibrated regulatory measures to navigate the platform economy toward a mutually beneficial pursuit of capital returns and societal welfare.

Initially, in an effort to promote private innovation and economic growth, regulatory authorities created a relaxed market environment conducive to the platform economy's development. Areas such as privacy protection, information security, and anti-monopoly efforts were approached with minimal intervention. However, this laissez-faire approach led to latent tensions, eventually manifesting in a surge of platform anti-monopoly activities, particularly in late 2020. Aligned with the directive of curbing unregulated expansion of capital, numerous platform companies' mergers and acquisitions underwent heightened scrutiny.

The regulation of platforms is poised to evolve into a routine practice. The platform economy, to a certain extent, epitomizes the trajectory of future economic development and stands as one of the rare domains in China with global leadership. Rather than being abandoned due to concerns, it should continue to be developed with government support, with emphasis placed on "accurately identifying key areas and entities potentially posing systemic risks, enhancing governance's foresight and agility, and detecting risks early for timely resolution and mitigation." The recent collective study undertaken by the Political Bureau of the CPC Central Committee not only shows support for the development of the platform economy but also sets high standards for standardization and directive work.

The platform economy tends to naturally exhibit a "winner-take-all" dynamic, where achieving significant capital scale is common rather than rare. While the vast scale of certain platforms may seem unfavorable for social stability, they are often engaged in intense real-world competition and face potential competitors, without actually controlling the market. Except for certain sectors, the overall market competition within China's platform economy remains relatively robust. Leveraging strong network effects, a select few platforms capitalize on their first-mover advantages to establish market dominance, posing challenges for new entrants and contributing to a monopolistic environment. Meanwhile, certain platforms heavily invest in constructing digital ecosystems, deeply integrating into various aspects of people's daily routines. While this integration brings about numerous conveniences, it also raises concerns regarding unregulated expansion.

Given the unique nature of platforms, there is a need to delve into formulating competition and regulatory policies tailored specifically for the platform economy. Unlike traditional economies, competition within the platform economy may not necessarily work in favor of companies leveraging network effects, necessitating striking a delicate balance in overseeing platform capital, finding a sweet spot between economies of scale and fostering fair competition, or exploring a market structure that accommodates both elements. For instance, implementing regulations such as "Platform Connectivity," which mandate compatibility among platforms, can help sustain or even amplify network effects while incentivizing platform firms to improve service quality, foster healthy competition, and mitigate the undue expansion of particular capital entities.

In the current era of socialism with Chinese characteristics, state power is entrusted with safeguarding the interests of the majority and remains impervious to the influence of capital. Through appropriate regulations and guidance, capital can be harnessed for the collective benefit, emerging as a key factor in the socialist market economy. Within this context, the platform economy assumes significant importance in the regulation and guidance of capital. However, while platform companies have made substantial contributions to economic development and the enhancement of people's livelihood, they are also confronted with various challenges. By examining the unique features of the platform economy and implementing effective government regulations and anti-monopoly measures, we can not only govern capital conduct but also advance platform growth and technological innovation. This will further fortify the socialist market economy with distinctive Chinese characteristics.

Financial Support for the Real Economy Is Not Simply About Giving Concessions

Xiaochun Liu

Financial support for the real economy is all about putting finance in its proper place within the economic and social landscape. Finance originates from the needs of the real economy; without a robust foundation within it, finance is just a house of cards. In the current context, emphasizing the reintegration of finance with its origins and reinforcing support for the real economy carries significant practical importance.

Historically, driven by profit-seeking, certain countries and regions have been focusing solely on dominating the economic hierarchy, which has led to a considerable concentration of resources in the financial sector. This excessive detachment of finance from the real economy has displaced real economic activities, resulting in the hollowing-out of industries, which not only precipitates in economic structural imbalances but also presents substantial challenges for societal governance. Furthermore, these socioeconomic risks extend globally, posing significant threats to the economies of other countries. This serves as a crucial lesson that warrants acknowledgment and assimilation.

The article was published in *Caijing Magazine*'s November 7, 2022 issue.

X. Liu (✉)
Shanghai Finance Institute, Shanghai, China

W. Xianqing (ed.), *Understanding China's Path to Modernization*,
https://doi.org/10.1007/978-981-96-7051-2_15

Furthermore, within China itself, finance plays a crucial role in supporting reform and opening-up policies, as well as driving high-speed economic growth. The financial sector has seen significant growth in both scale and operational capabilities. However, owing to limited regulatory experience during its development, certain issues such as regulatory arbitrage, shadow banking, and capital misallocation have emerged to varying degrees. These phenomena have diverted resources away from the real economy and also posed certain systemic risks.

Additionally, considering the prevailing international geopolitical dynamics and pressures from the United States, it is imperative for China to maintain a stable economic structure to withstand such pressures. A balanced relationship between finance and the real economy is not merely a fundamental requirement for ensuring a healthy and stable economy, but also forms the basis for economic resilience and the capacity to navigate external pressures.

Developing a Rational Perspective on the Real Economy

Financial support for the real economy involves effectively allocating market resources, accelerating capital accumulation, promoting expanded reproduction, advancing technology innovation, and industrializing technological achievements, which yield positive outcomes by curbing speculation, minimizing fund idling, and counteracting negative impacts that could impede the real economy, thereby ensuring the high-quality economic development. Conversely, the financial system is interdependent; only a stable real economic structure can ensure the stable operation of the financial system.

Financial support for the real economy requires us to have a rational perspective of the real economy. The concept of the real economy extends beyond manufacturing firms; it encompasses any industry or business that creates social and economic value, contributing to the realization of such value. Enterprises or industries engaged in activities such as capital speculation or unproductive trading, rather than creating social and economic value, do not align with the essence of the real economy. Even within primary and secondary industries, financial support should target healthy, innovative, profitable, and promising enterprises, rather than uniformly supporting all businesses within these sectors. This approach epitomizes the efficient allocation of market resources through finance.

This discussion ties into the prevalent issue that businesses have encountered in recent years regarding the difficulty and high cost of financing. However, these terms can be somewhat misleading.

Firstly, let's talk about the high cost of financing. People often intuitively believe that the cost of capital is determined by financial institutions. However, in reality, the fundamental pricing of capital is contingent upon the dynamics of supply and demand within the market. Financial institutions act as intermediaries between the supply and demand sides of capital, so the prices they offer are reactive rather than proactive. In this sense, financial institutions do not singularly determine capital prices. Moreover, in addition to the basic supply and demand dynamics, fluctuations in international capital markets also influence domestic capital pricing.

Furthermore, financing costs (such as loan interest rates) include a risk premium associated with the borrower, further influencing capital prices. Within the modern central banking system, the central bank's benchmark interest rate serves as a foundational reference for market capital prices. Adjustments to this benchmark rate by the central bank are rational responses to macroeconomic conditions. Therefore, from this perspective, market rates (capital prices) are neutral outcomes resulting from the comprehensive interaction of various factors; it cannot simply be classified as either high or low cost.

On the other hand, the price of capital itself plays a critical role in eliminating market entities that lack profitability (i.e., those unable to withstand market capital prices), facilitating the allocation of scarce resources to entities capable of effectively creating social value. For capital prices to fulfill this regulatory function, they must indeed be expensive. By understanding the underlying principles governing capital prices, it becomes easier to discuss the financing challenges.

Just as borrowers often complain about the high cost of financing, their desire for increased funds is universal. However, whether these needs belong to businesses or individuals, the mere requirement for capital does not necessarily translate into effective demand, which is demand backed by the capacity to pay. In the context of financing, it means that only financing demands with the ability to repay principal and interest are considered valid.

Presently, there is a lack of clear distinction between valid and invalid demands. Instead, people generally label it as difficult to obtain financing. Meanwhile, banks and financial institutions grapple with a scarcity of assets and struggle to find reliable borrowers. Motivated by profit, banks exhibit a strong inclination to extend credit, willingly extending loans to any market entity that can assure the safety of credit funds and pay a reasonable interest rate. Ensuring the security of credit funds essentially means safeguarding depositors' funds. Should the financial sector continue to support numerous inefficient, heavily leveraged, and disorderly expanding businesses in its backing of the real economy, it not only fails to comply with the standards of high-quality development but also weakens China's economic base, making it susceptible to external shocks.

Therefore, pinning the difficulty and high cost of financing solely to financial institutions overlooks the multifaceted nature of both the causes and potential solutions. The crux of the matter lies in borrowers continually improving their operational and managerial capabilities to earn the market's confidence. Concurrently, there should be increased emphasis on advancing reform and opening-up initiatives, reinforcing the rule of law in the market, and fostering a business environment conducive for borrowers.

Of course, it is also important to acknowledge that in the current era of heightened technological innovation, there exist significant differences in development models between emerging industries and traditional sectors. Consequently, traditional risk assessment models used by financial institutions may prove inadequate for these enterprises. This indeed contributed to the difficulty of financing, necessitating financial institutions to innovate and explore new business models and products.

For example, within the domain of bank lending, can new loan models tailored specifically for technology and innovation enterprises be developed? In this regard, proactive governmental involvement is essential. Regulatory and fiscal authorities must institute corresponding supportive policies to direct financial institutions toward actively pursuing innovation in this realm.

Banks Need Reasonable Profits

The prerequisite for fostering the high-quality development of the real economy through financial support necessitates a robust and healthy financial sector, and central to this support are commercial banks. As commercial entities, these banks need to achieve reasonable profits in market competition and interactions to ensure their sustained capacity to support the real economy.

The reasonable profits obtained by commercial banks are contingent upon market interactions and competition with all stakeholders, not solely limited to competitions between banks. It is imperative that all market participants earn their profits through competition, and not concessions from other sectors for revenue generation.

If Chinese enterprises, irrespective of their ownership—be it state-owned or private—lack market competitiveness and rely on concessions from other sectors, they will struggle to compete on a global scale. Such reliance also compromises their ability to achieve high-quality development standards. Therefore, the essence of enterprise growth lies in fostering entrepreneurial spirit, enhancing operational and managerial capabilities, promoting innovation, and expanding market reach.

In the current A-share market, listed banks exhibit a notably lower asset profit margin compared to non-bank listed companies, indicative of the banking industry's reliance on high-leverage operations. However, listed banks do have a slightly higher capital profit margin than the average level observed among non-bank enterprises. Even so, the profitability of listed banks only ranks 11th among all industries in the A-share market, placing them within the medium to upper echelon of profit levels.

This suggests that in China, the banking industry is not a lucrative or high-profit segment; rather, it earns average social profits. The substantial profits the banks generate are primarily attributed to their large asset sizes and significant presence in the A-share market, creating the societal perception that banks are making big money. This also indicates the prevalent issue of weak profitability among many listed companies in China, despite receiving substantial bank credit support; therefore, improving operational efficiency emerges as an imperative for them to enhance their profit margins.

Furthermore, China's banking industry exhibits a comparatively higher level of profitability compared to its counterparts in Japan and Western Europe, albeit slightly lower than that of American banks, indicating that the profit level of China's banking sector is, for the most part, reasonable. On the other hand, within the A-share market, banks' market value typically falls below their net worth, suggesting a lack of recognition by the market regarding the current and future profit-generating potential of banks. In reality, banks are more inclined and capable of supporting the real economy when they earn good profits. Their willingness to lend stems from a strong desire for profit, while their lending capacity is underpinned by their capacity to provide loans, including debt capacity and profit-making prowess. Banks are also emboldened to lend when borrowers exhibit sound operations, promising prospects, and sufficient repayment and interest payment capabilities. Their adeptness in identifying and managing risks further facilitate their aptitude in lending.

Of course, it is imperative for commercial banks to extend temporary and appropriate concessions to small and medium-sized enterprises grappling with operational hardships amid the unprecedented challenges posed by the COVID-19 pandemic. However, this necessitates proactive governmental involvement. Going beyond mere directives, policy interventions should emphasize guidance and incentives, harnessing market dynamics to afford commercial banks relatively advantageous developmental prospects amid these temporary concessions.

In essence, the pivotal focus lies in empowering banks to exercise their role in efficiently allocating resources within the market, thereby fostering conditions conducive for supporting the high-quality development of the real economy.

Standardizing the Direct Financing Market

Numerous tasks must be undertaken to facilitate financial support for the high-quality development of the real economy.

Foremost, there is a pressing need to vigorously develop multi-tiered capital markets. Beyond the stock market, a diverse range of policies should be formulated to incentivize and direct the growth of various forms of equity investment, including venture capital, aimed at fostering technological innovation and the industrialization of technological advancements. These policies should not only stimulate market dynamism to attract more participants into venture capital but also mitigate irrational speculation, thereby fortifying the groundwork for technological innovation and venture capital.

China's direct financing market entered the arena relatively late, and there remains a limited understanding among society and industry regarding the various financing methodologies, often perceiving them solely as a speculative tool. Participants in the direct financing market can be categorized into four groups: investors, fundraisers, traders, and intermediaries.

In theory, while traders are technically investors, their investment objectives and behavioral patterns deviate from those of traditional investors. Illustrated within the context of the stock market, investors allocate their investments toward listed companies, emphasizing the company's intrinsic value. Conversely, traders predominantly partake in stock trading, prioritizing market trends over the company's fundamental value. Fundraisers in the direct financing market pursue financing exclusively to address their operational capital requirements.

However, there is a discernible shift among today's investors toward a more transient, trader-oriented mindset, characterized by a lack of steadfast commitment to the companies they invest in. Simultaneously, certain fundraisers perceive listing and financing merely as avenues for profit generation. These trends disrupt the behavioral dynamics of the direct financing market and periodically give rise to market risks, consequently impeding the development of the real economy. Therefore, targeted interventions are imperative to formulate policies that regulate and guide the market, thereby enabling direct financing to more effectively serve the high-quality development of the real economy.

Additionally, the banking sector needs to enhance its asset-liability management capabilities. In the current landscape, commercial banks' assets and liabilities have become increasingly diversified. Credit assets now comprise only about half of total bank assets, implying that banks contribute to the real economy through avenues beyond credit provision. It is also crucial for society to shift away from the notion that banks solely provide loan services. Financial support for the real economy should not simply translate to soliciting loans from banks. Rather, banks should comprehensively and flexibly leverage a diverse array of functions including assets, liabilities, and payment settlement to offer comprehensive financial services to the real economy.

Bond business stands out as a vital avenue for banks to engage in the direct financing market, with banks serving as core liquidity providers within the bond market. It is imperative for banks of all types to further prioritize the establishment of internal bond business frameworks, foster diverse teams, and refine institutional processes. Specifically, there is a pressing need to rigorously separate the risks associated with trading activities from investment operations and to delineate the distinct logic and risk priorities between wealth management and asset management endeavors.

Wealth management services entail the management of assets for investors, where investment itself serves as a means rather than an end goal. Conversely, asset management services aim to invest assets by securing funds for said assets. Owing to these differing objectives, the approach to risk management diverges between these two service categories.

These two service types also differ in the operational methods when supporting the real economy. Presently, many departments or individuals, when discussing support for the real economy, often equate wealth management funds with credit funds, potentially introducing latent risks.

Furthermore, attention should be paid to the significant role of banking payment settlement and various innovative transactional businesses in supporting the high-quality development of the real economy.

It is also imperative to delve deeply into the new circumstances, developments, and characteristics of the real economy and to innovate financial products, service modalities, and risk management models accordingly. Particularly with the emergence of sci-tech enterprises and industries, there exist many operational characteristics and risk dynamics distinct from traditional sectors. Supporting these entities, including supporting the real economy, entails not merely lowering risk thresholds but thoroughly analyzing the operational characteristics and risk logic of these industries and sectors. This requires providing innovative and effective support methods and service offerings without compromising on risk management standards.

China's economy predominantly relies on indirect financing, despite efforts to develop multi-tiered capital markets, a process that will inevitably entail a protracted timeline. Confronted with unprecedented changes and complex international competitive landscapes, the rapid pace of technological innovation and the development of strategic emerging industries necessitate the exploration of new approaches for commercial bank credit provision. This endeavor demands not only initiatives from commercial banks but also proactive support from regulatory bodies and other governmental departments.

Emerging industries inherently harbor high failure risks and lack effective credit enhancement frameworks. Therefore, extending credit support to such enterprises demands the exploration of new revenue models and risk compensation mechanisms to cover potential losses. This entails policy acknowledgment of these new revenue models and risk compensation mechanisms, along with pertinent adjustments in fiscal, tax, and accounting practices. Additionally, governments must establish corresponding credit enhancement mechanisms to furnish commercial banks with adequate safeguards against risks.

Chinese Path to Modernization and Corporate Governance

Enterprise Strategy Amid New Global Changes

Gaoning Ning

When discussing the unprecedented changes of the century, many people would mention cross-cyclical and counter-cyclical adjustments in terms of business recommendations. However, there are few suggestions tailored to the unique circumstances of each company. In reality, every enterprise is caught in the vortex of the present cycle. How can they strengthen cross-cyclical and counter-cyclical adjustments? If a company today already has 75% debt, depreciated assets, and declining operations, how can it make cross-cyclical and counter-cyclical adjustments and adapt to the major changes? Its immediate priority is evidently to address survival issues and sustain operations. Whereas, for companies in slightly better conditions, their primary task is to maintain existing profits while improving their financial situation.

As the year draws to a close, every company must make budgets for the upcoming year. Budgeting for a company relies on forecasts, including

This article is derived from a speech delivered by the author at the Management Subforum of the 7th National Development Forum, "China's New Journey and National Development," held at the National School of Development of Peking University on December 18, 2022.

G. Ning (✉)
National School of Development, Peking University, Beijing, China

W. Xianqing (ed.), *Understanding China's Path to Modernization*,
https://doi.org/10.1007/978-981-96-7051-2_16

predictions about the economic situation, industry conditions, competitive environment, and product markets for the following year. Based on recent years' trends, it is advisable not to be overly optimistic about market prospects.

The Central Economic Work Conference held at the end of 2022 sent a clear and strong signal to boost the economy, indicating significant hope for better economic recovery in 2023. Some experts even optimistically projected an 8% economic growth rate for 2023, which is very encouraging for businesses. However, from the perspective of enterprises, it remains crucial to continue to adequately respond to economic cycle fluctuations and new global changes without becoming overly optimistic.

Understanding Economic Cycles

Each economic cycle represents a valuable learning opportunity for both the Chinese economy and its businesses. Since the 1970s, companies worldwide have faced significant economic cycles, including challenges such as the oil crisis, debt crises, the Asian financial crisis, the dot-com bubble, the subprime mortgage crisis, and the ongoing pandemic.

Over the past four decades, China's economy has seen almost linear growth, with businesses largely experiencing only minor cyclic patterns. Even when faced with fluctuations, the economy typically rebounded swiftly. Consequently, Chinese enterprises have not previously faced substantial demands for strategic adjustments and have managed to navigate these cycles based on their existing growth models.

However, the current scenario appears to be more complex. For Chinese enterprises, this is not merely another economic cycle but a monumental shift in industrial upgrading and the competitive landscape. Juggling an understanding of cyclical patterns while effectively managing internal operations presents a formidable challenge, and sustaining such an ideal state proves to be quite difficult for businesses.

In the case of Sinochem Group, the daily fluctuations in commodity and oil prices impact each shipment, refinery, and contract. These changes keep businesses on their toes, but they reflect broader trends in the oil industry. Despite this complex landscape, companies must still focus on every detail of their operations, including new chemical materials' research and development and sales, and continually improve their operational efficiency. This is certainly no easy task.

I recently studied a maritime logistics company that has been operating exceptionally well, primarily focusing on ship investments and cargo operations. Many shipping companies face similar challenges: while their core business is thriving, market fluctuations impact investment values. Balancing these trends while maintaining product quality presents significant difficulties.

Therefore, in face of these new circumstances, it is hoped that Chinese businesses can grasp major trends and economic cycle fluctuations, effectively aligning all aspects of their operations.

Understanding Global Changes

Under the current global shifts, what changes must companies navigate?

First and foremost are the macro-level changes in the broader environment. These include the rise of China, comparisons between the East and West, U.S. pressures on China, geopolitical tensions, and the slowdown of Western economies. I feel like the world has become more politicized, ideologically driven, regionalized, and racialized. In business management, these differences are starkly apparent—conflicts exist among various regions, beliefs, and races, including unexpected conflicts that have arisen. In terms of faith, conflicts between Christianity, Protestantism, Islam, and Confucian culture have notably increased, affecting employee dynamics as well as investment and trade policies.

Compared to five years ago or even earlier, businesses have experienced significant changes. Trade wars, tariffs, and shifting trade policies have led to frequent sanctions and listings for Chinese companies. Products may be banned one day and unbanned the next, often without clear reasons, primarily due to U.S. control. This environment has reduced the drive for growth and global expansion among companies due to increased external risks, resulting in a decline in international cooperation. Large joint ventures now struggle to succeed due to various uncertain factors, including political, economic, corporate, regional, and trade policy issues. Companies are subjected to extensive geopolitical scrutiny, exemplified by COFCO Corporation's overseas investments, which are continuously reviewed based on policy, trade, and industry considerations.

Restrictions on foreign partnerships in technology collaborations, put in place years ago, have now reached unprecedented levels. Projects involving cross-border technology transfers and cooperation face significant challenges, making it difficult to achieve inter-regional integration of key processes within the industry chain, even when those chains are controllable.

Additionally, there is an increasing cultural divide among employees from different countries, leading to increased distrust and insecurity among multinational employees. Chinese companies are facing numerous restrictions on international financing, with many countries imposing regulations that either raise financing interest rates or prevent local companies from participating in financing for projects in China.

Moreover, there is a global trend toward environmental, social, and governance (ESG) corporate evaluation systems. This trend not only requires companies to uphold their operational responsibilities but also places high demands on Chinese companies regarding their ESG responsibilities abroad. In the past, business operations focused on prioritizing shareholder interests, company profits, and employee benefits. Now, however, shareholder returns, operational efficiency, and employee income must take a back seat to social responsibility, social justice, and environmental governance, presenting a significant challenge for Chinese companies.

Effectively Transitioning Toward Innovation

Numerous experts and scholars argue that the global economic landscape is undergoing a transformation, necessitating companies to reconsider their strategic development in light of significant and novel changes. Chinese enterprises are currently developing, still some distance away from the relatively mature stages of their European and American counterparts. This implies that Chinese firms have limited choice of development pathway, as they can only progress forward, yet established companies ahead do not wish for them to continue their imitation and catching up efforts.

In the past, we used to focus on expanding company size, market share, and sales revenue.

In the past, we could somewhat easily rely on cost efficiencies and labor advantages to compete internationally.

In the past, our products went global, and we invested overseas to leverage international partnerships for domestic growth.

In the past, we acquired excellent foreign companies, utilizing their advanced technology and market advantages to facilitate domestic enterprise and industry development.

In the past, we operated under a high-leverage development model, benefiting from low interest costs and robust government backing, which enabled Chinese enterprises to engage in leveraged mergers and expansions.

In the past, we also bolstered our domestic enterprise capabilities by adopting, adapting, and integrating cutting-edge international technologies.

Yet, with the current landscape evolving rapidly, traditional models are becoming increasingly difficult to maintain. Collaborative international ventures have significantly dwindled, with many proposed joint projects now on hold due to uncertain future prospects.

In essence, these past development models cannot be sustained in the new changes, compelling Chinese enterprises to refocus on core corporate development principles: innovation, distinctiveness, heightened efficiency, and reduced costs. This stands as the only viable development path for companies to pursue.

Following the merger of Sinochem and ChemChina, the combined entity has adhered to the development principle of "prioritizing science," striving for leading research and development. All 26 research institutes within the entity are now fully aligned with industry needs, entering a state of company-wide innovation, and there would not be any investment if there is no innovation, research and development, and new products. Focusing merely on scale development is insufficient; true innovation must be embraced as the sole driving force for growth.

Chinese enterprises are compelled to adapt to these new changes, shifting from previous strategies such as rapid advancement, unconventional development, capital injection, and technology transfer, back to exploring the true essence of corporate growth.

I believe that a company's top priority should be innovation and envisioning the future. Innovation and exploration must become the company's core operational focus and belief, and at the same time, efficiency must be boosted, costs minimized, products enhanced, and management perfected. Improving efficiency is a form of innovation, representing innovative practices that cut costs. Having attended many seminars and learned about various company strategies, I can say that many state-owned enterprises now have a deeper understanding of innovation, research and development, and achieving high-quality growth.

Achieving Fundamental Transformation

What fundamental change are companies encountering in the face of new circumstances?

Previously, the Chinese nation's focus was on research and development and innovation. However, even after decades of developing new products, a gradual decline in the enterprises' market share is observed. This occurred because innovation used to be viewed simply as an aid for existing paths and products. Today, innovation in research and development is crucial for a company's survival, necessitating the continual innovation, upgrading, and breakthrough of old products as well. Innovation now serves as the foundation for companies and underpins every business aspect. Before making any investment, plan, or budget, it is crucial to evaluate the novelty, innovation costs, sales contribution of new products, and the potential for technological, process-oriented, or environmental leadership. If these criteria are not met, such investments, plans, and budgets should not be pursued.

In the past, enterprises focused on innovation by simply motivating their research departments and researchers, but this approach often had little to no effect. Today, driving innovation requires transforming the entire company rather than just a specific department. It involves changing the mindset for development and the business model of the organization, from top to bottom.

Innovation and research have become the core focus of many businesses. As a result, numerous companies may set up large research labs while only establishing small production workshops.

Moreover, a company's ability to achieve innovation heavily depends on whether it fosters an innovative culture. Many organizations inadvertently stifle their own innovation due to short-term performance demands, cultural constraints, and immediate evaluation requirements, forcing them to prioritize short-term gains over long-term innovation.

Determining who should drive innovation within a company might sound simple, but it is actually quite challenging in practice. Innovation operates on several levels: it is not just about researchers innovating within a company, but also about fostering innovation at the workshop level, headquarters level, and throughout the entire enterprise.

Managing a company's innovation path is incredibly complex, as it involves resource allocation, personnel management, and efficiency enhancement, all of which demand a scientific approach. Companies are also required to avoid focusing excessively on short-term results, a significant challenge, especially for state-owned enterprises with monthly reporting requirements, profit distribution obligations, and relentless pressure for profit growth. However, innovation inherently carries risks, complicating this balancing act. This dilemma has persisted for decades without a clear resolution. Some measures, such as reintegrating research and development costs, have been introduced to address this issue.

In light of the above-mentioned discussion, the Central Economic Work Conference outlined the economic development goals and strategies for 2023 and emphasized high-quality and innovative progress, which included openness, reform, global engagement, and the advancement of various industries. These directives have provided valuable insights for business operations. Companies should move beyond yearly plans and strategies; they should understand the economic cycles, long-term challenges, and innovation opportunities within broader trends, adjusting their resource allocation, investment strategies, and development models accordingly. In terms of business philosophy, companies must prioritize scientific methods and innovation-driven growth. They should refocus on the core principles of corporate development strategy, that is, innovative differentiation, high efficiency, low costs, and a steadfast shift toward high-quality development. The above points are a pivot paramount for businesses.

Building High-Quality Listed Companies and Contributing to the Chinese Path to Modernization

Zhiping Song

The 20th National Congress of the Communist Party of China (CPC) was convened at a crucial moment as the entire Party and people of all ethnic groups nationwide embarked on a new journey toward building a modern socialist country in all respects and advancing toward the second centenary goal. Currently, people throughout the country are diligently studying and implementing the guiding principles of the 20th CPC National Congress of. The report to the 20th CPC National Congress outlines the vision of building China's own modernization, emphasizing that high-quality development is the primary task in building a modern socialist country in all respects. It underscores the importance of promoting high-quality development, integrating the strategy to expand domestic demand with deepening supply-side structural reforms, enhancing the endogenous dynamics and reliability of the domestic economy, improving the quality and level of international circulation. Furthermore, we should speed up building a modern economic system.

This article is compiled from a speech delivered by the author at the 2022 Sohu Finance Annual Conference on November 16, 2022.

Z. Song (✉)
National School of Development, Peking University, Beijing, China

W. Xianqing (ed.), *Understanding China's Path to Modernization*,
https://doi.org/10.1007/978-981-96-7051-2_17

We will raise the total factor productivity, strengthen the resilience and security of industrial and supply chains, and promote the integrated urban–rural development and coordinated regional development, so as to propel qualitative and effective economic growth alongside reasonable quantitative growth.

The report to the 20th CPC National Congress plays a crucial role in guiding the future development of listed companies, serving as a beacon for their path ahead. These companies are shining examples of Chinese enterprises, representing the strong core of the economy, the foundation of the real economy, the engine driving economic development, and the pioneers in refining modern corporate systems and fulfilling social responsibilities. They also offer a fresh avenue for investors to partake in the benefits of economic growth. Evidently, in pursuit of high-quality development and in support of China's distinctive modernization journey, listed companies bear a direct and indispensable responsibility.

Current Landscape of China's Listed Companies

In 2024, China's capital market has developed for 34 years, evolving from a small and weak beginning to become the world's second-largest capital market. This growth has significantly contributed to China's economic development by supporting the reform and growth of state-owned enterprises, the rapid expansion of private enterprises, and the advancement of science and technology innovation initiatives in China. Recently, the capital market has emphasized supporting small and medium-sized enterprises through reforms in the National Equities Exchange and Quotations (nicknamed the New Third Board) and the establishment of the Beijing Stock Exchange, particularly fostering the innovative growth of specialized, refined, and new small giant enterprises.

As of November 16, 2022, there were 5003 listed companies on China's domestic stock market, surpassing the milestone of 5000 companies. The market expanded from 1000 to 2000 listed companies in a decade, from 2000 to 3000 in six years, from 3000 to 4000 in four years, and from 4000 to 5000 in just two years.

Looking at the ownership structure, there were 1336 state-owned listed companies (both central and local), 3164 privately owned listed companies, and 503 listed companies of other types. By listing platform, 3177 companies were on the main board, 486 on the Sci-Tech Innovation Board, 1217 on the second board market, and 123 on the Beijing

Stock Exchange. As of November 15, 2022, the total market value of domestic listed companies was RMB 80.57 trillion, with private listed companies representing 44.00% and state-owned listed companies making up 43.62%.

In the first three quarters of 2022, a total of 300 new companies were listed, raising over RMB 480 billion through initial public offerings (IPOs), a 29% increase from the previous year. Under the registration-based system, 246 new companies were listed on the Sci-Tech Innovation Board, the second board market, and Beijing Stock Exchange, collectively raising over RMB 360 billion. The number of A-share market companies listed under the registration-based system has now surpassed 1000, showcasing increased support from the capital market for innovative technology enterprises.

Furthermore, the delisting system has become a routine part of market operations, fostering an ecosystem based on the survival of the fittest and orderly progress. In 2021, a total of 28 companies were delisted in China, and this number increased to 46 in the first eight months of 2022.

In recent years, the overall performance of publicly listed companies has been on the rise, particularly in driving research and development innovation and optimizing capital structures. In the first three quarters of 2022, domestic listed companies collectively raked in RMB 52.37 trillion in revenue, marking an 8.51% year-on-year increase, accounting for 60.18% of the total gross domestic product (GDP). Net profits hit RMB 4.75 trillion, up by 2.46% compared to the same period last year. Notably, non-financial companies saw a 9% surge in revenue in the third quarter.

Looking at the figures by sector, the Beijing Stock Exchange led in revenue growth in the first three quarters of 2022, achieving a growth rate of 35%. The Sci-Tech Innovation Board led in net profit growth, reaching 24%.

Looking at the figures by industries, 11 out of 19 economic sectors experienced year-on-year revenue growth in the first three quarters, while nine saw increases in net profits. In the third quarter, industries such as electricity, heat, gas, water production, supply chain, wholesale, and retail trade witnessed over a 40% rise in net profits. Sectors like accommodation and catering, as well as agriculture, forestry, animal husbandry, and fisheries, rebounded, turning their net profits from negative to positive. Emerging industries, including photovoltaics, power batteries, and new energy vehicles, also showed outstanding performance.

In the first three quarters of 2022, listed companies' expenditures on research and development reached RMB 0.94 trillion, a year-on-year increase of 20%. Investment in research and development by companies listed on the second board market, the Sci-Tech Innovation Board, and Beijing Stock Exchange also grew significantly, with research and development expenditure growth rates of 32%, 54%, and 43%, respectively. The intensity of research and development was 4.59% for the second board market, 8.68% for the Sci-Tech Innovation Board, and 4.30% for the Beijing Stock Exchange. Significant progress has been made in transforming innovative achievements, as 720 out of the 1,777 listed companies on these markets reported year-on-year growth in both revenue and net profit in the first three quarters.

Listed companies rely on the capital market to achieve the accelerated development. As of October 2022, they have raised a total of RMB 19.1 trillion in funds, comprising RMB 4.72 trillion from IPOs and an additional RMB 14.38 trillion through subsequent financing. While benefiting from this financial support, listed companies also prioritize investor returns, sharing the fruits of development with their investors. The total cash dividends distributed by listed companies amount to RMB 10.65 trillion, with RMB 1.55 trillion distributed in 2021.

Furthermore, listed companies actively assume direct and primary responsibility for self-regulation, self-improvement, and self-enhancement. They reinforce integrity principles adhere to the "four respects"[1] and meet the requirements of the four bottom lines.[2] The overall image of listed companies has improved positively, with their barometer better utilized, providing strong support for the healthy and stable development of the capital market.

While acknowledging the significant achievements of listed companies, it is essential to focus on areas that require continuous improvement. This includes corporate governance practices that still need further enhancement, and the overall innovation capabilities remain insufficient and unbalanced.

[1] The "four respects" refer to the requirement that companies should respect the market, the rule of law, professionalism, and investors.

[2] The "four bottom lines" include not disclosing false information, refraining from insider trading, avoiding stock price manipulation, and safeguarding the interests of listed companies.

Significance of Establishing High-Quality Listed Companies

General Secretary Xi Jinping proposes the establishment of a well-regulated, transparent, open, dynamic, and resilient capital market,[3] while former vice premier Liu He emphasized the principles of "establishing systems, non-intervention, zero tolerance" to accelerate the development of the capital market. Achieving these goals involves enhancing the pivotal role of the capital market, fully implementing the stock issuance registration system, establishing a normalized delisting mechanism, and increasing the proportion of direct financing. A high-quality capital market relies on high-quality listed companies, which serve as the cornerstone for the sustainable development of the capital market. Therefore, it is of profound significance to establish high-quality listed companies.

Firstly, a high-quality listed companies will strengthen their role as the foundation of the capital market, further enhancing the vitality, resilience, and competitiveness. This continual improvement will bolster financial services' capabilities to support the real economy, provide robust guarantees for the development of a modern industrial system, and accumulate stronger momentum for China's economy to achieve long-term stable progress.

Secondly, a high-quality listed companies will set exemplary practices, driving quality improvements and efficiency enhancements in both upstream and downstream enterprises. This effort will facilitate industry transformation and upgrading, elevate overall market quality, and lay a solid foundation for promoting high-quality economic development.

Thirdly, a high-quality listed companies not only benefits investors and creates value for shareholders but also helps increase social wealth and residents' consumption. It is crucial for accelerating the formation of a new development paradigm where domestic circulation is the mainstay, complemented by the dynamic between domestic and international circulations.

In recent years, significant steps have been taken to enhance the quality of listed companies.

[3] Editor's Note: Reference: http://www.zqrb.cn/finance/hongguanjingji/2022-03-02/A1646167252754.html.

For example, in September 2018, the China Securities Regulatory Commission (CSRC) introduced the updated *Code of Corporate Governance for Listed Companies*, outlining new standards related to stable control mechanisms, the role of independent directors, performance evaluations for board members and senior management, and the importance of transparent information disclosure. Companies are now required to align their operations with new developmental principles, emphasize Party construction within corporate structures, and take a more active stance on environmental conservation and social responsibility.

The new *Securities Law of the People's Republic of China*, implemented in March 2020, introduces a particular chapter on the disclosure system, enhancing the basic information disclosure framework for listed companies. Key improvements include emphasizing the effectiveness of information disclosure, expanding the scope of obligations and specific disclosure items, establishing a voluntary disclosure system, instituting a public commitment disclosure system, and strengthening disclosure norms for acquisitions by listed companies.

In October 2020, the State Council released the *Opinions on Further Improving the Quality of Listed Companies*, which outlines 17 measures across six areas, focusing on improving the governance standard of listed companies, promoting their optimization and strengthening, enhancing the exit mechanism for listed companies, addressing outstanding issues, increasing the costs of illegal activities for listed companies and related entities, and fostering a collaborative effort to improve the quality of listed companies.

In December 2020, the CSRC initiated a special action on the corporate governance of listed companies to comprehensively improve their governance standards, aiming to establish a robust governance structure characterized by clear responsibilities and effective checks and balances. It facilitates the refinement of internal rules and regulations, building corporate governance systems based on the company's articles of association, the rules of the "three meetings",[4] information disclosure, management systems, and investor relations management systems.

[4] State-owned enterprises should establish a scientific and clear decision-making mechanism for the Party committee, the Board of Directors, and the general manager's office, collectively referred to as the "three meetings.".

It can be said that, through years of effort, Chinese listed companies have deepened their understanding of building high-quality listed companies and have made significant progress, improving the overall quality of listed companies in China.

Enhancing the Five Key Capabilities of Listed Companies

In the pursuit of establishing high-quality listed companies, it is not enough to improve the external institutional environment. Listed companies must also focus on their internal development and cultivate the internal strengths necessary for quality improvement.

Strengthening Basic Capabilities and Consolidating Governance

In recent years, China's listed companies have made significant strides in governance, but further consolidation and improvement remain necessary. Despite achieving good performance, issues such as financial fraud, major shareholder interest infringements, and governance dilemmas in the "dual board of directors"[5] still occur. Many of these issues stem from the inefficient operation of the corporate governance system. To enhance governance standards, efforts are required not only from external regulatory bodies but also from the listed companies themselves.

First, it is crucial to uphold the independence of listed companies and safeguard the legitimate rights and interests of both the companies and their investors. This involves emphasizing the independence of listed companies, optimizing the equity structure, ensuring major shareholders exercise due diligence and responsibility, and prohibiting actions that harm the company's interests.

[5] To elaborate, consider a scenario where shareholders propose convening a general meeting due to dissatisfaction with the existing board of directors and demand a re-election. Typically, the existing board may disregard these requests. If the proposing shareholders independently convene a meeting and elect a new board, a "dual board of directors" situation can occur.

Second, it is important to facilitate the effective performance of the "three meetings and one level".[6] This involves enhancing the rules for exercising powers in shareholder meetings, board meetings, and supervisory board meetings, ensuring the segregation of ownership and management rights, and decision-making and executive powers. Directors, supervisors, and senior management should diligently and faithfully fulfill their duties, fully leveraging the roles of independent directors and supervisors.

Third, it is essential to establish governance in accordance with regulations. This entails close alignment with the *Code of Corporate Governance Guidelines for Listed Companies* and other relevant legal requirements, continued improvement of the internal governance structure, and prompt rectification of any identified issues.

Strengthening Core Business and Enhancing Competitiveness

It is essential to focus on the core business without sidetracking in supporting the real economy. There are no backward industries, only outdated technologies and enterprises. Even in economic downturns and amid intense competition in saturated markets, companies can strive to become industry leaders and top players in segmented markets through market and product segmentation. It is crucial for companies to focus on their core business, as dedicated cultivation and operation in this area provide the foundation for sustained and stable development.

First, they should consolidate and strengthen the operations of core business. In uncertain internal and external business environments with escalating risks, listed companies must operate more prudently, placing greater emphasis on and reinforcing their core business.

Second, they should enhance the company's core competitiveness, which includes its core business, core expertise, core markets, and key clients. The core business is the foundation of the company's existence, core expertise, competitive edge, core markets, expansion goals, and key clients the primary source of its profits.

[6] The "three meetings and one level" in corporate governance refer to the general meeting of the shareholders, the board of directors, the board of supervisors, and the senior management level.

Third, they should strive to become champions in their respective fields. Large conglomerates should compete with world-class multinational corporations and work toward becoming globally leading enterprises known for outstanding products, remarkable brands, innovative leadership, and modern governance, whereas small and medium-sized enterprises should focus on niche operations, fostering specialized and innovative small giants, and becoming champions in specific areas, striving to be "hidden champions."

Fourth, they should enhance enterprise management. Effective management is essential and foundational for success and improved competitiveness. Regardless of the type of enterprise, weak management, poor product quality, or ineffective control of production and operating costs will ultimately lead to failure. Strengthening meticulous management is not a short-term strategy but a long-term commitment that requires effective methods and perseverance. During recent visits to companies such as CATL, Fuyao Group, Weichai Power, and Gree Electric Appliances, I was deeply impressed by their meticulous management.

Fostering Long-Term Growth and Enhancing Innovation Capability

Innovation is the primary driving force behind progress. Listed companies, as the backbone of innovation integration and technology transformation, play a crucial role in leveraging various tools in the capital market to support innovation and enhance competitiveness. This positions them to become important sources of research and development for innovation and emerging technologies, address critical challenges in core technology areas, and drive high-level circulation of technology, capital, and industry.

First, we should pursue purposeful, effective, and high-quality innovation to minimize the randomness of innovation. Throughout the innovation process, it is essential to adhere to market principles, prioritize efficiency, and conduct in-depth research and analysis. Efforts should be made to improve the quality and impact of innovation, continuously reduce innovation costs, and promote healthy enterprise development through innovation.

Second, we should support companies in their innovation efforts at various levels. Emphasis should be placed on the vigorous development of high-tech innovations while actively supporting innovation at different levels. High-tech innovation typically yields high returns but also involves relatively higher risks, making it suitable for a select number of capable companies. Although a significant portion of innovation occurs within medium, low, or even non-technical domains, their contributions to social progress should not be overlooked.

Third, we should effectively utilize the five models of corporate innovation. Independent innovation is original and self-driven, presenting significant challenges and requiring substantial investment. However, efforts must continue to advance key technological breakthroughs. Meanwhile, integrated innovation involves integrating various elements, drawing from mutual inspiration and independent innovation; continuous innovation entails the ongoing updating and iteration of existing technologies; disruptive innovation uses new technology to challenge traditional methods, whereas business model innovation, which may not appear to involve much technology, creates new value.

Enhancing Resilience and Improving Risk Management Capabilities

Listed companies need to enhance their risk awareness and strengthen their ability to handle crises and mitigate risks effectively.

Firstly, fully understanding the objective nature of risks is crucial. To establish robust risk management, companies need to develop an enterprise risk control mechanism. This involves studying, identifying, preventing, and mitigating risks through a comprehensive institutional framework. By creating a robust risk management system, businesses can build a defense against risks, enabling them to manage risks in a controllable and sustainable manner.

Secondly, fully understanding economic and industry cycles is essential. Aligning development strategies and growth paces with economic trends allows companies to explore moderate diversification based on their unique circumstances. By considering factors such as capital returns and corporate strategies, organizations can enter niche markets with high growth potential, counter-cyclical markets, or segments with less pronounced cyclicality. When venturing into sectors with distinct resources and operational capabilities, companies should emphasize hedging mechanisms within their business operations, ensuring protection from disruptive risks due to industry fluctuations while securing stable and enduring returns.

Thirdly, sustainable management for stable cash flow is imperative. Companies should operate within their means, reduce financial risks, consolidate fund usage, and minimize working capital, including inventory and accounts receivable, all while prioritizing their businesses' operational cash flow, aiming for profitable revenue and cash flow stability.

Fourthly, crisis preparedness and timely responses are important. Companies must prioritize early detection and proactive responses to crises, as businesses can prevent small crises from escalating by resolving issues in their early stages. The key principle in crisis management is to minimize losses for the company.

Maximizing Returns and Boosting Profitability

It is crucial for listed companies to prioritize the interests of small and medium shareholders at all times. Ensuring stable, long-term dividends is key to building trust and loyalty among investors, particularly for smaller shareholders who should feel valued and benefit from the company's growth.

First, companies should establish a shareholder-centric approach. Investors provide essential funding, and in return, companies should operate steadily, perform well, create value, and strengthen their position as listed entities. Enhancing communication with shareholders through various means, such as roadshows and reverse roadshows, can significantly boost shareholder confidence in the company's growth.

Second, companies should share profits with investors through dividends. Over the past three years, listed companies have distributed a total of RMB 4.4 trillion in cash dividends, marking nearly a 50% increase compared to the previous three years. Additionally, listed companies should prioritize societal benefits, fulfill social responsibilities, and engage positively with stakeholders such as employees, customers, suppliers, banks, communities, and the environment, fostering mutually beneficial relationships.

Third, companies should shift focus toward value creation over refinancing. By understanding market dynamics and aligning corporate strategies to enhance overall company worth, listed companies can not only repay shareholder trust but also generate substantial value for investors.

Fourth, companies should actively fulfill their social responsibilities. Listed companies should focus on ESG disclosure efforts, cultivate a culture of proactive disclosure, conduct performance briefings effectively, listen attentively to investors feedback, and strive to become trusted and respected entities by both investors and society.

In recent years, the China Association for Public Companies (CAPCO) has diligently implemented the directives from the Party committee of the CSRC, taking an active role in self-regulation, accurately defining its mission, strengthening its sense of responsibility, and working toward creating a welcoming environment for listed companies. With a focus on establishing high-quality listed companies, the association has undertaken a series of highly effective initiatives.

The current external environment presents listed companies with complex and profound changes. In response to the evolving landscape aimed at promoting the high-quality development of listed companies, the China Association for Public Companies will implement the directives put forth by former chairman Yi Huiman and actively fulfill its four key roles: serving as a communication bridge between listed companies and regulatory authorities, providing a primary platform for self-regulation among listed companies, offering a space for mutual learning and exchange, and promoting achievements in high-quality development. The association will also make efforts to enhance service delivery methods, promptly address members' concerns, and foster a dynamic environment conducive to the high-quality development of listed companies.

The report to the 20th CPC National Congress has identified high-quality development as the top priority in building China into a modern socialist country in all respects, outlining a new blueprint for Chinese path to modernization. Achieving high-quality economic development relies on the active participation of numerous listed companies, and establishing high-quality listed companies necessitates collaboration from all parties to create synergy. The China Association for Public Companies is committed to working with all stakeholders to elevate the quality of listed companies in China, aiming to help achieve the goals of Chinese path to modernization by enhancing their development quality.

In a Turbulent Era, Why Is Long-Term Development More Crucial Than Ever?

Yuzhen Gong

To begin, I will share two stories. The first is about Huawei's strategic choice between the Personal Handy-Phone System (PHS) and 3G technology.

At the end of the twentieth century, China Telecom launched PHS, which led to rapid growth for UTStarcom and ZTE. UTStarcom once achieved an annual sales revenue of RMB 10 billion, a figure that caught the attention of various enterprises at the time.

Huawei's management recognized this opportunity and promptly submitted a plan to enter the PHS market, which was unexpectedly vetoed by Zhengfei Ren.

Ren's rationale for rejecting PHS was that it was destined to be a transitional, short-lived technology, while 3G represented the future, believing that Huawei should avoid opportunistic ventures. In his opinion, missing out on PHS might lead to some profit loss for Huawei, which was acceptable, but missing out on 3G would significantly impact Huawei's

---

This article is based on a speech delivered by the author at the 42nd MBA Forum and Promotion Event of the MBA Program at the National School of Development, Peking University, on February 26, 2022.

Y. Gong (✉)
National School of Development, Peking University, Beijing, China

W. Xianqing (ed.), *Understanding China's Path to Modernization*,
https://doi.org/10.1007/978-981-96-7051-2_18

journey to becoming a great company—a fundamental mistake that was unforgivable.

As a result, Huawei invested most of its resources into the global, yet-to-be-commercialized, 3G business. In 2009, eight years later, Huawei finally obtained its first 3G license.

Since then, we all know the story well—Huawei rose to prominence, leaving its competitors trailing behind. It was the daring bet on 3G and sustained investments that shaped Huawei into what it is today.

In contrast, UTStarcom, once a dominant player in China's PHS market, is now a rare sight in the mainstream market landscape—a stark contrast to its former glory.

The other story centers around Jack Ma and Alibaba Cloud.

Today, Alibaba Cloud holds the top spot in the Asia–Pacific region and ranks third globally in cloud computing. Despite Baidu's supposed advantage in this domain, Baidu Cloud falls short compared to Alibaba Cloud.

Investing in cloud computing back then required substantial funds, amounting to billions annually, causing significant financial strain on Alibaba for years with little promise of success. Wang Jian, who led Alibaba's cloud computing efforts and is now an esteemed academician at the Chinese Academy of Engineering, faced skepticism during that period.

During those critical years, Alibaba's strategic meetings often centered around one pressing question: Should they halt the project and disband the team? The cloud computing team lived in constant uncertainty, unsure when their efforts might be terminated.

During one of the most challenging periods, Jack Ma visited the cloud computing team and declared, "We must pursue cloud computing, and I'm investing RMB 10 billion." This immediately lifted the team's morale, reassuring everyone that things would improve.

In 2012, Baidu, pessimistic about the future of cloud computing, disbanded its own cloud computing team, which was subsequently absorbed entirely by Alibaba, marking a decisive moment in the trajectory of cloud computing.

Jack Ma once remarked, "All decisions made by Alibaba today are geared toward strategic planning for seven to eight years down the road." Alibaba Cloud's ultimate triumph is rooted in this long-term strategic vision.

Three Types of Victories

We all want to make success, and the concept of "success" has become quite the buzzword these days. But what kind of success should we aim for, and what does success really mean?

Chen Chunhua, former dean of the BiMBA Business School of the National School of Development at Peking University, offers an intriguing perspective on the concept of "success." She categorizes it into three types: opportunists achieve only temporary success, pragmatists enjoy short-term success, but only those with a long-term vision secure lasting success.

I completely agree with her insight. With my background in history, I can back up her point by citing long-term patterns of rise and fall.

Historical evidence shows that no group of bandits or warlords has ever truly triumphed. When the dust settles, it becomes clear that those with a clear long-term vision emerge as the ultimate winners.

This tells us that sustaining long-termism is key to achieving enduring success.

Why Is Long-Termism So Difficult to Sustain?

Given its importance and benefits, why are there so few long-termists? Why do we still discuss long-termism today?

The answer is simple: sustaining long-termism is extremely challenging.

Consider Ren's decision regarding PHS. Today, we admire his foresight and strategic acumen. But who knows how much pressure he faced at that time?

He gave up on pursuing the PHS market, despite it experienced consistent growth from 2000 to 2003. UTStarcom transformed from a relatively unknown entity into a star company, while ZTE made significant profits in the PHS market and used those profits to challenge Huawei's market share. By 2003, ZTE's sales even reached 80% of Huawei's.

Huawei, as the leader among Chinese communication equipment manufacturers, saw little progress during that time. Missing out on claiming a piece of the PHS market and facing delays in 3G licenses, Huawei's substantial investments in 3G technology did not yield immediate returns for a prolonged duration.

In 2002, Huawei experienced significant losses for the first time, leading many to lose faith in the company. They believed Ren had made a grave and foolish mistake and, consequently, many left Huawei for what seemed like better opportunities elsewhere.

Ren later reflected, "I was really down back then, suffering for eight to ten years over PHS and TD (a type of 3G internet). I questioned whether not pursuing it would lead the company astray and toward collapse. On the other hand, if I did pursue it, would it mean sacrificing resources needed for strategic advantage?" Imagine being in Ren's position—facing immediate gains, mounting pressure, and uncertain future rewards. What would you do?

Feelings of anxiety, depression, doubt, wavering decisions, and contemplating giving up midway are realities that long-termists often confront.

In the 1960s, the well-known Stanford marshmallow experiment illustrated this challenge. Walter Mischel, a psychology professor at Stanford University, selected a group of kindergarten children for the study. Each child was asked to sit in a room for 15 minutes with a marshmallow, their favorite treat, placed on a table in front of them.

The rules were simple: if the child ate the marshmallow immediately, they would not get a reward. However, if they managed to wait 15 minutes before eating it, they would receive an additional marshmallow as a reward. Children who would not wait could ring the bell placed on the table to signal that they were giving up.

At the start of the experiment, researchers noted that a small percentage of children immediately grabbed and ate the candy. Some children rang the bell after only 30 seconds, while only around 30% waited the full 15 minutes before indulging in the candy.

In follow-up studies, researchers found that children who delayed gratification achieved greater success in later life, including professional achievements. Those who struggled to wait were more likely to be overweight in adulthood, achieve less, and a significant portion were prone to substance abuse.

This experiment introduced the concept of delayed gratification, emphasizing that those capable of delaying gratification tend to achieve greater success.

Zhang Yiming, the founder of ByteDance, frequently stresses the importance of delayed gratification. His success underscores the significance of this principle. However, why is it that so few businesses and individuals consistently embody the ideals of long-termists and delayed gratification? What makes long-termism particularly challenging to uphold?

This issue, intertemporal choice theory, is an important research topic in fields such as neuroscience, psychology, and behavioral economics, exploring how people choose between larger, later (LL) rewards and smaller, sooner (SS) rewards.

Research in this area consistently concludes that people tend to assign greater weight to immediate rewards over future ones. In simple terms, immediate rewards are valued more highly than future rewards.

The reason is straightforward: Humans evolved from animals, and despite our development of planning and strategic thinking, we, like other animals, still prefer immediate rewards when faced with intertemporal choices.

Researchers have also investigated the neural mechanisms behind these choices. In 2004, a seminal report in the journal *Science*, for the first time, demonstrated two distinct evaluation mechanisms in the human brain related to intertemporal choices: β and δ.

The β mechanism, concentrated in the early-evolved midbrain dopamine system, processes immediate options such as immediate decisions, current temptations, or immediate benefits. On the other hand, the δ system, situated in the relatively later-evolved frontoparietal network, handles delayed options and focuses on decisions involving delayed gratification.

The former represents a survival instinct, while the latter aligns with evolutionary needs. The relative activation levels of these two systems determine an individual's choices. If the β system is activated during the decision-making process, we tend to choose immediate gains; however, when the δ system is activated, we opt for delayed gratification.

Relevant to this is the cognitive mechanism theory of intertemporal choice, known as the "hot and cold cognition." The theory posits that the human brain consists of two sets of cognitive processing of information: hot and cold. Hot cognition is related to impulsive behavior driven by emotions, characterized by simple reflexes and faster response speed, maturing earlier. Conversely, cold cognition is associated with self-control, being cognitively driven and more cautious, thus slower and maturing later.

The interaction between the hot and cold cognition determines an individual's behavior in delayed gratification. When the hot cognition dominates, individuals tend to choose small, sooner rewards. Conversely, when the cold cognition takes control, individuals lean toward selecting larger, later rewards.

Building upon this, scholars have proposed the multiple self-theory for human intertemporal choice, involving concepts such as the myopic self and farsighted self, planner and doer, sophisticated self and naive self, among others.

While the theory itself may be complex—and I do not wish to delve too much into it—our primary interest is in what these research findings convey to managers.

We all possess dual aspects within ourselves and exhibit characteristics of short-termist. Valuing immediate gains is a fundamental aspect of human nature, particularly given the significant uncertainties of the future.

For the average person, the greater the immediate pressure or temptations faced, the easier it is for their short-sightedness to take precedence, leading to a more pronounced tendency toward short-term thinking.

Even long-termists can experience impulses toward short-term behaviors and moments of wavering. Every individual faces an internal conflict between their long-term and short-term desires. This is why Ren, despite committing to the long-term path of 3G technology, still felt depressed and under pressure when deciding to give up on pursuing the PHS market. I believe Li Yanhong (Robin Li) is also a proponent of long-term thinking, and Baidu is a company with long-term aspirations. Yet, why did they momentarily give up on cloud computing? The same principle applies here.

This illustrates the fundamental challenge of sustaining long-term thinking.

Short-Termism Leads to Long-Term Harm

Sustaining long-termism can be challenging, but why should we opt for it? Simply put, short-termism can lead to long-term harm for management levels and organizations.

The first harm of short-termism in management pertains to leadership. Leaders who embrace short-termism often lack foresight and exhibit self-serving behaviors. Those without foresight are destined to fail, and self-serving leaders will find it difficult to gain followers.

While everyone has their own interests, leaders must leverage the abilities of others, including those more capable than themselves, to achieve feats. Therefore, leaders must look beyond personal interests to reach greater goals. The consequences of self-serving behavior almost inevitably include alienation.

The second harm of short-termism in management lies in decision-making. Confucius succinctly highlighted the perils of short-termism with two sayings, "Pursuing small gains prevents major accomplishments" and "Those who lack long-term vision are bound to face immediate worries."

Making decisions is akin to playing chess; some individuals can foresee three to five steps ahead or even further, while others progress step by step, focusing solely on the present moment.

Why do some people struggle to become chess masters after reaching a certain level of mastery of chess skill? Often, it is because they lack a broad perspective, becoming easily caught up in immediate conflicts and regional battles, unable to grasp the entirety of the chessboard. While they might achieve small successes, they fail to understand how to leverage them effectively.

As the Chinese saying goes, "Those who lack long-term vision are bound to face immediate worries." Without long-term vision, individuals can become lost in the complicated realities, getting tangled in various issues and overly focused on short-term gains and losses. This applies to businesses as well. While they might win in the short run, they risk losing sight of the bigger picture, sacrificing overall success for temporary victories.

When companies prioritize current performance excessively, they risk neglecting crucial aspects that are vital for long-term success, creating more significant problems that can harm the company's long-term development.

The third harm of short-termism in management surfaces at the organizational level. Organizations accustomed to making quick profits may struggle to withstand tough challenges in the future, as rushing into actions inevitably leads to disarray.

The biggest mistake organizations can make is adopting a "boom or bust" approach—achieving rapid success one day, only to suffer catastrophic failure the next. Throughout history, many organizations have followed this path. Figures like Huang Chao, Li Zicheng, and Zhang Xianzhong rose as leaders of peasant uprisings but failed to achieve lasting success. Their common characteristics included focusing on capturing territories, recruiting soldiers, moving aimlessly through regions, and surviving off the land by constantly seeking new resources wherever available. They all overlooked a critical factor: the importance of building a solid organizational foundation, ultimately falling into the trap of what can be called "the ideology of roving rebel bands."

In the business world, the ideology of roving rebel bands manifests as quick profit-making schemes, such as companies focusing solely on acquisitions without developing core competencies or those seizing every opportunity without building sustainable advantages.

Historically, victories achieved through such methods were always temporary and lacked a solid foundation, destined to be forgotten as mere fleeting moments of glory. On the surface, short-term actions may seem like a rational choice, but in the long run, they are actually irrational, as they trade tomorrow's costs for today's gains.

The history of evolution makes it abundantly clear that short-term behaviors are driven by survival instincts, while long-termism is a hallmark of true maturity. This principle applies equally to individuals and organizations.

Living solely by instinct without the ability to contemplate and plan for the future is what sets humans apart from other animals.

The presence and depth of this future-oriented mindset serve as distinguishing factors between outstanding individuals and organizations from mediocre ones. Each of us harbors limitations and vulnerabilities. It is only through acknowledging and confronting these weaknesses can we transcend them and break free from the confines of short-termism.

The Value of Long-Termism

Choosing between short-term and long-term strategies is essentially about resource allocation. Short-term actions involve investing resources in the present and reacting passively to changing circumstances, while long-term thinking entails investing resources in the future and actively shaping one's destiny.

Both individuals and organizations always face resource limitations. The allocation of your resources will invariably lead to corresponding outcomes. Long-termism allows you to break free from immediate concerns, develop unique abilities and strengths, and steer both yourself and your organization toward a better future from a broader perspective.

Why should we attach importance to long-termism? This can be examined from the following perspectives:

Firstly, in terms of goal setting, someone who focuses solely on short-term gains may struggle to sustain success, even with clever planning and hard work. A fixation on quick wins can box themselves into a corner, leading to increasingly challenging situations and missed opportunities for a brighter future. Long-termism, on the other hand, provides clear direction and ongoing motivation for our lives, which are crucial for achieving success in both personal and organizational endeavors.

Secondly, from a cognitive standpoint, short-termism caters to impatience with immediate responses and tackles short-sightedness with quick fixes. In contrast, long-termism offers a broader perspective, allowing us to see beyond present distractions and recognize what truly matters in the bigger picture. This helps us remain calm, composed, and focused amid the hustle and bustle of our ever-changing world.

In the *Great Learning*,[1] it is said, "The point where to rest being known, the object of pursuit is then determined; and, that being determined, a calm unperturbedness may be attained to. To that calmness there will succeed a tranquil repose. In that repose there may be careful deliberation, and that deliberation will be followed by the attainment of the desired end." This process encapsulates the journey from understanding to eventual success. By comprehending future needs, we gain the perseverance required to remain calm, fostering thoughtful consideration and enabling us to find optimal solutions and achieve the best results.

Chinese culture often emphasizes the concept of "power and profit," stating that influence and profitability go hand in hand. Achieving significant gains requires recognizing and leveraging overarching trends rather than focusing solely on immediate benefits. Therefore, it is essential to first establish a strong position. Pursuing short-term gains may yield only minor rewards, but seizing long-term opportunities can secure substantial advantages.

The Art of War by Sun Tzu teaches that true masters "seek opportunities in the situation, not faults in others," highlighting the importance of capitalizing on circumstances and devising strategies rather than blaming team members or subordinates. This philosophy is equally applicable to business management. When facing challenges, it is crucial to maintain a

[1] The *Great Learning* is a short text generally attributed to Confucius for the first chapter and his disciple Zengzi for the subsequent ten commentaries. It is the first of the four books selected by Zhu Xi during the Song dynasty as an introduction to Confucianism. It was originally a single chapter within the *Li Ji* (*Classic of Rites*).

long-term perspective and adopt a broader view to avoid getting caught up in assigning blame to individuals or specific incidents.

These represent entirely different ways of thinking. Long-termism allows for decisions based on future outcomes, embodying the essence of cognition.

Thirdly, from an actionable standpoint, long-termism imbues our present actions with profound meaning, ensuring consistency and coherence in our efforts.

Long-termism does not disregard short-term actions or immediate decisions. As with chess, each move must be made step by step. However, without considering the long-term implications, each move loses its value. Only by linking each piece to a clear strategic plan can the true strategic value and significance of each move be fully realized.

Engaging in long-term thinking and planning allow us to consider how our current actions will impact the future. By integrating long-term goals into our immediate decisions, we align our short-term behaviors with our overarching objectives.

This approach helps us understand the purpose behind each step and how achieving specific objectives contributes to our overall and long-term goals. It enables us to navigate present actions without succumbing to short-term temptations or falling into the trap of short-termism.

By adopting this mindset, we can turn tactical opportunities into strategic victories and seize current opportunities for lasting success.

Fourthly, from a competitive standpoint, embracing long-termism is crucial to avoid getting caught in cutthroat competition.

Not all individuals or organizations will adopt long-termism, which is why, in the end, those who do will ultimately emerge victorious.

According to former Amazon CEO Jeff Bezos, "If everything you do needs to work on a three-year time horizon, then you're competing against a lot of people. But if you're willing to invest on a seven-year time horizon, you're now competing against a fraction of those people, because very few companies are willing to do that."

Jeff Bezos asked Warren Buffett, "Your investment thesis is so simple. Why don't more people copy you?" Buffet replied, "Because nobody wants to get rich slow."

In reality, long-termism contradicts basic human survival instincts. Not everyone can or will embrace long-termism. However, it is known that the best path is often the least traveled one. Adopting long-termism, you will encounter few competitors, making it the optimal choice to break free from the current trend of intense competition.

How to Become a Long-Termist?

Firstly, long-termism requires an awakening.

To embrace long-termism, one must recognize that both individuals and organizations operate with two systems, each with a short-term aspect.

This is the reality we must first acknowledge. Therefore, we must always be vigilant against short-term impulses, consciously choosing and continually reinforcing our long-termist characteristics.

Long-termism needs to be activated and strengthened, and it can be. It is a set of values that can also become habitual patterns of thinking and behavior.

In other words, both individuals and organizations are malleable. Short-termism exists like gravity, and our task is to consistently use long-termism to correct our actions, ensuring we do not deviate from its main path. As an ancient saying goes, "I daily examine my personal conduct on three points." If you do not recognize the two systems within yourself and your organization, it is easy to unconsciously slide toward short-termism.

Secondly, long-termism is a belief.

Long-termism is about making choices for the future, which is inherently uncertain and not yet a reality. When people lose faith in the future, they abandon long-term thinking and pursue short-term gains. Hu Dayuan and I teach a course at the National School of Development, where we take students on a field trip to the site of the Battle of Chishui River, illustrating how decisions are made and teams are led in uncertain environments. The Battle of Chishui River is part of the Long March, a significant historical event. However, not everyone who participated in the Long March reached the end.

Some left, some betrayed, some surrendered, and even some prominent in the earlier stages faded into the background. The common trait among these departures was shaken beliefs.

Pessimists tend to focus on the present, while optimists are more inclined to believe in the future.

Only with confidence in the future can people set aside immediate rewards in pursuit of greater long-term benefits. The stronger our belief in the future, the more we lean toward long-term thinking, and the greater our ability to endure loneliness and pain. Some even find joy in this perseverance, viewing it as a process of self-transcendence and self-realization, achieving a sense of great accomplishment by surpassing others.

As a long-termist, you must hold firm to your convictions to truly envision and realize the future. Long-termism is the sole foundation for enduring and sustainable development for both individuals and organizations.

In particular, we need to embody the following six beliefs:

First, we should hold belief in the power of long-term thinking. Have faith in your long-term rationality. Prioritize significant matters over trivial ones, and opt for the long term over the short term. Long-term rationality enables you to address problems from a broader framework, a higher perspective, and over extended timelines, thereby enabling the most rational choices.

Do not let short-term rationality lead to long-term irrationality; trust that your long-term rationality is correct. Restraint and patience are among humanity's noblest qualities. By believing in the power of long-term thinking, you can cultivate these qualities.

Second, we should hold belief in the power of conviction. Previous studies on intertemporal choice have shown that positive, hopeful emotions can enhance an individual's self-control in such decisions. The more positive and confident you are, the stronger your self-control becomes during the decision-making process.

Belief means trusting that positive ideas can be realized. Strong belief is the primary source of power for both individuals and organizations. Whether in wars in the past or today's entrepreneurship, one of the core reasons why a small organization can ultimately triumph is having a strong belief from the beginning and maintaining that belief.

A crucial aspect of sustaining belief is creating a supportive environment, as the viewpoints and behaviors of team members can influence and inspire one another.

An interesting phenomenon is that long-termist leaders will attract long-termist followers, while short-termist leaders will inevitably attract subordinates or team members who pursue only short-term gains. From this perspective, beliefs, trust, confidence, and faith can positively reinforce each other.

Mutual trust within a team leads members to align with the overall belief of the team. When a group of people share a common belief, they attract and inspire each other, unleashing boundless potential, ultimately turning belief into reality. This is the power of belief.

Zeng Ming once said something I strongly agree with: The vision of an organization is meant to be believed in, not challenged. If members doubt and question the organization's vision, progress simply cannot be accomplished. Belief is essential for turning vision into reality.

Thirdly, we should believe in the power of symbiosis. In any field, competitive and adversarial thinking can shape your strategy and mindset. If you are locked in an unending struggle with your opponents, even a victory is pyrrhic.

When you view the future from the present, your focus is limited to competing for resources, seeing only opponents. However, if you view the present from the future, from the lens of long-termism, your focus shifts to creating the future landscape. In this way, even current competitors can become partners in the grand scheme of co-creating the future.

Therefore, do not just focus on temporary victories and losses, but keep your eyes on the constantly evolving bigger picture. Believe in the power of symbiosis, and only then you can transcend momentary gains and losses.

Fourthly, we should believe in the power of fundamentals. Core aspects of management, such as talent, culture, strategy, organization, leadership, and execution, are essential strengths. Whether in times of conflict or today's commercial environment, individuals and organizations often find themselves in chaotic conditions, where they can easily lose their way. In such scenarios, it is the most basic, simple, common, and authentic elements—and their dynamic alignment—that determine how far one and their organization can progress. A solid organizational foundation enables better performance and sustained victories.

We often contrast short-term performance with long-term organizational investment, prioritizing immediate gains while neglecting long-term development. However, a truly effective organization and genuine long-term strategy create opportunities for better and greater performance by building organizational capabilities and solidifying fundamentals. In the long run, strengthening one and their organization's fundamentals is necessary for establishing a strong foundation, allowing the organization to remain resilient in a turbulent environment.

Fifthly, we should believe in the power of focus. Continuously investing and accumulating in a clear direction is crucial. Long-term value creation is undeniably a continuous process. When the general direction is correct and you commit to consistent investment in that direction, the probability of achieving significant success is much higher than pursuing multiple directions.

Lastly, we should believe in the power of kindness. While industries and markets today are constantly changing, humanity's inclination toward kindness and altruism remains steadfast. From an evolutionary perspective, this is essential for the survival and development of humanity, as behaviors that benefit the overall interests of society are rewarded in the long term. Only a society that embraces cooperation, altruism, and kindness can thrive and develop in the face of competitive evolution.

Almost all religions and philosophical theories across the world aim to inspire people to do good deeds. This principle extends to businesses as well. The ultimate goal of a business is to create social value and drive human progress, and only those that embody these values earn societal approval and respect, fostering positive interactions and mutual benefits with society.

While profit is undeniably important for businesses, those lacking ethical principles cannot thrive in the long run. Sustainable success is rooted in strong values, and truly exceptional companies are those that promote ethical behavior. This core belief fortifies individuals and organizations, enabling them to weather any challenges and adhere to the fundamental principle of achieving lasting survival and continuous growth. This marks the greatest distinction between mediocrity and excellence.

Businesses that contribute long-term value to society will ultimately receive enduring rewards from society.

Long-Termism Is a Practice

Recognizing the importance of long-termism is easy, but putting it into action is extremely challenging. We must acknowledge this reality because human nature has its weaknesses, and we constantly face the conflict between two cognition processes in our brains. Knowing what to do is simple, but actually doing it is difficult. When confronted with critical moments of conflict between long-term and short-term goals, global and local perspectives, or pursuing a mission and seeking immediate benefits, one's decisions in these pivotal moments will reveal their deepest desires and ultimately determine the destiny of both the individual and their organization.

Throughout the journey of embracing long-termism, one will experience doubts, hesitations, and wavering, all of which, surprisingly, contribute to their personal and organizational growth and maturity.

How does one become a proponent of long-termism? It is quite simple: do what is difficult yet right. Management involves taking on challenging yet correct tasks, and life demands the same.

Coming back to our discussion: In this fast-paced era, why do we need to embrace long-termism? Because it is the only thing that is challenging yet right.

There is a quote that I greatly appreciate, "True light is never a time without darkness, but simply never being overshadowed by darkness. A true hero is never devoid of base emotions, but simply never succumbing to them."

In that spirit, I would like to state that a true advocate for long-termism is not immune to the impulses of short-term choices but steadfastly resists being swayed by those urges. The path lies before us, and as humans, we have the power to choose. The choices we make will shape the life we lead.

Chinese Path to Modernization and Population Trends

Coping With Negative Population Growth Ahead

Fang Cai

This article presents recent observations and studies on the upcoming era of negative population growth. Although the terms "finance" and "wealth" are not explicitly mentioned, individuals involved in investment or financial wealth management should consider a change in mindset.

Let's start by examining the latest population data, which unveils a recent shift in population dynamics. Previous turning points in population trends have manifested in various ways—such as the peak of the labor force in 2010—leading to labor shortages, inadequate human capital, a slowdown in productivity growth, and a decline in capital returns. This resulted in a corresponding slowdown in both potential and actual economic growth rates between 2010 and 2019. To tackle this, we implemented supply-side structural reforms, addressing it as a supply-side shock. The new population turning point we are now observing is likely to bring about fresh challenges.

The population statistics of recent years have consistently surprised us. The first shock came with the seventh National Population Census

This article is based on the author's speech delivered at the 2022 China Wealth Forum, held in Qingdao on July 30, 2022.

F. Cai (✉)
Chinese Academy of Social Sciences, Beijing, China

W. Xianqing (ed.), *Understanding China's Path to Modernization*,
https://doi.org/10.1007/978-981-96-7051-2_19

in 2020, revealing that China's total fertility rate had plummeted to 1.3—one of the world's lowest and significantly below the average for high-income countries. What does this mean? Those studying population dynamics understand that such a drastic decline does not happen overnight; it is the culmination of long-standing trends. With fertility rates dropping below the replacement level of 2.1, it signals that, after a period of population stability, we are inevitably heading toward a peak followed by negative growth. By 2021, the natural population growth rate had dwindled to 0.34‰, nearing statistical zero growth and potentially already there, according to adjustments by the Ministry of Civil Affairs. Additionally, the proportion of individuals aged 65 and above now exceeds 14%. What is the significance of this? According to the World Health Organization, surpassing 14% indicates an "aged society," a stage Japan has already reached and one we are likely to follow within a decade. The World Health Organization defines an "aging society" as one where the elderly make up more than 7% of the population; a "super-aged society" when that figure exceeds 14%; and a "severely aged society" when it surpasses 21%. Japan is currently a "severely aged society," and we are projected to reach this stage in about 10 years.

These revelations have surfaced much earlier than the 2019 population forecasts by the United Nations, with China's actual trajectory outpacing their projections by several years. Various indicators clearly show that China's population peak and the onset of aging exceeding 14% will arrive sooner than anticipated, a situation closely mirrored by the United Nations' 2022 update.

According to the latest forecasts, China's population is set to reach its peak and then start declining around 2022 or 2023—a milestone that coincides with India surpassing China in population, marking the end of China's era as the world's most populous country. This signifies a significant shift into an era of population decline, which is not just a temporary phase but rather a long-term trajectory. Moreover, between 2023 and 2035, the working-age population is expected to shrink rapidly each year by about 1.5%, a rate faster than initially projected. Picture this: every year, millions of individuals in the prime working-age bracket of 20 to 45 years are dwindling in absolute numbers, all while the population ages further. This paints a novel scenario, supported by all observed trends.

As mentioned earlier, the population dynamics of the past decade have primarily impacted the supply side, resulting in a slowdown in economic growth—a phenomenon called the "new normal." This new normal, rooted in supply-side factors, can be addressed through structural reforms. However, unlike in the past when shocks were predominantly supply side, it is now the demand side—especially household consumption—that will constrain China's economic trajectory.

Population is a crucial economic variable that has often been overlooked, with many focusing on short-term economic fluctuations or cycles. About 20 years ago, a Japanese institution predicted that the sole variable of long-term economic growth was the rate of population growth. Japan's economic trajectory, aside from short-term blips, has closely mirrored changes in its population, which further supports the aforementioned forecasts.

The three effects of China's population are currently having adverse impacts on consumption. Back in 2010, when the Chinese nation was dealing with supply-side shocks, China adjusted its demand structure accordingly, shifting away from excessive reliance on external demand and exports, as well as from over-dependence on investment and capital formation. Instead, the country gradually turned toward boosting consumption, especially household consumption, which became the primary driving force.

Historically, both China's population and economic growth slowed down, wherein the overall population effect is the first factor leading to subdued consumption. People are consumers, and when population growth slows or turns negative, it inevitably affects consumption.

The second is the growth effect, or income effect. When economic growth slows, the rate of income improvement also slows, directly impacting consumption. Therefore, the population growth, per capita GDP, and household consumption are all moving downward in tandem. With a future outlook of negative population growth and even lower GDP growth rates, these factors will significantly restrain household consumption.

The third is the age structure effect. China's situation in this regard differs from that of developed countries. In many developed countries, the wage levels of elderly individuals are determined by their years of work. As they age, their income tends to be higher, and they often maintain a decent level of financial security even after retirement, sometimes supplemented by income from investments. Consequently, elderly individuals in these countries generally possess higher income levels compared to younger population. However, they also tend to exhibit a reluctance to spend, giving rise to what scholars term the "retirement-consumption puzzle." In contrast, this scenario does not occur in China because the overall income levels of the elderly population are typically lower than those of younger individuals. Moreover, retirees in China often harbor concerns about supporting their children and grandchildren, prompting them to prioritize saving over spending. Consequently, both the capacity and inclination for consumption among the elderly are relatively diminished. Consumption levels decline with age, and excluding healthcare expenses, the elderly rank lowest in terms of expenditure among all demographic groups. From both cross-sectional and individual perspectives, as the population ages, insufficient consumption among the elderly contributes to an overarching trend of inadequate consumption, illustrating the age structure effect.

In the future, more countries are expected to experience negative population growth, particularly in the wake of the COVID-19 pandemic, as people's desire to have children weakens. The decision to delay having children may become the new normal in the short term, leading to a global trend of aging populations, negative population growth, or population stagnation. There are differing viewpoints on these predictions. Charles Goodhart suggests that with aging populations and labor shortages emerging as new trends, inflation will reemerge, marking the end of the deflation era. However, this is difficult to predict, as there are underlying reasons behind the current inflation not previously encountered by China, or the United States, Europe, and Japan, all of which have experienced high inflation in the past. The root causes lie in supply chain disruptions and issues related to factors such as crude oil prices. As a result, scholars like Lawrence H. Summers give weight to the significance of inflation and critique U.S. policies, while Paul R. Krugman views inflation as a transient and short-term phenomenon. The long-term trend of aging populations may lead the global economy into a period of prolonged stagnation characterized by low interest rates, low inflation, and low growth, potentially resulting in high levels of debt worldwide. In China, given the trend of aging before prosperity, we foresee that consumption will emerge as the key, consistent, and long-lasting constraint on future economic growth. This shift in mindset is imperative for us.

In response, we can analyze the economic situation with a long-term perspective on growth trends. We can gain valuable insights by considering both short- and long-term factors, as well as supply and demand dynamics and macro and micro dimensions. In reality, population dynamics may present long-term macroeconomic shocks on the demand side, but immediate short-term impacts must also be addressed. The ongoing effects of the COVID-19 pandemic continue to impact economic growth and recovery, especially from the demand side. Meanwhile, consumption issues can be examined from a micro perspective. Therefore, China's efforts on policy should focus on continuously expanding domestic demand, particularly consumption, which will emerge as a primary factor in maintaining a reasonable range of future economic growth. Over the past decade, China's primary task has been to improve and stabilize its potential growth rate. Looking ahead to the next 10 or 20 years, the most crucial task will be aligning demand-side factors to meet the potential growth rate. While achieving the potential growth rate, we should also focus on addressing short-term shocks.

When we consider both long-term and short-term measures, we can see this period as a transition into an era of negative population growth.

In an age of negative population growth, national policies, business decisions, and individual choices may shift their focus. It is well known that population plays a crucial role in mobilizing and allocating resources, and its fluctuations ultimately manifest in various ways. Therefore, negative population growth implies a decrease in the incremental mobilization of resources, making economic development more dependent on how resources are reallocated. While discussions around wealth management and finance used to aim at expanding the pie in the past, today, the focus is on distributing the pie more effectively. This shift from mobilization to allocation and reallocation changes the traditional constraints of economic growth, moving the focus from the supply side to the demand side, thereby presenting a fresh challenge that requires new adjustments in many critical decisions.

We also pay attention to the short term because it impacts the long term. Short-term effects are not merely temporary; they leave scars that can influence long-term outcomes. In studying cyclical issues or the impacts of crises, researchers often encounter the "hysteresis effect," a term borrowed from physics. This effect implies that each shock leaves scars that prevent a return to the previous normal state, pushing us onto a new trajectory, typically a lower new norm. Many significant historical turning points and long-term trends have unfolded this way. A single chance event could prematurely accelerate changes, ushering in a new normal before you can adapt.

The COVID-19 pandemic has disrupted employment, household incomes, and spending habits. This reduction in spending has become a significant constraint on economic growth, establishing a new normal. When combined, these factors cause lasting impacts, leading to a hysteresis effect. In discussing response strategies, such as the "33 measures,[1]" we primarily put emphasis on market players. These market entities encompass not only producers but also consumers and households, with the latter being a key in determining whether demand can rebound, economic recovery can be sustained, and long-term growth can continue.

Meanwhile, in response to the current insufficiency in household consumption and income, and to address long-term demand constraints, it is essential for the government to play a larger role and adjust the structure and direction of its involvement. This necessitates new and more extensive government spending.

For a period of time, I have been particularly concerned about whether the government should increase the proportion of spending relative to GDP and whether it should raise the share of social expenditures in total spending. Observing various countries, I have noticed that as per capita income levels rise, the proportion of government spending to GDP also increases. This observation aligns with Wagner's law, a principle established many years ago by German economist Adolph Wagner. According to related research, the fastest increase in the proportion of government spending occurs when per capita GDP reaches USD 12,000 to USD 24,000. This range is China's goal for the period from now until 2035, having exceeded a per capita GDP of USD 12,000 in 2021. I refer to this 13-year span as the "Wagner acceleration period," during which China should significantly increase the proportion of government expenditure relative to GDP, while also adjusting the structure of government spending, reducing direct economic activities, and focusing more on social security, social provision, and social welfare. In a certain sense, this period can also be called the "welfare state construction period," especially in the short term, where direct financial support and consumption vouchers for Chinese residents are reasonable measures. These measures

[1] "33 Measures" refer to a circular released by China's State Council in May 2022, urging the implementation of a package of detailed policy measures aimed at further stabilizing the economy. This package includes 33 measures covering policies on investment, consumption, food and energy security, and industrial and supply chains.

are inherently part of the government's responsibilities during this period. In other words, without restoring resident consumption to normal levels, achieving a genuine economic recovery will be challenging.

So, what does this mean for financial development? While I cannot provide a direct answer, an analysis of the previous discussion reveals several significant changes that should inform our future financial development, models, operational mechanisms, and product innovations.

Firstly, there is a notable shift from supply-side constraints to demand-side constraints. This change must be considered even when designing the simplest financial products. China's level of financial innovation has currently reached a high point. The events leading up to the 2008 subprime mortgage crisis demonstrated that both positive and negative outcomes are possible. With advancements in information technology and the digital economy, China's capabilities have significantly improved. Therefore, regardless of the development direction, China will have ways to respond. However, the more forcefully you act on a judgment, the higher the likelihood of mistakes.

Secondly, fiscal policy will become more crucial compared to monetary policy in the future, with changes in the direction of fiscal expenditures. In other words, fiscal spending will be more closely tied to people's livelihoods and social welfare, impacting China's financial and wealth management strategies.

Thirdly, there is a shift from a market-oriented perspective focused on producers and operators to a household-centric approach. The family, as the fundamental unit of population reproduction and consumption, significantly influences demand factors, offering potential valuable insights.

Lastly, given the significant income disparity in the past, many wealth managers have focused on the middle-income group. However, considering China's population of 1.4 billion, the future middle-income group remains relatively small. Taking a longer-term perspective, the next decade is crucial for achieving basic modernization. During this period, special groups such as the elderly, recently impoverished rural populations, and migrant workers are transitioning from low-income to middle-income brackets. This transitional phase should also serve as a target for China's financial and wealth management strategies and profit sources.

Impact of an Aging Population on Economic Growth: Pressure and Motivation

Bo Zhao

The aging population is often viewed as a "trouble" for economic growth, particularly affecting high-income countries the most, as these countries with higher per capita income typically have a higher proportion of elderly individuals due to better healthcare and improved health conditions. Furthermore, higher per capita income is associated with lower total fertility rate, as the opportunity cost of childbearing and child raising increases with income growth.

The economy influences population dynamics, which, in turn, impact economic development. This article will discuss the population's influence on economic growth across four key areas: the labor market, capital accumulation, total factor productivity, and economic structure.

This article is based on the author's speech at the 152nd NSD Policy Talk on May 16, 2021.

B. Zhao (✉)
National School of Development, Peking University, Beijing, China

W. Xianqing (ed.), *Understanding China's Path to Modernization*,
https://doi.org/10.1007/978-981-96-7051-2_20

Labor Market

The significant impact of population aging on the country's labor supply is widely recognized. According to the Seventh National Population Census in 2020, China's working-age population (aged 16 to 59) stood at 880 million, a decrease of over 40 million compared to the Sixth Census in 2010, marking a 6.8 percentage point decline as a share of the total population. This trend shows an initial increase in the working-age population, followed by a decline, indicating that the turning point has already passed.

It is important to note that the working-age population does not directly translate to the actual workforce, so we should also take into account employment figures. Data reveals that China's employment numbers experienced a turning point around 2017.

Both these indicators convey the same message: the demographic dividend, as measured by the working-age population, has been largely exhausted, which will negatively impact China's production.

Capital Accumulation

Capital accumulation is another crucial factor influencing economic output. A country's growth heavily depends on a rapid influx of investments, primarily driven by domestic savings, which is, in turn, directly impacted by the demographic structure: Retirees experience a decline in income post-retirement while maintaining their consumption levels, leading to a reduction in the savings rate and slowing down capital accumulation. Therefore, countries with a significant elderly population will witness a continued decrease in savings rates. Consequently, maintaining a robust savings rate is essential for sustaining high-speed investment growth.

In the case of China, one challenge lies in the 5% decrease in the savings rate between 2010 and 2022, exacerbated by the aging population. Without an increase in the savings rate, China may need to rely on international balance adjustments to support strong investment growth, which could gradually reduce the long-standing surplus and potentially result in a deficit. Consequently, it might become necessary to facilitate rapid domestic investment growth by attracting foreign capital.

Total Factor Productivity

Total factor productivity (TFP) measures how efficiently inputs like labor, capital, and land are utilized in production. Successfully tackling the challenges of an aging population hinges on boosting TFP, with key focuses on technological progress and human capital.

Technological progress can help compensate for labor shortages and even replace some low-skilled jobs with automation. Concurrently, investing in education can enhance workforce skills, increasing labor value and transitioning from a "demographic dividend" to a "talent dividend."

Our research shows that countries with significant aging populations are more inclined to invest in technology research and development and human capital enhancement; there is a strong positive correlation between the elderly population and the proportion of national R&D investment in GDP, as well as between the elderly population and the human capital index. Countries with higher degree of population aging tend to excel in R&D investment and human capital accumulation.

China's Seventh National Population Census revealed positive trends: the average years of schooling among the working-age population (16–59) was up to 10.75 years in 2020 from 9.67 years in 2010, and the illiteracy rate decreased from 4.08 to 2.67%.

Economic Structure

Population aging also impacts the economy through changes in consumption patterns, as different age groups exhibit distinct consumption preferences. Analyzing the composition of national residents' consumption reveals that as the population ages, there is an increased demand for services such as healthcare. These shifts in consumption patterns further influence China's industrial structure.

Elderly individuals primarily prioritize non-tradable goods, including medical services, wealth management, and retirement provisions. When these goods cannot be sourced through trade, domestic production must increase to meet demand. As the population ages, the demand for such services rises significantly, leading to a corresponding increase in their relative prices. This dynamic attracts production factors, gradually transitioning them from the primary and secondary sectors toward the service sector. This evolution increases the service industry's contribution to the economy and boosts employment within this sector, ultimately shifting the economy from industrial dominance to a service-oriented focus.

While developed countries have undergone similar processes, it is not necessarily the ideal path. During this transition, we must be cautious of Baumol's cost disease, a phenomenon that occurs in sectors with slow technological progress, like the service industry, which often attract significant input but experience persistently high prices, such as continuously rising healthcare costs. When sectors with limited scalability and slow technological progress dominate the service industry, they can hinder the overall economic growth.

Even though certain areas within the tertiary industry are experiencing rapid advancement, the overall pace of technological progress and growth in this sector tends to lag behind that of the primary and secondary sectors, particularly in areas like education, urban services, and healthcare. Baumol's cost disease can lead to premature deindustrialization, causing an early downturn in the overall rate of technological advancement. Given that technological progress largely dictates long-term per capita income, this can subsequently diminish overall economic growth rates. The elimination of the target for the share of value-added in the service industry in China's 14th Five-Year Plan is, in my view, a prudent decision.

Aging is both a challenge and an opportunity for reform. To address the aforementioned concerns, we can comprehensively lift birth restrictions to invigorate the labor market; enhance financial markets and attract foreign investment to bolster capital accumulation; foster innovation and increase expenditures on R&D as well as education to elevate total factor productivity; modernize the services sector while avoiding premature deindustrialization; and consistently uphold a robust export advantage to optimize the economic structure.

Distinctive Features of Aging in China and Policy Recommendations

Xiaoyan Lei

Since the release of the results of the Seventh National Population Census, there has been considerable discussion on the topic of aging and population policy. This article aims to offer insights into observed trends from a data-driven perspective.

Aging in China

Population Size and Structure

When examining the population size and its structure, this article exclusively utilizes data from five national population censuses (1982, 1990, 2000, 2010, and 2020) to ensure comparability, rather than relying on annual one-thousandth sample survey data. Analysis of Fig. 1 reveals several noteworthy observations.

First, China's total population has steadily grown, reaching 1.41 billion in 2020.

This article is based on the author's speech delivered at the 152nd NSD Policy Talk on May 16, 2021.

X. Lei (✉)
National School of Development, Peking University, Beijing, China

W. Xianqing (ed.), *Understanding China's Path to Modernization*,
https://doi.org/10.1007/978-981-96-7051-2_21

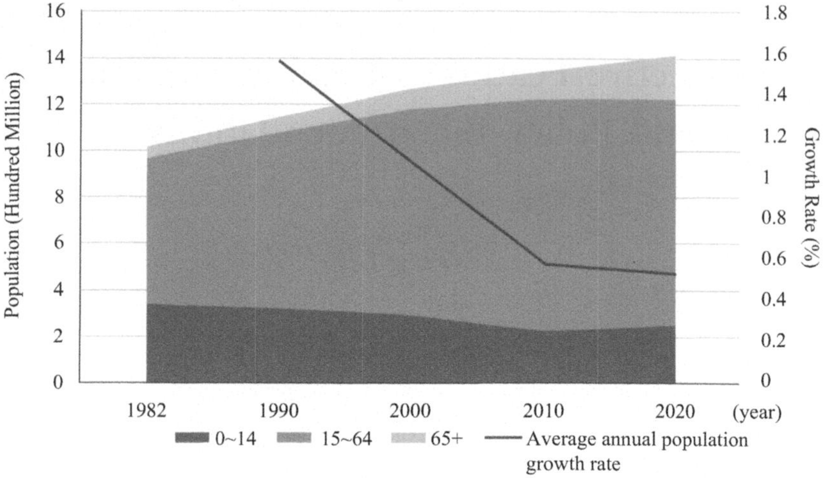

Fig. 1 Population size and structure

Second, the population growth rate has decelerated, dropping from an average annual growth rate of 1.56% between 1982 and 1990 to 0.53% between 2010 and 2020.

Third, the elderly population (aged 65 and above) has been steadily increasing both in number and proportion, reaching 191 million in 2020. This accounts for 13.5% of the total population, approaching the threshold for severe aging (14%).

Fourth, the population of children (aged 0 to 14) has seen a slight uptick in the past decade, possibly due to relaxed birth policies.

Dependency Ratio of Population

The dependency ratio, which indicates the proportion of the non-working-age population to the working-age population, has witnessed changes. From 1982 to 2020, the working-age population, serving as the denominator, has slightly decreased, reaching 968 million in 2020. Meanwhile, the total dependency ratio (the sum of elderly and child dependency ratios) has been on the rise since 2010, climbing from 34.2% to 45.9% over the decade. This increase is predominantly attributed to a significant rise in the elderly dependency ratio, which surged from 11.9%

in 2010 to 19.7% in 2020. In contrast, the rise in the child dependency ratio has been comparatively modest, increasing from 22.3% in 2010 to 26.2% in 2020.

Fertility

Official data indicates that China's total fertility rate has persistently remained below 1.6, indicating a prolonged low level and continuous decline. Despite a brief rebound following the relaxation of birth policies, the rate dropped to 1.3 by 2020. Additionally, the number of women of childbearing age (15 to 49 years old) has consistently decreased since 2011. The combined effect of these factors has led to a noticeable downward trend in China's population growth in recent years (as illustrated in Fig. 2).

There are also significant urban–rural disparities in China's fertility rate, with urban areas having lower fertility rates than towns, and even lower rates than rural areas. Following the implementation of the universal two-child policy, fertility rates in both urban and rural areas initially increased but subsequently declined, to a certain extent, with cities experiencing a faster rate of decline.

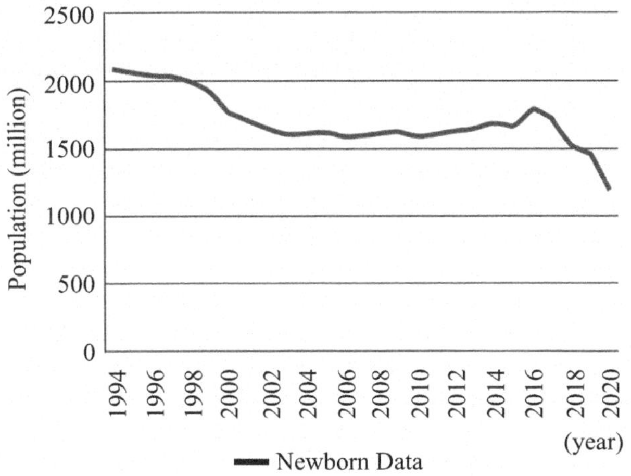

Fig. 2 Newborn data

The fertility trend also shows distinct differences based on the number of children. From 2000 to 2019, the fertility rate for first-born children consistently decreased, while the fertility rate for second children initially increased following the relaxation of the birth control policy but subsequently declined. Whereas fertility rates for families with three or more children saw a slight increase, although their overall proportion remains very small.

In terms of fertility intentions in urban and rural areas, according to the China General Social Survey (CGSS) conducted by Renmin University of China, from 2010 to 2017, women of childbearing age (15 to 49 years old) expressed a desire to have between 1.7 and 1.9 children. Urban women consistently reported very low fertility intentions, remaining below 1.75. Similarly, rural women's fertility intentions were around 1.9, with a noticeable downward trend in 2021.

Examining the fertility intentions of women across different generations—those born in the 1960s, 1970s, 1980s, and 1990s—reveals a clear preference for fewer children among younger cohorts. In recent years, fertility intentions among women born in the 1980s and 1990s have declined, with a particularly sharp decrease observed among those born in the 1990s.

An analysis of fertility intentions based on the desired number of children and urban–rural divides shows that while the proportion of women not wanting to have children remains small (less than 5%), there is a growing trend in recent years. This trend is more prominent among urban women who do not wish to have children. At the same time, the percentage of women desiring to have one child, which had previously been declining, has increased in recent years in both urban and rural areas. Despite over two-thirds of women still hoping to have two or more children, this proportion has declined in both urban and rural areas in recent years.

The findings on fertility intentions among various age groups and birth cohorts are indeed noteworthy. Notably, a significantly higher proportion of women born in the 1990s express no desire to have children compared to those born in the 1960s, 1970s, and 1980s. Furthermore, this percentage has been rapidly increasing in recent years. Among those born in the 1980s and 1990s, there is a growing trend toward expecting just one child, while the preference for having two or more children is diminishing.

Finally, when examining the mismatch between fertility intentions and actual childbirth rates, it is crucial not to solely concentrate on women in their reproductive years (15 to 49 years old), as younger age brackets often have not yet started families. We can gain clearer insights by directing our focus to individuals aged between 35 and 49. According to data from the 2017 CGSS survey, which captured details on both fertility intentions and the actual number of children, a considerable gap emerges between these two aspects. On average, the actual number of children falls short by 0.42 compared to the desired figure, underscoring a prevalent shortfall in achieving one's envisioned family size. This contrast is notably divergent across urban and rural regions, with rural women exhibiting a difference of 0.33, whereas their urban counterparts show a higher discrepancy of 0.62.

All in all, the current demographic landscape in China reveals several significant trends: a rapidly aging population, a growing dependency ratio, a shrinking working-age population, declining fertility rates, and fewer newborns. There are also notable urban–rural disparities in fertility rates and intentions, with urban areas reporting the lowest rates. Younger generations are showing reduced interest in having children, with a noticeable decline in fertility intentions. Furthermore, actual birth rates are falling significantly below desired levels, especially evident in urban settings.

Policy Recommendations

The 2020 *Report on the Work of the Government* called for "optimizing the fertility policy, promoting a moderate level of fertility, and developing a universal childcare and basic elderly care service system,"[1] and various discussions have taken place regarding adjustments to the fertility policy. Given the current demographic trends in China, as indicated by the data, I would like to propose some policy recommendations.

First of all, it is recommended to adjust the birth policy at the appropriate time. Specifically, it is suggested to fully lift birth restrictions. Concerns about a surge in births are unfounded, as the desire to have three or more children is low among the population.

[1] Editor's Note: Report on the Work of the Government——Delivered at the Third Session of the 13th National People's Congress of the People's Republic of China on May 22, 2020. (Ref: http://www.gov.cn/gongbao/content/2021/content_5593438.htm).

Secondly, it is crucial to lower the cost of childbirth. Why is there such a low willingness to have children? Why do many people who express a desire to have children end up not doing so? The answer to these questions is largely cost, which includes the expenses of childbirth, child raising, and education. Currently, the cost of childbirth is primarily borne by women. To reduce this burden, the cost must be shared more equitably between women and men. For example, in addition to providing maternity leave for women, paternity leave should be increased and properly implemented. The childbirth allowance currently provided by the government is also inadequate.

Thirdly, it is important to reduce the child raising cost. More access should be increased to childcare services for children aged 0 to 3, as these early years of child raising involve high expenses. Additionally, incorporating pre-school education into compulsory education could alleviate a major concern for many women.

Lastly, it is vital to increase investment in education. The current educational system is highly competitive, and the primary solution is to boost national-level investment in educational resources and ensure a more equitable distribution. Reducing disparities in school quality across different regions and levels would lessen the intense competition among students.

China's Private Pension Scheme: Its Significance and Challenges

Yaohui Zhao

On April 21, 2022, the General Office of the State Council issued the *Opinions on Promoting the Development of Private Pensions* ("*Opinions*"), outlining three main principles: government policy support, voluntary participation by individuals, and market-oriented operation. The document clearly defines the private property nature of private pensions, which I believe is its most significant highlight.

The private property nature is primarily reflected in four aspects:

Firstly, the right of possession is emphasized through the implementation of a private pension scheme. Contributions are made by participants individually, ensuring complete accumulation. The key element is the "individual account."

Secondly, the right to profits is evident in the closed operation of these accounts, where equity belongs to the participants and withdrawals are not allowed unless specified otherwise. Participants can use the funds in

This article is based on the author's speech delivered at the 156th NSD Policy Talk on April 24, 2022.

Y. Zhao (✉)
Department of Economics, National School of Development, Peking University, Beijing, China

W. Xianqing (ed.), *Understanding China's Path to Modernization*,
https://doi.org/10.1007/978-981-96-7051-2_22

their accounts to purchase bank financial products, savings, and invest in funds and other financial products, assuming the associated risks.

Thirdly, the right of disposal allows for the transfer and replacement of funds within individual pension accounts or even transferring them to other accounts. This marks a breakthrough, as such operations were previously prohibited.

Finally, the right of use ensures that, once the age for receiving benefits is reached, the accumulated funds in the individual pension account are solely for the individual's use.

In my view, while private pensions may not be entirely private property, they are very close to it. Except for the provision that prohibits early withdrawals unless otherwise specified, the other aspects resemble private property rights.

The *Opinions* also clearly positions the private pension scheme as complementary to basic pension insurance and enterprise (occupational) annuities, serving as additional supports for pension insurance. China's pension insurance system currently has two main pillars. The first pillar is basic pension insurance, which includes urban employee pension insurance and rural and urban resident pension insurance. The second pillar is enterprise supplementary pension insurance, available only in some well-performing large institutions, with limited coverage.

In my opinion, the significance of the private pension plan is by no means limited to supplementing the first and second pillars of pension insurance.

Issues Faced by China's Pension System

General Secretary Xi Jinping addressed the challenges facing China's pension system in his article, "Promoting High-Quality and Sustainable Development of China's Social Security System," published in the 8th issue of *Qiushi* magazine on April 16, 2022, in which he highlighted significant issues within the pension and social security systems in China. As society evolves, marked by rapid urbanization, an aging population, and diversified employment, the primary contradictions have shifted, exposing persistent deficiencies in the country's social security system. These deficiencies can be broadly categorized as follows:

Firstly, the social security system requires enhanced coordination. Complete system integration has not been achieved, resulting in insufficiently smooth transitions between systems.

Secondly, there is significant pressure to balance regional income and expenditure conflicts, with some regions at risk of depleting their social security funds.

Thirdly, certain groups, such as migrant workers, flexible employees, and those engaged in new forms of employment, are not fully covered by social security. This leads to inadequate coverage, loss of coverage, and discontinuation of coverage.

Lastly, disparities in treatment among urban and rural areas, regions, and different groups remain unreasonable.

These issues underline the necessity for the introduction of private pension plans. As a response to these challenges, China has implemented the private pension scheme.

Moving forward, let's delve into the specific problems currently present in China's pension system.

Decentralized Administration and Challenges in Transitioning Between Social Security Systems

Currently, the employee pension insurance system and the resident pension insurance system operate independently and are managed locally in different regions without connectivity. Over the years, there has been an ongoing effort to enhance coordination between these two systems. At present, provincial-level coordination for employee pension insurance has largely been achieved, with efforts moving toward nationwide integration. Similarly, efforts are being made to promote city-level coordination for resident pension insurance, which initially started at the county level.

With 334 prefecture-level administrative units in China, there are potentially at least 33 pools for employee pension insurance and over 300 pools for resident pension insurance, each operating independently. Population and labor mobility have become significant social trends, leading to individuals transitioning between resident pension insurance and employee pension insurance, including reverse and cross-regional movements. While transferring within the employee pension insurance system is relatively convenient, inter-regional transfers for resident pension insurance and transitions between employee and resident pension insurances remain inadequately implemented. Previous solutions have been proposed but were not the most favorable for participants.

Huge Regional Differences in Pension Pressure

In the context of pensions, the "dependency ratio of pension insurance" refers to the ratio of retirees receiving pensions to working employees paying contributions. In Guangdong Province, this ratio is 9:1, meaning nine working employees support one retired worker. However, in Jilin and Heilongjiang provinces, approximately 1.2 employees support one retired worker, indicating significant pension pressure.

This disparity undoubtedly reflects the effects of labor force mobility. The results of the 2020 Census reveal labor migration patterns, such as the net influx of population into economically developed provinces like Guangdong. I believe that these regional differences in pension pressure are not due to varying birth rates but rather unbalanced economic development, which drives people to move from low-income to high-income areas. Consequently, provinces experiencing large population outflows face the risk of their social security funds being depleted.

Therefore, the solutions outlined in the *Opinions* are quite reasonable. In my opinion, addressing deficit risks should not be left to individual provinces but should be centrally coordinated nationwide. For instance, if Heilongjiang Province experiences a deficit, it should not bear the burden alone, especially since many young people have migrated to Guangdong Province.

The concept of comprehensive coordination was proposed in the late 1990s. Despite over 30 years having passed, achieving national coordination remains a challenge, highlighting the difficulty of this issue.

The difficulties of national coordination can be attributed to two main factors:

First, local interests pose a significant obstacle. Regions like Heilongjiang, which experience population outflow, may be very willing to support the coordination policy, but provinces like Guangdong, Zhejiang, Shanghai, and Beijing, which receive a population influx, may be reluctant.

Second, there is a moral hazard. Once the policy is implemented, provinces currently in deficit will likely expect short-term financial assistance to offset their deficits. Previously, many regions allowed "retroactive payment of social security," where individuals could pay tens of thousands of yuan to continue receiving retirement benefits for decades. Due to the ethical risks involved, this policy has been banned.

Inadequate Coverage, Loss of Coverage, and Discontinuation of Coverage

With the rise of new economic models, flexible employment is becoming increasingly common. Currently, there are 200 million flexible workers in China, accounting for more than a quarter of the national workforce. Among these, delivery riders, who play a crucial role in our daily lives, amount to a staggering 84 million, representing approximately one-tenth of the national workforce—a number continues to grow.

The majority of these platform-based flexible workers do not participate in employee pension insurance, which has become a prominent issue online. In recent years, China transferred the responsibility for collecting social security contributions from social security departments to tax authorities, increasing pressure on companies to ensure coverage for their employees. However, the current method of forcibly enrolling individuals in insurance is no longer effective. Despite pressure from tax authorities, it remains challenging to ensure that platform-based flexible workers join employee pension insurance schemes. Consequently, a significant portion of the population lacks social security coverage, leaving many, especially young individuals, without pension security for their old age.

In my opinion, the primary purpose of introducing private pension plans is to assist those lacking necessary security to prevent them from losing coverage, rather than solely safeguarding high-income groups.

Significant Disparities in Benefits

The horizontal axis in Figs. 1 and 2 represents different types of social insurance, while their vertical axis indicates insurance coverage rates. The different colored bars represent data from 2011 to 2018. It is evident from the graphs that urban and rural residents have almost achieved full social security coverage. Furthermore, urban residents primarily participate in employee insurance, with a coverage rate of approximately 66.8%, while rural residents mainly partake in the new rural insurance scheme.

Resident insurance provides very limited funds, resulting in significant differences in the annual pension amounts across different core pension insurances.

As depicted in Fig. 3, the gray bar represents the median pension amount for employee pension insurance, which was around RMB 32,000

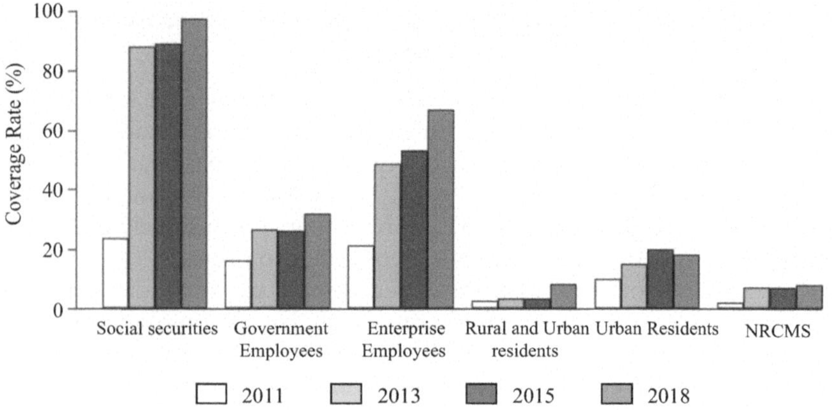

Fig. 1 Social insurance and pension scheme coverage rate among urban elderly residents

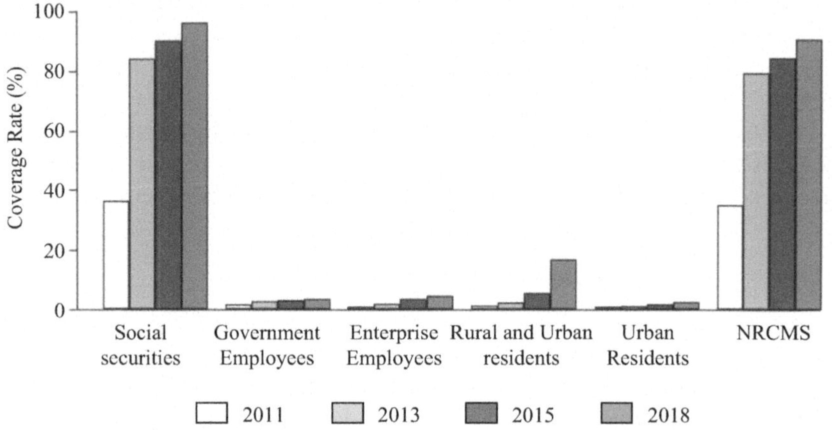

Fig. 2 Social insurance and pension scheme coverage rate among rural elderly residents

in 2018. In contrast, the dark gray bar represents the median pension amount for rural resident pension insurance, which was approximately RMB 1,000 annually. This vast difference is primarily due to the differences in the types of insurance.

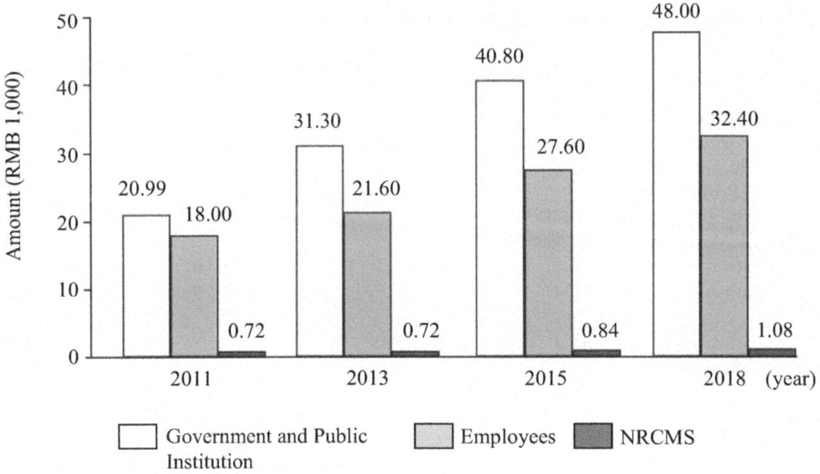

Fig. 3 Pension amount (median)

Is the pension level adequate for retirement? In 2015, we performed a simple calculation on a sample of individuals aged 50 to 60 who had not yet retired. The results are presented in Table 1.

We first assessed the current wealth of individuals and then discounted the expected social security pension to its present value. Using the poverty line standard, we evaluated whether this group could maintain a living standard above the poverty line after retirement, relying solely on their pension. The calculations revealed that about 88% of rural residents would fall below the poverty line after retirement if they depended solely on social security. When other sources of wealth were considered, this percentage decreased to around 38%, indicating that relying solely on pensions is insufficient for the aging population. This is a significant issue. If young people today retire with inadequate savings through social security, they will face similar problems. With insufficient pensions, elderly individuals will be forced to continue working to make ends meet.

Table 1 Financial situation of the retirees

	Rural residents	*Urban residents*	*Female*	*Male*	*Total*
Social security wealth	88.8	36.5	75.8	72.9	74.4
Social security wealth + Durable consumer goods + Productive fixed assets + Working capital	73.8	29.2	65.3	57.6	61.5
Monetization of land	63.2	28.1	57.6	49.2	53.5
Monetization of housing	46.4	17.7	42.8	33.9	38.5
Monetization of both land and housing	38.1	17.0	36.8	27.5	32.3

Note Aged 50 to 60, assuming specific discount rate and growth rate, with weighted percentages (%) Housing-for-pension is likely to play an important role in reducing elderly poverty
Families will continue to be a significant source of economic support for the elderly, even as the government's role expands. However, it remains crucial to emphasize the protective role families play in elderly care

Establishing the Pension System

The urban employee pension plan began in the 1950s and underwent reform in the 1980s, when the pension systems for enterprises and public institutions were separated. In 2015, the pension scheme for public institutions was integrated into the urban employee insurance.

Meanwhile, the resident pension plan was initiated in 2009 with the new rural pension plan, covering rural residents. In 2012, the urban resident pension plan was introduced, extending coverage to urban residents without security or employment. By 2014, urban and rural resident insurances began merging, a process completed by 2020. Since then, all residents of the People's Republic of China can access a basic pension, provided they are willing to join the plan.

Design of the Employee Pension System

The design of the employee pension system has faced significant challenges. From the 1960s until 1986, employers were primarily responsible for providing pensions. However, with the bankruptcy of state-owned and collective enterprises, a shift toward social pensions became necessary.

Starting in 1986, state-owned enterprises began implementing comprehensive pension plans that included industry-wide pooling and regional coordination. Personal contributions to the pension system were introduced in 1991.

In 1997, the State Council issued the *Decision of the State Council on Establishing a Unified Basic Pension System for Enterprise Employees*, which established a consensus on combining unified accounting with contributions and benefits formulas. The "unified" component is funded by employer contributions, which have decreased from a maximum rate of 20% to 16%. In some regions, the employer contribution rate is 14%, while individual contributions is at 8%.

Original Intent for the Combination of Social Pooling with Individual Accounts

The term "combination" refers to the integration of social pooling with individual accounts. The original intent behind this design was to encourage individuals to contribute by providing them with individual accounts. However, these individual accounts do not function as personal property, as funds do not accumulate in them; they remain inactive, individuals do not have ownership of the funds, and transfers are not allowed. Furthermore, under this design, 20% of pension contributions are pooled and disconnected from individual interests, which I believe is a significant reason for the low participation enthusiasm among residents.

Active participation is crucial for the success of the pension insurance system, a topic we have long researched. In 1999, Professor Xu Jianguo and I published two papers pointing out that "the current transition model avoids addressing payment motivation, resulting in widespread non-payment and evasion behaviors," and suggested a move toward marketization. Our specific recommendations included, among others, defining the implicit debt of the pension and allocating it to individuals in an account-based manner, transforming the pension fund accounts into real accounts, and transferring them to market management. Essentially, these measures align with the objectives of the new private pension scheme.

In 2001, we conducted a comprehensive analysis of incentive mechanisms. Our careful calculations led us to conclude that the key to effective incentive design is to reduce the reliance on communal-pot distribution,[1] and instead deposit both employer and employee contributions into individual accounts, and have them managed by professional investment institutions to achieve secure and reasonable returns, comparable to or exceeding individual investment returns. "Under reasonable assumptions, allocating 1% of GDP annually could eliminate the current pension debt over 50 years, equivalent to a 5.6% payroll tax. Contributing a total of 10.2% of wages to individual accounts could ensure full accumulation in these accounts and provide a 60% replacement rate for pension income. Combined, these contributions would account for only 15.8% of wages." This underscores the critical importance of motivation in the success of the pension system.

Unlike employee pension insurance, the resident pension insurance has always been based on a fully funded private pension scheme. All contributions, including personal contributions and government subsidies to attract contributions, go into individual accounts from the beginning. However, there are fundamental differences between this and the individual accounts discussed today. Residents cannot control their accounts themselves, mainly manifested as the inability to choose investment management institutions independently, interest rates determined by the government, and restrictions on portability. Therefore, despite the presence of individual accounts and fund accumulation, allowing residents to check their balances, the system still fails to increase residents' willingness to participate. I believe that the main reason for this lack of enthusiasm is the insufficient control and security over their accounts provided to individuals, which leads to a lack of trust in the resident pension insurance system.

Enhancing Pension Payment Enthusiasm

In today's flourishing new economy, higher enthusiasm for contributing to old-age insurance becomes more important than ever. The rise in flexible and platform-based employment has led many young people to disconnect from traditional employee social security systems. At the same

[1] The communal-pot distribution method refers to a system where resources or rights are centralized and then uniformly allocated without considering individual differences. This approach can result in a lack of motivation, reduced efficiency, and issues with fairness.

time, a significant number of retirees within the system rely on continuous financial support from younger contributors in terms of pension payments.

Currently, China has around 84 million platform-based flexible employees, accounting for 10% of the workforce. If a large number of young workers transition to flexible employment and leave the social security system, who will support the current elderly population? This scenario will inevitably lead to a growing deficit in social security funds, escalating the overall pressure on the system.

For young people, not saving for retirement during their peak earning years can lead to insecurity if gaps in their social security coverage emerge post-retirement.

Additionally, excessive pressure on social security can accelerate the informal employment. Policy-related payments, including pensions, healthcare, unemployment, and maternity benefits, collectively account for approximately 36.8% of payroll costs, with housing provident fund contributions adding an additional 10% to 24%. Altogether, these contributions can total about 46.8% of payroll costs. Consequently, if businesses diligently fulfill these payment obligations, labor costs can become significant. This means that for every RMB 1,000 in wages paid by enterprises, they also incur about RMB 400 in social security costs.

As a result, enterprises may resort to reducing the formality of employment to cope with the financial burden. Formalizing platform-based employment would be beneficial but is hindered by the overwhelming payment pressures. Consequently, actual payment rates by companies are significantly lower than mandated, achieved through strategies like lowering the number of employees or reducing their wages to minimize contribution levels. Such practices inadvertently disincentivize compliance, propagating a cycle where dishonest practices prevail over ethical conduct. To counter these issues, traditional methods like increased monitoring and inspections prove ineffective. Instead, it is imperative to incentivize participation by making it profitable. People act rationally and out of self-interest, so making participation appealing is a fundamental economic tactic.

The Choice of Pension Schemes

There are two main types of pension schemes: defined benefit (DB) and defined contribution (DC). In a DB scheme, the insured person knows in advance how much they will receive each month after retirement. In a DC scheme, the insured person knows how much they need to contribute, but the amount received after retirement depends on the investment returns. The latter essentially operates on a private pension scheme.

Both DB and DC schemes can be further subdivided into "with fund accumulation" and "without fund accumulation." For example, a DB scheme without fund accumulation is similar to a pay-as-you-go system, simply meaning no funds are accumulated. When employees retire and funds are needed, they are collected from current employees. This is known as a pay-as-you-go system.

In the private pension scheme, there are also nominal accounts and real accounts. In a nominal account, if current employees deposit RMB 100 into their account, this RMB 100 is immediately used to pay retired employees. Although the funds are not actually retained in the account, it is reflected in the balance. In contrast, a real account system means that the funds in the account are both visible and tangible.

Factors to Consider When Choosing a Plan

When selecting a pension insurance system in China, we should take several key factors into account.

Firstly, it is important to consider whether the plan effectively addresses the challenges of population aging. The increasing number of elderly individuals creates a substantial demand for transition, posing hidden risks related to changes in age demographics. It is also necessary to evaluate whether the plan encourages the postponement of retirement.

Secondly, it is crucial to assess whether the system can increase active participation. Many systems fail to address motivational issues. Regardless of whether it is a pay-as-you-go system or a fund accumulation system, most countries require mandatory participation, primarily to prevent short-sighted behavior. Some individuals focus solely on their present needs, neglecting their future financial security, which can lead to poverty in old age and ultimately burden society. Since society ultimately bears this cost, some people may exploit societal support by deliberately not saving and spending all their money. They rely on the expectation that the state and society will support them in their poverty-stricken old age. However, implementing mandatory participation can be challenging in many countries.

Thirdly, it is essential to consider whether the system promotes common prosperity and avoids a huge wealth gap.

Which System is More Reliable?

When it comes to resisting population aging, let's first take a look at the pay-as-you-go system. In this system, the retirement income of elderly individuals depends entirely on contributions from the younger working population. As the dependency ratio worsens, the financial burden on younger generations increases. In China, the change in the dependency ratio is notable. This ratio measures the number of people aged 60 and above who rely on support from those aged 20 to 59. It is evident that the dependency ratio has been deteriorating rapidly in recent years. In 2000, the ratio was 5.5:1; by 2020, it dropped to 3:1; and by 2050, it is projected to decrease further to 1.2:1.

Therefore, if we adopt a pay-as-you-go system and assume everyone retires at 60 years old, the working population would need to contribute half of their income to support retirees. This scenario is highly unsustainable and discourages active workforce participation.

Now, let's look at the private pension scheme. If we implement a nominal account system where money cannot accumulate, it essentially mirrors the pay-as-you-go system. However, with a fund accumulation system, where the elderly rely on their own savings for retirement rather than on contributions from younger generations, these issues are mitigated. Therefore, the fund accumulation system is more sustainable and better suited to an aging population. In my view, this is also a key reason why many regions are adopting the fund accumulation system (Fig. 4).

Which System Encourages Prolonged Employment?

As life expectancy rises, countries must consider delaying retirement to maintain economic stability, as retiring at the traditional age of 60 can quickly lead to a certainly unsustainable 1:1 dependency ratio. With a life expectancy of 90 years, raising the retirement age to 70 would significantly improve this ratio. Therefore, extending the retirement age

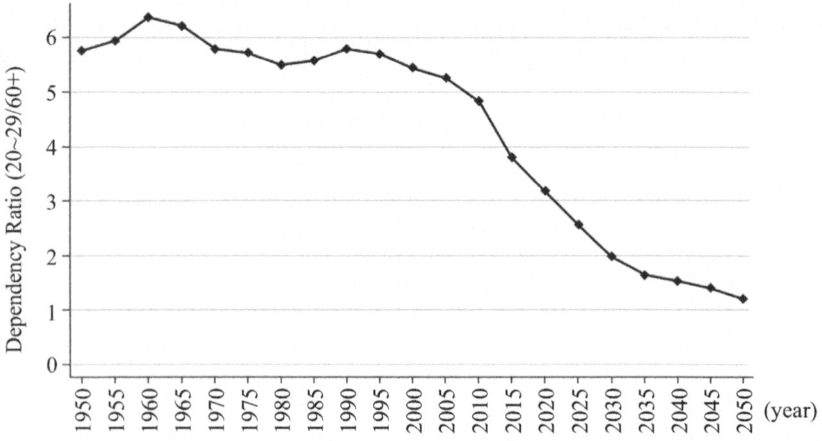

Fig. 4 China's dependency ratio (1950–2050)

becomes a primary tool for most countries to tackle the challenges of an aging population.

In a pay-as-you-go system, contributors often view their pension as an earned right. If the government changes regulations midstream, contributors might perceive it as a breach of trust and potentially resist delayed retirement. Conversely, a personal account system operates differently. Here, the funds are individual assets, and opting for early retirement means spreading limited funds over a longer period, resulting in lower annual payouts. Delaying retirement, therefore, increases the retirement income. Therefore, with rising life expectancy, people may be more inclined to delay retirement. From this perspective, a personal account system appears more favorable.

Developed countries typically employ a pay-as-you-go system, which is now under strain due to aging populations and significant deficits. These systems were not designed with current demographic challenges in mind, leading to difficulties in raising retirement ages, exacerbated by political pressures during elections, as candidates often promise to maintain retirees' welfare without delays. Therefore, developed countries have recognized the limitations of the pay-as-you-go system.

At present, in the United States, the reliance on social security as the first pillar has significantly decreased, with supplemental insurance and corporate pensions becoming more prominent. Corporate pensions, in particular, have grown to be a stronger second pillar, surpassing social security. Both Republicans and Democrats have advocated for the privatization of social security, though this goal has not yet been achieved. However, the United States has substantially reformed its pension system by expanding the third pillar.

Which System Encourages Contributions?

Under the current pay-as-you-go system, contributions are made to secure entitlements, but additional payments do not yield extra benefits. Once the contribution period meets the required standard, participants become eligible for retirement benefits. This setup tends to encourage minimal contribution practices, as participants aim to "game the system" by simply meeting the minimum contribution requirements. Consequently, the entire distribution system favors low contributors, with funds from higher earners subsidizing them. While this structure promotes participation, it fails to incentivize higher contributions.

Conversely, the private pension scheme sees each account as personal property, where increased contributions lead to greater returns. This system not only fosters contributions but also motivates participants to contribute more.

Which System Promotes Common Prosperity?

At first glance, the pay-as-you-go system seems ideal for promoting common prosperity due to its redistribution mechanism that supports low-income contributors. In contrast, the private pension scheme lacks such redistribution capabilities, making the pay-as-you-go system appear more beneficial for achieving common prosperity on the surface. Nonetheless, due to widespread non-participation or minimal contributions, many may end up with lower-than-expected pension benefits. Consequently, participants might only receive basic pension benefits or opt out of the system entirely, forgoing their pensions, ultimately leading to increased numbers of individuals with lower incomes.

While the private pension scheme is not without flaw, it can be enhanced with complementary initiatives.

Firstly, maximizing participation through incentives is crucial to preventing elderly poverty. Encouraging universal contributions, irrespective of income levels, can help avert elderly poverty among all beneficiaries.

Additionally, support measures should specifically address individuals with persistently low incomes.

It is imperative to keep these two aspects distinct, ensuring that support measures do not undermine the incentive structure of the pension scheme.

The Appeal of Individual Pension Accounts

Individual pension accounts have the potential to alleviate poverty if managed effectively. This potential is grounded in the natural tendency of individuals to save. As people age, their earning capacity decreases while their consumption needs increase. Eventually, a point is reached where personal income can no longer cover consumption, making savings essential.

One might ask, "Why should my money be held in a government account when I can place it in my own savings account?" The primary reason is that the returns on personal savings are typically limited, and individual investors are vulnerable to exploitation. Investment institutions, being experts in maximizing investment returns, offer a better alternative. However, these institutions often have high minimum investment requirements that low-income earners struggle to meet. Therefore, in most cases, ordinary people rely on banks for financial management. Yet, under the system of individual retirement accounts, small contributions from many individuals are pooled together and entrusted to institutional investors for financial management, thereby yielding higher returns. For the average person, this is the primary appeal of individual retirement accounts.

Causes of Elderly Poverty

Elderly poverty can be attributed to the shortcomings of private pension schemes. People who have spent their lives in low-income brackets are more likely to fall into poverty in old age, even if they consistently contribute to their pension accounts, which may still be insufficient to meet their retirement needs. In such instances, I believe it is crucial for the government to provide support rather than relying solely on pension schemes. Singapore's Workfare program exemplifies an effective approach. It not only subsidizes low-income earners but also encourages employment. Those who remain employed receive more substantial subsidies, with a significant portion directed to their personal accounts, thereby helping them better prepare for retirement.

This approach appears highly effective. Often, those who have never contributed to pension funds are individuals overlooked by social security systems, typically self-employed and engaged in flexible work arrangements. Mandatory insurance schemes do not easily cover them due to the challenges of assessing their income and collecting contributions. In contrast, developed countries have a lower proportion of self-employed individuals, making it easier to implement mandatory social insurance programs. However, middle- and low-income countries have a sizable population of self-employed workers, including farmers. Therefore, finding ways to incentivize self-employed individuals to participate in social insurance is crucial. In this regard, Chile and Singapore have adopted different approaches, leading to diverse outcomes.

The Pension System in Chile

In 1981, Chile introduced a fully funded individual account pension system, a groundbreaking reform compared to the previous pay-as-you-go system, which was already in crisis. By 1971, Chile's pension expenditure had reached 17% of GDP, and over 100 different pools made reform efforts complex due to conflicting interests. To address this, the Chilean government increased the savings rate and promoted financial market development, facilitating economic growth.

The solid line in Fig. 5 represents Chile's per capita GDP, while the dashed line represents the per capita GDP of South America. It is evident that since the reforms of the 1980s, Chile has experienced an economic miracle, achieving remarkable economic growth and significantly distancing itself from other Latin American countries. As a result, Chile has become a model praised by the World Bank for its economic policies.

In the 1990s, many countries, including Argentina, Peru, Colombia, Uruguay, Mexico, Poland, Russia, and India, implemented pension systems similar to that of Chile. Chile's system was undeniably successful at the time, becoming a global model for pension reform.

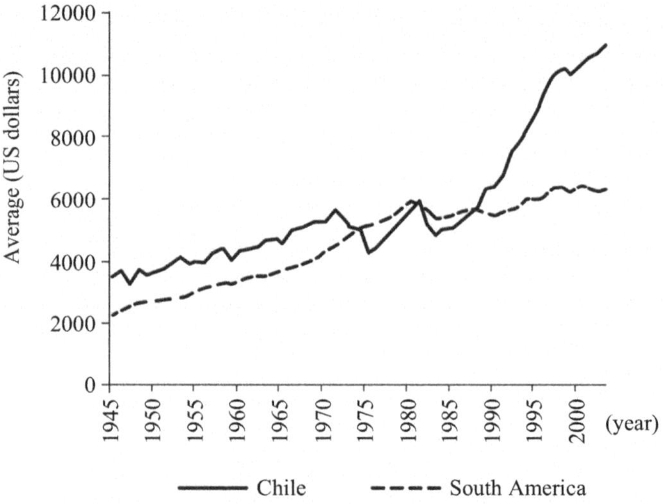

Fig. 5 Average GDP per capita (1945–2003)

However, Chile's system has two major design flaws. First, the participation rate is low. Many South American countries have a significant number of self-employed individuals, with nearly one-third being flexible workers. These workers do not enter formal social security systems and are not mandatory contributors. Over 20 years later, the Chilean government found that nearly half of the population did not participate in the system. Among those who did, half contributed at a low level or inconsistently. As a result, many Chileans have realized that their pensions are very meager after retirement.

In 2008, Chile established a solidarity-based pension to provide a minimum pension to those who were uninsured or had low coverage. However, this pension covered nearly 60% of the population, essentially using contributions to distribute welfare universally rather than providing targeted assistance. In 2015, Chile significantly increased the coverage level again, far exceeding the poverty line. These measures greatly dampened contributors' enthusiasm, as many people became unwilling to participate, believing that being insured might result in not receiving any money.

During the COVID-19 pandemic, many insured individuals in Chile requested the government to return their earlier pension contributions. The government permitted multiple withdrawals from these funds. However, once withdrawn, this money will not return.

As a result, Chile's system of mandatory individual retirement accounts is currently facing disintegration, as are many Latin American countries. Most Latin American countries have dissolved their private pension schemes and reverted to a pay-as-you-go system.

The Pension System in Singapore

In 1955, Singapore established its own retirement system, known as the Central Provident Fund (CPF). This system was created during the period of British colonial rule, as the British refrained from shouldering the retirement burden of the local populace and instead passed on that responsibility to the residents of their colonies.

Today, Singapore's adoption of this system has proven to be highly resilient and operating effectively, with minimal impact from an aging population.

The crux of this system lies in mandatory contributions by employees to individual accounts under a fully funded accumulation scheme. Participants can choose their investment institutions or opt for government-guaranteed risk-free investments. In the 1950s, there was also a significant number of self-employed individuals in Singapore. The government did not enforce participation among low-income or self-employed persons; instead, it attracted this group through interest subsidies for those partaking. According to recent data, if a Singaporean's individual retirement account reaches SGC 60,000, the state subsidizes an additional percentage point on the interest accrued. Simultaneously, the government incentivizes the children of low-income elderly parents to contribute by offering tax exemptions.

The Singaporean government also intervenes to assist only elderly individuals without caregivers who have experienced consistently low income throughout their lives. For low-income elderly individuals with caretakers, Singapore emphasizes strengthened filial responsibility. Assistance is not merely monetary; at times, it involves practical support like medical aid or free education for their children. In my perspective, the successes of the Singaporean government lies in emphasizing individual and familial responsibilities, employing a shrewd design where the government acts solely as a safety net.

Advantages of the Private Pension Scheme

A comprehensive examination reveals that the private pension scheme helps to improve the universal coverage of social security, facilitate integration across different systems, and address regional imbalances and benefit discrepancies, all within the framework of individual accounts.

For instance, to improve the coverage, if an individual's accumulated pension rights are incorporated into their personal account history and then transferred to a centrally managed social security institution, the individual's control over their pension account will no longer be restricted by local government regulations. Additionally, the remaining balance of residents' pensions can be directly integrated into their individual accounts, as these balances are clearly defined. This direct integration ensures that the individual's assets are no longer under local government control.

Once the first two issues are resolved, the transfer process becomes straightforward. The disparity in benefits primarily stems from differences in contributions, necessitating individuals to take responsibility for their own pensions.

In conclusion, the private pension scheme is not merely a supplementary pillar but a potentially revolutionary approach.

The private pension scheme, by reinforcing individual responsibility and increasing initiative, helps mitigate the risks associated with an aging population and enhances the level of pension security. Successful implementation in the initial years could lay the groundwork for subsequently establishing an individual account of unified national basic pension insurance.

Following the introduction of the private pension scheme, the immediate integration of resident pension insurance is most suitable. Gradual integration of employee pension insurance would also effectively address long-standing issues such as transfer continuity, overall coordination, and participation levels that have plagued social security.

A critical principle to emphasize is that the private pension scheme must include a minimum living guarantee for elderly people as a safety net. Of course, the issue of implicit debt remains a challenging matter that requires our utmost attention.

Furthermore, I believe additional incentive measures should be implemented. The private pension scheme primarily targets flexible workers who are either uninsured or have low insurance coverage. However, these individuals often have limited investment options and may not have substantial funds to contribute to their accounts. Currently, residents' pension insurance comes with payment subsidies. In some regions, saving RMB 1,500 can yield a subsidy of up to RMB 100, along with an interest subsidy. Combined, these benefits often exceed the actual interest from a three-year fixed deposit.

For China, I suggest converting these subsidies into interest subsidies for individual pension accounts instead of cash subsidies. We can adopt a model similar to Singapore's, where the government provides upfront subsidies. For example, if a person invests RMB 100,000 in their account, the government can subsidize this amount. This approach ensures that everyone has a fixed balance of RMB 100,000 to 150,000 before retirement, securing their basic living needs after retirement. Additionally, high-income individuals should be allowed to pay premiums for other low-income family members, such as non-working spouses and low-income parents, to receive tax benefits.

Finally, encouraging participation requires certain necessary conditions, with transparency being the most important. The Ministry of Human Resources and Social Security can establish a platform providing historical investment performance records of various optional fund management institutions, allowing investors to understand different risk-return combinations and make informed choices. Regarding personal accounts, insured individuals should be able to check their balances and investment returns at any time, preferably accessible on mobile devices.

Currently, several details regarding fund management need to be finalized. These include reducing management fees, specifying account transfer frequencies, effectively controlling risks for fund management companies, and providing priority for purchasing national bonds for those with low risk tolerance, among other considerations.

We also need to promote financial literacy nationwide. This is because individual pension accounts are a relatively new investment option, and it is essential to educate everyone on how to use and manage these accounts effectively.

Chinese Path to Modernization and Urban-Rural Development

The Intrinsic Logic of China's Urbanization 2.0 and Rural Revitalization

Yang Yao

First, let's look at urbanization's contribution to China's economy.

Urbanization represents a structural transformation in China, shifting from low-productivity sectors to high-productivity ones. Cities benefit from agglomeration and innovation effects, which inherently bring about economic growth. Based on my calculations, urbanization has contributed approximately 10% to China's economic growth over the past three to four decades.

Urbanization also contributes greatly to consumption, as urban residents' per capita consumption is more than 2.3 times that of rural residents. By 2035, with an urbanization rate of 75%, the resulting increase in consumption will be sufficient to offset the decline caused by an aging population.

At the Fifth Plenary Session of the 19th Central Committee of the Communist Party of China (CPC) in 2020, President Xi Jinping used the terms "metropolization" and "urbanization" together in his report

This article is a compilation of the author's speeches delivered at the 56th session of the China Economic Observation on March 18, 2021, and the 2021 Enterprise Strategy Decoding Forum on March 20, 2021.

Y. Yao (✉)
National School of Development, Peking University, Beijing, China

W. Xianqing (ed.), *Understanding China's Path to Modernization*,
https://doi.org/10.1007/978-981-96-7051-2_23

on the 14th Five-Year Plan, marking a significant shift in direction. Previously, official documents generally referred only to "urbanization," not "metropolization." Concerns were primarily focused on the rapid expansion of large cities, excessive population concentration, and the emergence of issues such as big city syndrome.

In the document *Major Issues Concerning China's Strategies for Mid-to-Long-Term Economic and Social Development*, President Xi Jinping outlined two future trends for urbanization in China: the further concentration of the population in central urban areas in the eastern coastal regions and the common phenomenon of farmers buying houses and congregating in county towns among the existing 1881 counties and cities in China.[1] Regarding the second point, I believe that there may be a future fusion between county towns and villages.

Trend One: Population Concentration

The first trend, "population concentration," refers to the migration of populations from third- and fourth-tier cities to first- and second-tier cities, followed by dispersion within these urbanized areas. I term this phenomenon, seen globally, as "urban concentration with limited dispersion".[2]

For example, in the United States, which has a land area comparable to China and a population of over 300 million, it is apparent that the population is concentrated in a few specific areas, such as the East Coast, West Coast, Great Lakes region, and Florida, while other regions are sparsely populated. Similarly, in Japan, despite its small land area, there is significant population concentration, with 60% to 70% of the population residing in the narrow region connected by high-speed trains, linking Tokyo, Nagoya, and Osaka within less than two hours.

In the future, China will also develop several urbanized regions. The government has already announced a list of nine central cities, including Beijing, Tianjin, Shanghai, Guangzhou, Chongqing, Chengdu, Wuhan,

[1] Editor's Note: "Xi Jinping: Some Key Issues in the National Mid-to-Long-Term Economic and Social Development Strategy" (Ref: http://politics.people.com.cn/n1/2020/1031/c1024-31913885.html).

[2] It is characterized by populations gathering in cities to create large urban centers, with residents living in various dispersed locations within these cities.

Zhengzhou, and Xi'an. Surrounding these nine cities, seven major urbanized regions will form, including the Pearl River Delta, Yangtze River Delta, the middle reaches of the Yangtze River, Sichuan Basin, the Xi'an–Xianyang, the Zhengzhou–Kaifeng, and the Beijing–Tianjin–Hebei regions. By 2035, it is expected that China's urbanization rate will exceed 75%, with over 60% of the population residing in these seven urbanized regions.

This development trend holds significant economic implications for China.

First, increased agglomeration will bring greater benefits. The Guangdong–Hong Kong–Macao Greater Bay Area is poised to become a new growth pole for both China and the world, with Shenzhen likely emerging as a high-tech innovation center on par with Silicon Valley.

Second, there will be a significant adjustment in economic geography. The economic contribution of urbanized areas will increase, while that of non-urbanized areas will decrease.

Third, it will impact the real estate industry. Although China's total population is projected to start declining between 2025 and 2028, overall housing prices are not expected to experience significant growth. However, the new urbanization path will drive continued population growth in urbanized areas, potentially maintaining or even increasing housing prices in these central cities. In contrast, non-urbanized areas, especially those experiencing population outflow, will struggle to maintain their housing prices.

Therefore, we need to implement several supporting measures, including reforming the household registration (*hukou*) system, equalizing public services, and reforming *gaokao* (Nationwide Unified Examination for Admissions to General Universities and Colleges). The reform of the household registration system has been a topic of discussion since the spring of 2012 and was reiterated at the Third Plenary Session of the 18th CPC Central Committee in 2013. However, successful implementation has not been achieved. One significant reason is that the proposed reforms are too radical, such as fully opening up cities at the county level and below, allowing anyone with stable employment and residence to apply for household registration. This approach is unprecedented globally; even the United States maintains a household registration system. A potential solution is to use a residence permit instead of household registration, thereby reducing the public service attributes associated with household registration. During this process, equalizing public services will be a crucial direction—one also emphasized during the 14th Five-Year Plan period. Given that *gaokao* is a major benefit associated with the household registration system, we propose combining local entrance examinations with the national unified exam, which will benefit students whose household and school registrations are separated, facilitating the implementation of open household registration in major urban areas.

Trend Two: Development of the County Economy

Another trend of Urbanization 2.0 is the migration of rural residents toward county towns, which is becoming increasingly common. Therefore, the development of the county economy is gaining importance. As shown in Fig. 1, since 2014, labor mobility has stabilized, with the number of inter-provincial migrants essentially ceasing to increase. Additionally, a trend of returning to hometowns for entrepreneurship has emerged. This trend also highlights the rise in hidden unemployment in rural areas, as China's unemployment statistics only account for urban areas, excluding rural regions.

In 2020, China achieved a decisive victory in poverty alleviation. The next step is to prevent those who have been lifted out of poverty from falling back into it. Therefore, the Chinese nation's focus should shift

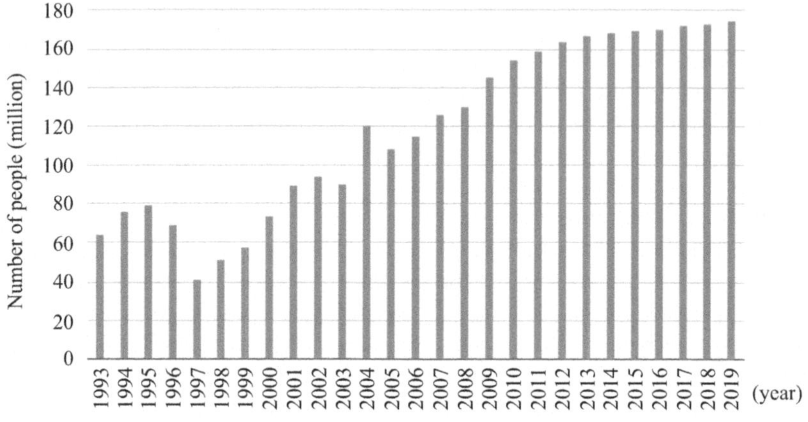

Fig. 1 Number of Chinese migrant workers moving into cities (*Source* China statistical yearbook)

from poverty alleviation to comprehensive rural revitalization to continue developing rural areas. By 2035, approximately one-quarter of China's population, or around 300 to 400 people, will still reside in rural areas. Even with complete urbanization, I estimate that one-fifth of the population will continue to live in rural areas nationwide. Consequently, the central government has proposed the strategy of rural revitalization, which I believe is the correct decision, validated by the future trajectory.

What is the core of rural revitalization? It is not about developing agriculture, as agriculture only accounts for 8% of China's gross domestic product (GDP). Fifteen years ago, the primary income source for Chinese farmers had already shifted to non-agricultural activities. To achieve full rural revitalization in the future, we should prioritize providing rural residents with high-quality non-agricultural employment opportunities. In the central and western regions, it is essential to implement local urbanization, with labor-intensive industries remaining the main driving force. For example, my hometown, Xin'gan County in Jiangxi Province, has achieved rapid development over the past decade. In recent years, Jiangxi Province has climbed the national GDP rankings, moving from the bottom to the middle positions, owing to its integration into the Yangtze River Delta and a large number of people returning to start businesses in their hometowns.

There are currently 350,000 residents in Xin'gan County. The main industries are luggage and lighting fixtures, both in the mid-to-low-end sector. Notably, the luggage industry alone accounts for 80% of the mid-to-low-end luggage market in the country. Although the profit margin for luggage is very low, earning only about RMB 5 per bag, it provides the local people with stable employment. Factory workers earn a basic monthly income of around RMB 4000 to 5000, with diligent workers potentially earning over RMB 10,000. Over the years, the standard of living in the village where I am from has greatly improved, with many families now owning cars. In rural areas, owning a car is a sign of prosperity, as these cars are not used for transportation but purely as consumer goods.

Counties with below-average development levels can achieve rapid progress through industrial transfer, maintaining labor-intensive industries as their main focus. Therefore, having robust industries is crucial to ensure the success of poverty alleviation efforts and to provide a foundation for rural revitalization, ultimately leading to the realization of urban–rural integration.

In the future, rural areas will become agreeable living spaces for many Chinese people, striking a balance between buying houses in county towns and residing in villages. With increased income levels and improved transportation, basic infrastructure such as tap water, sewage systems, and flush toilets can become widespread in rural households. By transforming rural areas into livable spaces, we can successfully implement the national rural revitalization strategy.

Key Policies for Implementing the Rural Revitalization Strategy

Fang Cai

After successfully overcoming poverty, we immediately turned our attention to the rural revitalization strategy. However, some local governments are uncertain about how to effectively implement this new strategy. In particular, grassroots leaders who are accustomed to following direct and tangible policy measures require clear guidance to advance their work.

Rural revitalization covers a wide range of areas. Without clear direction, local governments may feel their efforts futile and may become superficial, focusing only on improving the physical appearance of villages. While these efforts are part of rural revitalization, concentrating solely on one or two aspects is too narrow. Therefore, this article will focus on identifying the key policies for effective rural revitalization.

Key Points for Advancing Rural Revitalization

In my view, here are several key points to help understand the direction and timing of rural revitalization:

This article is compiled by Caixin Net based on the author's speech at the 2022 Caixin Summer Summit.

F. Cai (✉)
Chinese Academy of Social Sciences, Beijing, China

W. Xianqing (ed.), *Understanding China's Path to Modernization*,
https://doi.org/10.1007/978-981-96-7051-2_24

First, rural revitalization is an ongoing process that has been discussed for many years. The latest phase begins as China achieves success in poverty alleviation and consolidates those achievements. In other words, it is essential to build on the gains made and ensure their sustainability.

Second, the ultimate goal of rural revitalization is to modernize agriculture and rural areas. By 2035, China aims to achieve fundamental socialist modernization, which includes the modernization of the agricultural sector and rural communities.

Third, successful rural revitalization will be evident through robust agriculture, beautiful villages, and prosperous farmers. Key indicators include: robust agriculture, which is essential for prosperous industries; beautiful villages, including access to basic public service and improved village appearance; and prosperous farmers, which is fundamental for achieving common prosperity.

Fourth, the fundamental approach to rural revitalization is to bridge the economic and social gap between urban and rural areas. Achieving rural revitalization involves multiple approaches, and, in my opinion, the most fundamental is to dismantle the economic and social divide between urban and rural areas. This dual structure has been a long-standing issue. Despite significant progress since the reform and opening-up, the gap has not been fully closed. The next decade presents a critical window to address this disparity effectively.

Based on my analysis, countries with per capita GDP ranging between USD 12,000 and USD 24,000 can serve as valuable benchmarks for China as it strive to narrow this gap and achieve its goals of modernization.

China aims to join the ranks of high-income countries by 2025 and become a moderately developed country by 2035. Specifically, this means surpassing a per capita GDP of USD 12,000 by 2025 and reaching a per capita GDP of USD 24,000 by 2035. According to the World Bank criteria, a country with per capita GDP of USD 12,600 is defined as a high-income country, a threshold we are close to achieving. As China enters the high-income category, the country's 2035 goal corresponds to the middle tier of high-income countries, defined as having per capita GDP of approximately USD 23,000 to USD 24,000. Consequently, over the next decade or so, China's development will encompass the range of USD 12,000 to USD 24,000 per capita GDP, and countries currently within this range can serve as benchmarks for China to strive toward.

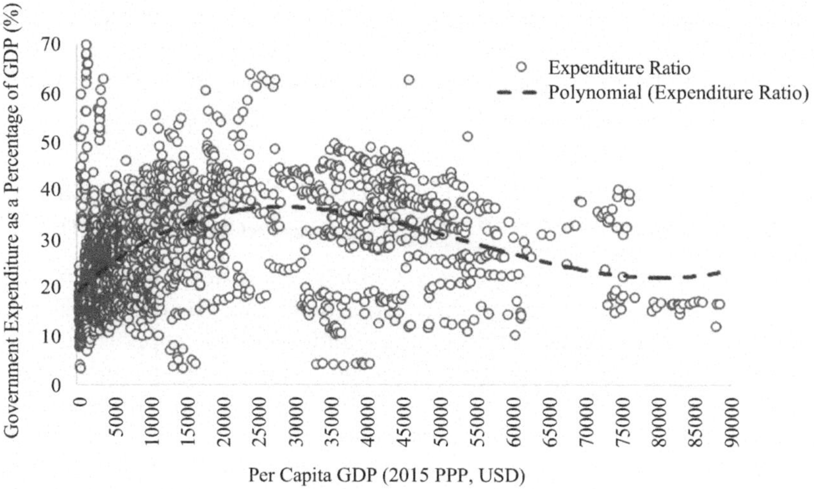

Fig. 1 The wagner acceleration period

Furthermore, my research reveals that within the USD 12,000 to USD 24,000 per capita GDP range, there is a notable characteristic: governments display the greatest determination toward modernization, accompanied by the most rapid growth in public expenditure as a percentage of GDP. This phase can be referred to as the Wagner acceleration period (see Fig. 1).

Wagner's Law and the Wagner Acceleration Period

Wagner's law suggests that as per capita income increases, government expenditure, particularly on social services such as social protection, mutual aid, and welfare, also increases as a percentage of GDP. However, the rate of this increase varies across different stages of economic development.

The period during which a country's per capita GDP increases from USD 12,000 to USD 24,000 is marked by the fastest growth in government expenditure, meeting the basic requirements for social welfare spending. Essentially, achieving the growth rates and expenditure levels associated with this range means creating a welfare state. This phase is referred to as the Wagner acceleration period. In the year to 2035, China will fall squarely within the Wagner acceleration period. Therefore, this range serves as a crucial benchmark; guiding overall socialist modernization efforts and aligning rural revitalization initiatives with these standards is essential to achieving the desired development outcomes.

Drawing from International Best Practices and Continue Supporting Low-Income Groups

After successfully combating poverty, China's next major task is to prevent from large-scale relapse into poverty. To achieve this, the country should draw from international best practices and continue supporting low-income groups. Securing the gains from the country's anti-poverty efforts requires an active approach. By "active," I mean setting ambitious goals to achieve substantial results. This involves not only preventing a widespread return to poverty but also focusing on the lowest 20% of rural residents by income, as identified by the National Bureau of Statistics. Targeted policies are needed to ensure steady income growth for these groups. Building on the foundation of preventing a relapse into poverty, we must also expand the middle-income group to achieve the highest possible goals.

In 2021, the average income growth rates for the top four income groups among rural residents were 11.8%, 10.9%, 12.5%, and 11.5%, all showing double-digit increases. However, the lowest income group's growth was only 3.7%. While this positive growth helps prevent a large-scale relapse into poverty, we should aim higher. We need to elevate this low-income group, or at least a significant portion of it, into the middle-income bracket. This means their income growth rate needs to match or exceed that of the other groups to reduce income disparities. Currently, due to the impact of the COVID-19 pandemic, many rural workers are unable to migrate for work, making this low-income group particularly vulnerable. Therefore, we must adopt more proactive measures to boost their income growth, ensuring we meet our long-term goals.

In consolidating the achievements of poverty alleviation, we can look to international standards for guidance.

First, the poverty line used in China's poverty alleviation efforts was higher than the World Bank's original standard of USD 1.90 per person per day (purchasing power parity), ensuring that the country's poverty reduction achievements were substantial and credible. However, in 2022, the World Bank raised its poverty thresholds, with new standards expected to be adopted in November. For low-income countries, the international poverty line will rise from USD 1.90 to USD 2.15 per person per day; for lower-middle-income countries, from USD 3.20 to USD 3.65; and for upper-middle-income countries, from USD 5.50 to USD 6.85. These adjustments reflect changing conditions and are valuable benchmarks for China in the post-poverty alleviation phase.

Additionally, OECD countries typically use a relative poverty standard, defining the poverty line as 50% of the median income. Applying this standard, the relative poverty line for rural residents would be approximately RMB 8,451, denoted by half of the median of Chinese rural residents' per capita income. The lowest income group generally falls below this threshold, indicating a significant number of low-income individuals. It is important to note that the OECD's relative poverty standard focuses on median income, addressing relative poverty, which aligns with China's goal of expanding the middle-income group. By adopting this standard, we can better support low-income populations and work effectively toward increasing the middle-income demographic.

Promoting New Urbanization and Facilitating Rural Labor Transfer

A key component of rural revitalization is promoting new urbanization and facilitating the rural labor transfer. It should be noted that while the promotion of rural revitalization relies on the efforts of every participant—farmers, workers, and primary-level officials—it also necessitates the implementation of supportive public policies, which serve as a public good. Therefore, this discussion will take a relatively macro-level perspective.

There is a common saying that agriculture should become a promising industry that attracts workers. To achieve this, agriculture must provide reasonable comparative returns and become a self-sustaining industry. However, as of now, it can be said that agriculture struggles to offer reasonable comparative returns, making it essential to explore why agricultural relative returns remain persistently low.

Relative national income, or comparative labor productivity, is a descriptive statistical indicator that represents the ratio of value added to the labor force in each of the three industries. Since the reform and opening-up, China's rural labor productivity has significantly improved, accompanied by a large-scale transfer of labor. However, the relative national income of agriculture has consistently remained low, primarily due to the large portion of the labor force contributing only a small share of industrial value added, making it difficult for agriculture to achieve income comparable to other industries. Clearly, the excessive labor force in agriculture has led to sustained low comparative returns. Therefore, the fundamental solution is to continue promoting the rural labor transfer to other sectors.

To promote the rural labor transfer, it is necessary to advance a new type of people-centered urbanization, which involves facilitating the continued migration of surplus rural labor to cities as migrant workers and enabling these workers to swiftly become urban residents.

Now, let's consider the urgency of advancing urbanization and promoting labor transfer using the aforementioned reference frame. If we were to draw a graph with the horizontal axis starting with China and listing countries and regions in order of their per capita GDP, placing countries with higher per capita GDP than China to the right, we would observe that China has the highest proportion of employment in agriculture among these countries. Additionally, China's urbanization rate is significantly lower than the average level of other countries. Even when compared with countries having an average per capita GDP between USD 12,000 and USD 24,000, China shows a 5.5 percentage point difference in urbanization rate and an 18.2 percentage point difference in the proportion of employment in agriculture. Furthermore, within China, there is an 18-percentage point gap between the urbanization rates of registered residents and permanent residents, a significant difference that needs to be narrowed down. These disparities highlight the need for reform in the household registration system to advance urbanization and accelerate labor transfer. Such reforms can significantly increase labor supply and consistently achieve resource reallocation efficiency, thereby supporting productivity improvement. This will also help raise the wages of migrant workers, increase household income, and substantially boost consumption.

A study conducted by a team from the OECD specializing in researching the Chinese economy indicates that after rural labor transfers to urban areas, even if other conditions remain unchanged, their consumption can increase by 30%. Furthermore, if these individuals obtain urban household registration after moving to the city, their consumption can increase by an additional 30% after alleviating concerns about future consumption. This demonstrates substantial reform dividends on both the supply side and the demand side, highlighting the importance of narrowing the gaps in urbanization and labor structure.

Expanding Land Management Scale and Boosting Labor Productivity

One of the key factors limiting the increase in agricultural comparative benefits is the small size of land holdings. The inadequate transfer of labor and limited liquidity of land result in relatively small-scale land management, leading to lower labor productivity.

According to data from the World Bank, China's rural labor productivity—measured as the value added per agricultural worker—exceeds the global average and the averages for low-income and lower-middle-income countries. However, it remains significantly below the levels seen in upper-middle-income countries and even further behind high-income countries. Specifically, China's productivity is only 77% of the average for upper-middle-income countries and a mere 12% of that of high-income countries. As the country is now on the path to becoming a high-income country, it is crucial to significantly narrow the gap in rural labor productivity between us and these higher income countries. It is important to note that China boasts relatively advanced agricultural technology and equipment, especially in plain regions where, despite small farm sizes, mechanized operations are prevalent through leasing and hiring services. This demonstrates that the primary reason for low rural labor productivity lies in the high proportion of the workforce engaged in agriculture and the small size of individual operations.

China has one of the smallest average farm sizes globally, which has remained relatively unchanged at around 0.67 hectares for over four decades. Furthermore, land holdings are often fragmented across multiple locations, divided into five or six, or even more, separate plots. As a result, the operational scale of each plot becomes even smaller. The World Bank defines smallholders as those with land holdings of less than 2 hectares, while China's average is only around one-third of that threshold. Recent agricultural census data reveals that approximately 80% of agricultural workers manage plots smaller than 0.67 hectares. This limited scale of land ownership constrains labor productivity and prevents us from achieving economies of scale in agriculture.

Bridging the Income and Public Service Gap Between Urban and Rural Areas

Despite some progress, the income disparity between urban and rural areas in China remains significant. Over the past decade, the national Gini coefficient has declined, and the urban–rural income gap has somewhat narrowed. However, both metrics remain high compared to reasonable standards. Notably, the Gini coefficient remains above the levels seen in comparable countries, with the urban–rural income gap contributing to nearly half of the overall income inequality. This means that to achieve common prosperity and substantially reduce the Gini coefficient, we need to focus on redistributive measures and bridging the urban–rural income gap. Future efforts to enhance redistribution should align with the general principles of Wagner's law or the Wagner acceleration period.

The dual economic structure is both a systemic arrangement and an outcome of its operational dynamics. Over time, this structure crystallizes into a dual social structure. The existing household registration system creates a significant statistical gap between the urbanization rates of permanent residents and those with official urban registration, which manifests in the disparity of basic public services between urban and rural areas, and between migrant workers and urban residents. Even compared to the unemployed or informally employed in cities, migrant workers have less access to basic public services.

The dual structure within urban and rural areas, particularly regarding unequal access to basic public services, is evident in many instances. Currently, disparities in social pension insurance levels result in 56.6% of recipients of basic social pension insurance receiving only 5.9% of the total pension payments. Additionally, migrant workers who have not settled in cities face significant inadequacies in children's education, social security, and subsistence allowances. Despite significant expansions in basic public services coverage and improvements in protection levels, there remains a considerable gap compared to the requirements for equalization. Therefore, dismantling the dual economic structure is urgent, and we must seize the opportunity within the coming decade.

Implementing Rural Revitalization Through Public Goods Provision

The urban–rural divide is a legacy of the old system, and reforms now increasingly depend on top-down public policy adjustments. Therefore, to eliminate this dual structure, we should focus on the provision of public goods. Rural revitalization cannot rely solely on the ingenuity of participants or be entirely regulated through market mechanisms. While market mechanisms should play a decisive role in resource allocation and maximize participant enthusiasm, public policy decision-making is crucial as a means to enable better government involvement and provide necessary leverage to address the divide effectively.

First, the fundamental constraint on industrial revitalization is not a lack of resources or the inherent weakness of agriculture as an industry. Instead, it stems from insufficient market returns, leading to inadequate incentives. Low market returns in agriculture result from low labor productivity, which in turn, lead to lower relative income. This requires the government to engage in top-down design and assume necessary expenditure responsibilities by accelerating rural labor transfer and land circulation through household registration system reform and expanding the scale of agricultural operations. Agriculture should not be relegated to a non-competitive industry, nor should the government's role in providing public goods be neglected.

Second, reforms and policy adjustments related to the provision of public goods are not zero-sum games; they can bring tangible, increased returns, improve China's potential economic growth rate from the supply side, and enhance the economy's capacity to support growth from the demand side. This reform dividend should serve as a continuous driving force for further reforms. Therefore, we should seize opportunities to accelerate the pace and intensify the efforts of reform in areas where the reform dividend is most significant and evident.

Third, the key to eliminating the urban–rural divide lies in achieving equal access to basic public services. To accomplish this, the government must address the institutional disparities in public service provision. Additionally, there should be a significant increase in government expenditure on social protection, solidarity, and welfare. Ensuring equal provision of basic public services between urban and rural areas does not contradict market mechanisms; instead, it is a fundamental principle of providing public goods.

Fourth, the rural labor productivity is not only crucial for modernizing agriculture and rural areas but also serves as a fundamental basis for the entire economy. The notion that rural labor productivity underpins the national economy, a concept we learned from Marxist political economy, remains valid today. As agriculture's share in the overall economy diminishes, the significance of rural labor productivity as a foundation becomes even more pronounced. Without improvements in agricultural productivity, the modernization of agriculture and rural areas cannot be achieved. This failure will not only hinder China's comprehensive modernization but also weaken the resilience of the entire economy.

Advancing Rural Development Steadily and Prudently to Implement the Rural Revitalization Strategy

Jikun Huang

Rural development is vital for farmers' well-being, agricultural modernization, and long-term rural growth. Implementing the rural revitalization strategy requires steady progress in rural development. The No. 1 Central Document[1] places greater emphasis on advancing rural development steadily and prudently, including improving the implementation mechanism for rural development, improving rural living conditions, building rural infrastructures in key areas, promoting the construction of digital countryside, and strengthening the coordinated provision of basic public services within counties.

[1] Editor's Note: i.e., The Opinions of the Central Committee of the Communist Party of China and the State Council on Doing a Good Job in Comprehensively Promoting the Key Work of Rural Revitalization in 2022.

This article was first published in the 5th issue of *Rural Work Communication* in 2022.

J. Huang (✉)
New Rural Development Institute, Peking University, Beijing, China

China Center for Agricultural Policy, Peking University, Beijing, China

Academy of Sciences for the Developing World, Trieste, Italy

W. Xianqing (ed.), *Understanding China's Path to Modernization*,
https://doi.org/10.1007/978-981-96-7051-2_25

Improving the Implementation Mechanism for Rural Development

To steadily and prudently advance the rural development, a robust implementation mechanism is crucial. By executing projects tailored to local needs and actively engaging the enthusiasm and initiative of farmers and villages, we can achieve remarkable results in rural development. Therefore, a sound implementation mechanism is pivotal in enhancing the rural living environment, improving rural infrastructure, promoting construction of digital countryside, and providing basic public services. Establishing a well-functioning implementation mechanism is also essential to uphold the principle of developing rural areas for the benefit of farmers, so as to ensure the effective and organized progress of rural development.

To make substantial progress in rural development, the No. 1 Central Document places special emphasis on the implementation mechanism for rural development. Compared to previous years, this year's document pays more attention to the needs of farmers, advocating that "rural revitalization should be centered around farmers, and rural construction should be designed for farmers," and introducing an implementation mechanism promoting a "bottom-up approach, village self-governance, and active farmer participation." Specifically, it highlights the importance of accelerating the development of village planning for eligible villages based on demand, initiating the execution plan for rural construction activities, managing risks associated with village-level debts, streamlining approvals for small-scale village construction projects, and clarifying property rights related to rural construction projects. Additionally, it calls for the creation of a comprehensive list outlining county-level responsibilities for overseeing village public infrastructure, among other specific measures. Regarding the preservation of traditional villages, the primary focus for 2022 is the "Village Restoration Plan."

While rural development has made significant strides in various regions in recent years, many construction projects have not aligned well with the urgent needs of farmers. According to a January 2022 survey by the China Center for Agricultural Policy at Peking University ("the PKU survey"), which included 1768 households across 169 administrative villages in five provinces, farmers identified their top five most urgently needed construction projects as road transportation, elderly care, healthcare, education, and drinking water. However, the projects implemented between 2019 and 2021, except for road transportation (which received 46% of total rural construction funds), deviated significantly from these needs. Although road transportation construction projects generally aligned with farmers' preferences, the top three desired projects—village roads, village bus stops, and intra-village roads—differed considerably from the actual projects undertaken. Of course, it should be noted that farmers' needs vary greatly across different regions.

To realize the overall goal of "rural revitalization should be centered around farmers, and rural construction should be designed for farmers," rural construction projects must be tailored to local conditions and dynamically aligned with the urgent needs of local farmers. Therefore, it is extremely important to fully consider farmers' actual needs, harness their initiative, and adhere to the principles of "bottom-up approach, village self-governance, and active farmer participation" when developing science-based plans for short-term and long-term rural development suited to each village. This requires local governments to shift from their previous top-down approach in planning and implementing rural construction projects and to promote effective practices that involve farmers in these projects.

Improving Rural Living Conditions by Advancing the Five-Year Action Plan

Building beautiful and livable rural areas is crucial for comprehensively advancing the rural revitalization and directly impacts the fundamental well-being of many farmers. This initiative represents a significant endeavor to bridge the urban–rural divide and achieve seamless urban–rural integration. However, basic public services in rural regions have historically prioritized infrastructure related to production and daily life, resulting in a long-standing deficiency in essential residential environment facilities. Despite increased investment and ongoing improvements in rural living environments in recent years, the overall situation remains relatively subpar.

Strengthening the improvement of rural living environments has been a key focus of central policies in recent years. Following the three-year action plan for improving rural living environment unveiled in 2018, the Central Committee's No. 1 Central Document proposed the Five-year Action Plan for Improvement of Rural Human Settlement Environment

(2021–2025) ("the Five-Year Action Plan"), in a bid to addressing issues such as toilets in rural areas, sewage treatment, black and odorous water bodies, household waste, village cleanliness, and green initiatives. Building upon this, the Central Committee's No. 1 Central Document emphasizes continuing the Five-Year Action Plan and outlines key priorities for the year ahead. For toilet upgrades, the emphasis is on "addressing the actual needs of farmers." For sewage treatment, the focus is on "prioritizing treatment in densely populated villages." Regarding household waste, the document emphasizes "source sorting and reduction, encouraging on-site utilization and processing," whereas for village cleanliness and beautification, it underscores "comprehensively implementing actions for village cleaning, greening, and beautification."

According to the PKU survey, despite visible improvements in the overall rural living environment due to recent actions, there remain issues with inadequate remediation and significant regional disparities. By the end of 2021, 90% of rural households were using sanitary toilets, and 95% had implemented centralized waste management, following a model of "collection in villages - transportation in townships – disposal in counties," which has notably improved the appearance of villages. Nevertheless, regional disparities persist, with some rural areas still lacking toilets that meet farmers' needs and displaying limited utilization of fecal resources. Furthermore, efforts to enhance village appearances often prioritize superficial improvements over fundamental concerns. Many regions continue to face challenges such as the absence of source-based waste sorting, sluggish progress in domestic wastewater treatment, and difficulties in addressing polluted water bodies.

To continue implementing the Five-Year Action Plan, housing facilities must be developed in accordance with local environmental factors and the specific needs of farmers. Regarding toilets, existing issues should be addressed based on actual circumstances. For sewage treatment, areas with suitable conditions and demands should be integrated into urban sewage networks or equipped with self-built sewage network facilities. In regions unsuitable for centralized treatment, small-scale ecological treatment solutions should be implemented. Concerning garbage management, efforts should focus on promoting the classification and reduction of household waste at the source. Clear goals must be established for remediating black and odorous water bodies, and village cleanliness and greening initiatives should consider the genuine needs of farmers, leveraging the self-governing capabilities of villagers to ensure effective implementation of cleanliness, greenery, and beautification efforts.

Building Rural Infrastructures in Key Areas Through Focused Efforts

Well-developed rural infrastructure is essential for advancing rural revitalization and modernizing agriculture and rural areas. Strengthening rural infrastructure is crucial for supporting agricultural and rural development and for narrowing the urban–rural gap to achieve common prosperity. General Secretary Xi Jinping has emphasized the importance of prioritizing public infrastructure construction in rural areas, promoting the integrated development and connectivity of urban and rural infrastructure, and advancing the upgrade of rural infrastructure.[2] The No. 1 Central Document clearly identified key projects to address rural infrastructure shortcomings during the 14th Five-Year Plan, including improving rural road connectivity, ensuring reliable rural water supply, developing rural clean energy, advancing the construction of digital countryside, and enhancing village-level comprehensive service facilities.

The No. 1 Central Document placed special emphasis on "concrete advancement of rural infrastructure construction," with more specific priorities, requirements, and measures. For instance, besides continuing to emphasize the need to pave roads in larger natural villages (groups), it clearly outlined the orderly promotion of constructing highways of Grade III or higher in townships, implementing rural road safety protection projects, renovating dangerous bridges, and carrying out pilot reforms in rural road management and maintenance systems. Additionally, it stressed the need to improve supporting purification and disinfection facilities and equipment, and further implement the rural power grid consolidation and enhancement project, and introduced the promotion of photovoltaic projects in rural areas. It also proposed implementing a project to enhance the quality and safety of rural housing and strengthening the rectification of safety hazards in self-built houses used for business purposes in rural areas.

[2] Editor's Note: "Writing a New Chapter in Agricultural and Rural Reform and Development: An Overview of General Secretary Xi Jinping's Important Discourse on 'Three Rural Issues'" (Ref.: http://www.xinhuanet.com/mrdx/2021-09/23/c_1310204090.htm).

Although rural infrastructure construction in China has developed rapidly in recent years, significant challenges across key areas and regional disparities remain. According to the PKU survey, as of January 2022, 80% of villages are now within 1 km of township-level road networks, household tap water coverage has reached 69.8%, and 87% of rural residents report satisfactory drinking water quality. However, the development level of some villages in China's western region and mountainous areas remains low, with substantial shortcomings. Regarding domestic energy sources, only 25% of rural households primarily use electricity for cooking. Furthermore, 46% of rural houses were built before the year 2000, with some provinces exceeding 60%, highlighting the urgent need to improve the quality and safety of rural housing.

To effectively promote rural infrastructure construction, it is essential to tailor measures to local conditions and focus on key areas. Based on existing infrastructure and farmers' needs, it is important to determine the key areas and sequence for rural infrastructure projects suitable for each region, particularly in terms of roads, water supply, energy, and housing. It is also crucial to implement practical initiatives and ensure tangible results, while adopting innovative approaches for construction and maintenance, and establishing a robust institutional mechanism to guarantee the construction and management of rural infrastructure.

Promoting the Construction of Digital Countryside

Driving transformative changes in rural production, lifestyle, and governance through digital technology is crucial for enhancing agricultural productivity, optimizing resource flow and allocation between urban and rural areas, fostering high-quality agricultural development, and modernizing rural governance systems. Key aspects of building digital countryside include developing digital infrastructure and digitizing the rural economy, governance, and daily life. To effectively harness digital technology for rural modernization, it is essential to address market demands, bridge gaps in rural economic digitization, enhance the farmers' digital literacy and skills, and accelerate the digital transformation of rural governance and public services.

The No. 1 Central Document dedicates a comprehensive section to vigorously promoting the construction of digital countryside, emphasizing solving practical problems, and expanding the application scenarios of agricultural and rural big data with a market-driven approach. It continues to stress the importance of advancing smart agriculture and integrating information technology with agricultural machinery and techniques to overcome shortcomings in economic digitization. For the first time, the document introduces the Digital Commerce to Boost Agriculture project, aimed at promoting healthy and regulated live-streaming sales of agricultural products. It also emphasizes accelerating the Express Delivery to Villages project and extending Internet+ government services to rural areas. Additionally, the document underscores the need to strengthen digital literacy and skills training for farmers. Meanwhile, to explore standards and evaluation systems for construction of digital countryside, it proposes accelerating the standardization of digital countryside, developing an evaluation indicator system, and continuously conducting digital pilot projects in rural areas.

When promoting the construction of digital countryside, we should focus on addressing development gaps and ensure that farmers are the primary beneficiaries. According to the *Index of Digital Rural County 2020*, jointly compiled by Peking University's New Rural Development Institute and Alibaba Research Institute, China's digital rural counties have established a solid foundation for growth. Despite the impact of the pandemic, they maintained a steady growth rate of 6% in 2020. However, the study also highlights the need to address regional disparities and development gaps, particularly in achieving balanced regional development in rural economic digitization. At the same time, the PKU survey confirms that digital infrastructure in rural areas has been continuously improving, with 99.9% of surveyed villages having full 4G network coverage, 23% having e-commerce service stations, 35% having express delivery services, and 37% having established one-stop service platforms offering online services. Nevertheless, there is still room for improvement in the accessibility of digital technology at the farmer level. As of the end of 2021, less than 1% of farmers were engaged in online sales of agricultural products. This is addressed by the *Development Plan for Digital Agriculture and Rural Areas (2019–2025)*, which proposes to increase the proportion of online retail sales of agricultural products from 9.8% in 2018 to 15% by 2025.

Therefore, in vigorously promoting the construction of digital countryside, it is essential to focus on key areas while addressing existing gaps, with particular attention given to ensuring that farmers benefit from these advancements. The construction of digital countryside should be phased and systematically implemented, adopting an inclusive and equitable regional development strategy while fully leveraging both the government's public functions and the market's resource allocation role. Farmers should be regarded as crucial participants in construction of digital countryside. This involves enabling more farmers, especially those with low incomes, to participate in the digital business-driven agriculture revitalization project, which can be achieved through training and other measures to increase their share in the e-commerce pie. In developing new formats for agricultural product distribution, we should establish innovative institutional mechanisms, thus ensuring that the majority of farmers gain greater benefits from adding value to the upstream agricultural supply chain.

Strengthening the Coordinated Provision of Basic Public Services Within Counties

Strengthening basic public services is one of the government's crucial responsibilities, as it ensures the fundamental needs for survival and development for all citizens. The improvement of these services is closely linked to the level of economic and social development. Given the significant disparity between urban and rural basic public services in China, it is essential to enhance the provision of such services in rural areas. However, developing basic public services requires time, and at this stage, it is pragmatic and feasible to prioritize coordinated efforts.

The No. 1 Central Document outlined tasks to "enhance the level of basic public services in rural areas" and to "accelerate the integrated development of urban and rural areas at the county level," elevating these tasks by integrating them into a single goal, that is, to strengthen the coordinated provision of basic public services within counties. This integration takes into account the dual constraints of the household registration system and the fiscal decentralization system, which hinder urban–rural integration in China. The document continues to stress the need to address shortcomings in the medical and health sectors, with a particular focus on public services for the elderly and children. It emphasizes implementing new plans for preschool education and improving services in nursing homes. Additionally, for the first time, it proposes shifting the focus of basic public service provision from merely covering administrative regions to serving the resident population, highlighting a trend during the 14th Five-Year Plan period, transitioning from spatial urbanization to people-centered urbanization. The document also reaffirms the commitment to advancing the construction of urban–rural school communities and introduces a project to upgrade village-level comprehensive service facilities.

Despite recent increases in investment in rural basic public services, achieving equal access to essential services such as education, healthcare, and comprehensive services between urban and rural areas remains a significant challenge. The PKU survey found that only 54% of the sampled villages have primary schools, 43% have kindergartens, and just 28% have public kindergartens. Although medical infrastructure has improved, with clinics in 96% of villages, 16% of the sampled villages still lack standardized clinics. Furthermore, facilities for elderly care are limited, with only 20% of sampled villages having nursing homes.

To address the insufficient and uneven supply of basic public services in rural areas, development should be coordinated at the county level. China needs to transition from a system that serves administrative regions to one that serves the resident population, ensuring equal access to public services. This requires meticulous planning to meet the needs of rural residents and advance the equalization of basic public services. Given the significant disparities between urban and rural areas, it is essential to strengthen the construction of these services in rural regions. In the context of coordinated county-level development, the central, provincial, and local governments must prioritize and increase investment in basic public services in underdeveloped counties.

Chinese Path to Modernization and Ecological Civilization

Understanding Three Dimensions of the Carbon Peaking and Carbon Neutrality Goals

Jintao Xu

In 2015, the Paris Agreement, a legally binding international treaty, was adopted at the Conference of the Parties in Paris. I believe this agreement produced two pivotal outcomes.

First, all participating countries agreed to limit the global surface temperature rise to 2 °C, with an ideal target of 1.5 °C, by the end of the twenty-first century. This signified a resolution of both scientific and political disputes over climate change.

Second, major carbon-emitting countries pledged voluntary emission reductions. This was a significant shift, given the historical divide between developing and developed countries, which was notably evident prior

This article is based on the author's speech delivered at the "Towards a New Era of Carbon Neutrality: Industrial Transformation and Capital Opportunities" Yangtze River Delta Forum, organized by the National School of Development at Peking University on April 17, 2021.

J. Xu (✉)
Department of Economics, National School of Development, Peking University, Beijing, China

China Center for Environmental and Energy Economics, National School of Development, Peking University, Beijing, China

W. Xianqing (ed.), *Understanding China's Path to Modernization*,
https://doi.org/10.1007/978-981-96-7051-2_26

to the 2009 Copenhagen Climate Change Conference. These voluntary commitments from countries like China and India enabled global climate cooperation.

However, these achievements were tempered by shortcomings: the collective impact of voluntary emission reductions fell far short of the 1.5 °C to 2 °C target. Instead, projections indicated a potential temperature rise of 3 °C to 6 °C by the end of the century if only these commitments were met. Therefore, the conference stipulated that major emitting countries reevaluate their pledges by 2020 to better align with the 1.5 °C goal.

In 2020, China made a significant leap in its commitment to reducing emissions. During the United Nations General Assembly, President Xi Jinping announced that China aims to peak carbon emissions before 2030 and achieve carbon neutrality by 2060.[1] While this may not seem drastically different from previous commitments in wording, the substance of the pledge is profoundly transformative.

This marks the first time a specific end goal for carbon neutrality has been explicitly stated. In fields such as resource economics and dynamic planning, it is known that changing the endpoint condition significantly impacts actions throughout the entire planning period. Setting a target for carbon neutrality means a dramatic change in the approach to achieving it. If the goal were only to peak carbon emissions before 2030, companies might consider this a growth period for high-carbon industries until then.

However, with the carbon neutrality goal in place, the likelihood of further developing high-carbon industries before 2030 is significantly reduced. Investors and businesses will recognize that achieving carbon neutrality and near-zero emissions by the mid-twenty-first century requires a much stronger shift toward low-carbon industries, renewable energy, and non-fossil fuel sources well before 2030.

The carbon peaking and carbon neutrality goals merit examination from three key perspectives.

Firstly, the energy mix is set for a significant overhaul.

Historically, the energy sector has made strides in adjusting its structure, with a focus on increasing the use of renewable energy sources. However, due to the intermittent nature and uneven distribution of

[1] Editor's Note: "President Xi Jinping's Speech at the General Debate of the 75th Session of the United Nations General Assembly" (Reference: https://www.ccps.gov.cn/xxsxk/zyls/202009/t20200922_143558.shtml).

renewable energy, thermal power plants have also been developed to provide peak load support for renewable energy sources. Some regions have traditionally relied on conventional energy sources to fuel economic growth. With the introduction of the dual carbon goals, a reevaluation of fossil fuel development becomes imperative.

From a national strategic perspective, the development of renewable energy presents immense opportunities. President Xi Jinping emphasized the importance of transitioning to a primarily renewable energy-based system during the 14th Five-Year Plan period at a meeting of the Central Committee for Financial and Economic Affairs.

I remember seeking advice from experts at an energy conference five or six years ago about the feasibility of non-fossil fuels dominating energy consumption by 2050. At that time, they expressed skepticism. However, with the target now established, it will undoubtedly shape future actions and strategies significantly.

Despite the brief passage of time, China is increasingly equipped to meet these goals, having made substantial advancements in technology and cost efficiency. In 2012, at a World Bank conference, I was struck by the Chief Economist of the Green Party of Germany's vision for the country's energy future: transitioning to an economy predominantly powered by renewables by 2050, phasing out fossil fuels, and completely abandoning nuclear energy. This ambitious goal resonated deeply with me. Following his speech, the Chief Economist of the World Bank in Europe and Central Asia highlighted that while Germany's aspirations were commendable, the foundation for achieving these targets lies in Chinese technology, as Germany sources its renewable energy equipment, such as solar panels and wind turbines, from China.

Some alumni from the National School of Development currently hold positions at Goldwind, the world's third-largest wind turbine manufacturer with operational footprint across over 30 countries and regions worldwide. This highlights that China's technology and equipment are already playing a key role in supporting green and low-carbon development worldwide and are well-positioned to lead China's transition to green and low-carbon energy. In fact, China's current technological capabilities, combined with corporate efforts, have been steadily reducing costs, providing us with a competitive advantage. Since 2021, the phase-out of renewable energy subsidies indicates that these technologies have become market-competitive and economically viable.

However, it is undoubtedly that the development of renewable energy still faces significant challenges. To quickly make renewables a major part of China's energy system, two major institutional breakthroughs need to be made.

The first breakthrough involves building a unified national market. Previously, experts often cited the State Grid Corporation's monopoly as the main issue, suggesting it be broken into smaller grids. However, our current findings suggest a different problem—local protectionism is the real barrier to renewable energy development. Renewable resources are unevenly distributed across China, with less economically developed areas often having richer resources. Electricity generated in these regions also struggles to secure long-distance orders due to regional barriers. To tackle this issue, the National Development and Reform Commission has introduced policies in recent years.

The second breakthrough pertains to establishing distributed energy systems. For energy reforms in North China, enhanced national support can accelerate the development of rooftop solar power. In rural areas, where households own their rooftops, property rights issues are nonexistent for installing solar panels. Increased national support could also address the challenges in transitioning from coal to gas or electricity, significantly advancing China's energy structure reform. At this point, technology and cost are no longer the primary obstacles; the critical next step is overcoming institutional barriers.

Secondly, it is crucial to integrate carbon emission reductions with natural carbon sink strategies.

Some developing countries, such as Brazil, aim to reduce 30% to 40% of their carbon dioxide emissions by addressing deforestation and forest degradation, as degraded forests release carbon dioxide rather than absorb it. China excels in this area. In 2019, China made the largest global contribution to greening efforts, accounting for 70% to 80% of the total.

China has also been rapidly expanding its artificial forest cover. The annual increase in carbon sinks from these planted forests could potentially contribute 5% to 10% toward reducing the country's carbon emissions intensity. Achieving carbon neutrality requires prioritizing nature-based solutions, with forest carbon sinks potentially becoming a mainstream tool for reducing carbon dioxide levels. This is particularly significant for China, as it could profoundly impact rural development and regional economic growth.

In the past, we underestimated the contributions of ecosystems. Many policies appeared environmentally friendly but actually hindered climate action. For example, during the planned economy period, extensive tree felling in Northeast China led to the "two crises" (resource shortages and economic difficulties) in the 1980s. In response, the government introduced various policies, culminating in a comprehensive ban on logging natural forests in 2016, a move environmentalists celebrated as a significant step forward in environmental protection and soil erosion prevention.

From the perspective of carbon sinks, tackling deforestation is not enough. Only healthy forest ecosystems can serve as effective carbon sinks; degraded forests may actually turn into carbon sources. Many of China's natural forests are in decline and might have already become carbon sources. Therefore, active human intervention is needed to enhance forest productivity, supporting the country's carbon neutrality goal.

Consider Northeast China, where we need to rethink the management of natural forests. This requires significant institutional reforms, similar to those needed in the old industrial regions of Northeast China, which have long-standing systemic issues. Over the past two to three decades, these areas have developed substantial reform and innovation experience. Therefore, I believe China should promptly lift the blanket ban on logging and restart reforms of state-owned forests in Northeast China and nationwide. By introducing market mechanisms and actively managing state-owned forests with the dual carbon goals in mind, we can significantly support national climate action.

In addition, proactive forest management can continuously supply the country with green materials, supporting transitions in other sectors. Forests hold immense potential for biomass energy. By relaxing natural forest protection policies and providing adequate support, we will witness significant growth in biomass energy from forests. Given that Northeast China's natural conditions are similar to those in Northern Europe and Canada, there is no reason China cannot perform just as well. Sweden, for instance, sources 30% of its primary energy from forests, a model worth emulating.

The government currently provides substantial subsidies to the fossil fuel, steel, and cement industries, which should be quickly phased out and redirected toward supporting renewable energy and resources. For

China to achieve carbon neutrality, it must enhance ecosystem contributions and find cost-effective methods for low-carbon, green development, as relying solely on fossil fuel emission reductions would undoubtedly be more costly in the long run.

Thirdly, global linkage is inevitable due to policy influence.

Historically, China has leaned heavily on administrative measures and central government resources for environmental protection and energy reform, rather than fully embracing market mechanisms and economic policies.

However, the current conditions are now favorable. A case in point is the environmental tax system implemented in 2018, whose tax rates have been widely criticized as insufficient to create meaningful behavioral changes among corporations and local governments. A higher tax rate could prove more effective to meet energy efficiency and emission reduction goals. In 2020, China announced the nationwide launch of a carbon market targeting the power sector, introducing a carbon price that underscores the concept of emission costs.

Several factors now exert considerable influence on carbon pricing, investment, and industrial structure.

Recently, the European Union introduced border adjustment policies to accelerate climate action, which are likely to drive up carbon prices. Rapid price hikes could prompt European companies to advocate for carbon tariffs on imports, such as Chinese wind turbines and solar panels, based on their emissions. This pressure might push China to raise domestic carbon prices and potentially implement a carbon tax.

While carbon trading offers a mechanism for setting carbon prices, it currently applies only to the power sector. Since electricity is not exported, determining carbon pricing for exported goods remains a challenge. Consequently, it is crucial to expand the national carbon market swiftly from electricity to all sectors. However, keeping pace with the border adjustments of the European Union and the United States poses significant challenges. The pressure to align with these global standards is, in my opinion, substantial.

One of the simplest strategies for China might be to implement a carbon tax on exported products. Historically, carbon trading pilots have seen prices peak at around RMB 70, approximately USD 10. If a scenario with a USD 20 carbon tax is considered, the cost of carbon would rise dramatically, significantly impacting traditional industries while benefiting emerging ones. Given that the United States is the world's largest trader, it is increasingly likely they will adjust their border policies in response.

A major aspect of US President Biden's campaign platform was climate policy. One question to consider is that his administration may restart the 2009 energy bill. Furthermore, one of his biggest domestic challenges in international trade is unfair competition. If the United States adopts a carbon pricing mechanism, it will naturally lead to border adjustment measures, such as carbon tariffs on imports, pressuring exporting countries to impose their own carbon taxes.

In China, I believe the government is steadily expanding its carbon trading system. With the European Union and the United States poised to implement border adjustment policies, the impact on China's export-driven industries could be substantial. In 2021, China's gross domestic product (GDP) growth was largely driven by exports. If the European Union and the United States start imposing carbon tariffs, it would exert considerable pressure on China's climate policies. From my perspective, a carbon tax is an achievable tool and could potentially be reconsidered in China. This would have profound implications for the economy, investments, and industrial structure moving forward.

Carbon Neutrality and Transition Finance

Jun Ma

The term "green finance" has been a frequently discussed topic in the past, but "transition finance" is now gaining prominence. This article will delve into this subject from three perspectives:

First, we will explore the background and market practices related to transition finance. Next, we will break down the five fundamental elements of the transition finance framework as discussed by the G20 Summit. Finally, we will review the current progress of transition finance in China and outline the next steps moving forward.

This article is adapted from the author's speech delivered at the 3rd session of the Chengze Forum, organized by the National School of Development at Peking University on July 10, 2022.

J. Ma (✉)
Macro & Green Finance Lab, National School of Development, Peking University, Beijing, China

Institute of Finance and Sustainability, Beijing, China

W. Xianqing (ed.), *Understanding China's Path to Modernization*,
https://doi.org/10.1007/978-981-96-7051-2_27

Background of Transition Finance

The Climate and Energy Research Center at the Institute of Finance and Sustainability (IFS) once conducted an extensive review of policies related to the carbon neutrality sector, encompassing existing policies in areas such as energy, transportation, construction, and industry, as well as those that should be implemented to achieve carbon neutrality. These policies are crucial for China to meet its carbon neutrality goal by 2060. The study also identifies the technological measures needed to achieve carbon neutrality, drawing from key documents from relevant government ministries and recommendations from industry experts, organizations, and associations.

From a policy perspective, two categories stand out as particularly important: economic policies and non-economic policies, with the latter primarily involving administrative interventions.

Economists argue that economic policies are crucial for achieving the dual carbon goals through effective resource allocation using market mechanisms. These policies include fiscal measures, taxation, carbon markets, and financial regulations. Fiscal policy involves government spending on green subsidies, guarantees, procurement, and industrial funds to support the transition to a low-carbon economy. Beyond the current focus on large emitters, there is ongoing discussion about extending carbon tax policies to cover small and medium-sized enterprises. China's carbon market policies are also evolving, featuring the national carbon trading market in Shanghai, seven regional markets, and the soon-to-be-revived China Certified Emission Reduction (CCER) voluntary carbon market. These mechanisms aim to incentivize low-carbon enterprises and apply pressure on those lagging in emission reductions. Meanwhile, financial policy refers to the green finance system established over the past seven to eight years, including standards for green and transition finance, disclosure requirements, and monetary policy tools from the central bank to support carbon reduction projects with low-cost funding. Furthermore, large banks are required to conduct risk analysis and management for high-carbon industries while promoting innovation in green financial products.

Beyond economic policies, administrative measures are also essential. These measures involve breaking down the national carbon emission reduction goal into local quotas.

Therefore, it is necessary to achieve a mechanism to coordinate between economic policies and administrative measures, and such efforts are ongoing.

Demand for Green and Low-Carbon Investment

In the context of the financial landscape in China, what is the country's actual demand for green and low-carbon investment?

In December 2021, the Green Finance Committee (GFC) of the China Society for Finance and Banking released a report titled *Roadmap for Financing China's Carbon Neutrality*, which concluded that, in the pursuit of carbon neutrality, the cumulative demand for green and low-carbon investments in China over the next 30 years will reach RMB 48.7 trillion (at 2018 constant prices). This figure is significantly higher than predictions from other institutions, primarily due to different statistical approaches. The GFC's estimate is primarily based on financial criteria, while other institutions focus mainly on low-carbon energy criteria.

Where should all this money be invested? The primary areas for investment are energy, transportation, construction, and industry.

Take the energy sector as an example. According to Professor Zhang Xiliang from the Institute of Energy, Environment and Economy at Tsinghua University, by 2045, 95% of the energy used in China's electricity industry will come from renewable sources, with a small portion from coal-fired power with carbon capture and storage (CCS). This suggests a substantial investment in new energy sources in China over the next 20 years. In the transportation sector, new energy vehicles are definitely a key investment opportunity and a primary technological pathway for achieving low-carbon and zero-carbon objectives. According to the Greentech Innovation and Investment Research Center at the Institute of Finance and Sustainability, the sales of new energy vehicles in China are expected to increase significantly by 2030.

Green buildings are another key focus area. Globally, buildings account for 40% of energy consumption and carbon emissions. The State Council has proposed that within the next decade, most new buildings in China must meet high standards for energy and water efficiency, which will qualify them as green buildings. However, achieving these green standards does not necessarily lead to significant reductions in emissions, as many certified green buildings show only limited improvements in this area. Looking forward, more buildings are expected to meet near-zero emission requirements. From the perspective of industry sustainability, zero-carbon buildings are economically viable in major cities.

There are also significant opportunities for green and low-carbon investments in sectors such as industry, negative emissions, materials, and digitalization. However, the technologies in these areas are still developing and require investment from institutions capable of tolerating higher risks, such as private equity or venture capital (VC). The report *Towards Carbon Neutrality 2060: Embracing New Opportunities for Low-Carbon Development*, jointly released by the Institute of Finance and Sustainability and Hillhouse Academy, provides a detailed analysis of investment opportunities across various fields. It highlights the need for investment in industrial electrification, scrap metal utilization, utilization of electric arc furnaces, and alternatives to cement limestone in the industrial sector.

Significance of Transition Finance

After roughly seven years of development, China's green finance system has experienced rapid growth, establishing the country as the largest green finance market globally. By the end of March 2022, China's outstanding green loans had reached RMB 18 trillion. In the last six years, approximately RMB 2 trillion worth of green bonds have been issued, making China the second-largest green bond market in the world. Additionally, China now boasts over 700 green funds and various innovative green financial products, such as asset-backed securities (ABS), exchange-traded funds (ETFs), green insurance, and carbon finance.

In short, the expansion of China's green finance sector has been remarkable, with notable surges in 2021 when green loan balances grew by 33% and green bond issuance jumped by 170%.

However, there remains a pressing need to develop transition finance, as traditional green finance frameworks have not sufficiently supported transitional activities.

Firstly, traditional green finance tends to focus on "pure green" or "near-pure green" projects. In the realm of climate change, this means supporting initiatives such as clean energy, electric vehicles, and key inputs for these industries, such as batteries.

Second, the current system falls short in providing financial support for economic activities aimed at transitioning high-carbon industries to low-carbon ones. This gap exists because the green finance taxonomy does not fully encompass transitional economic activities. Research shows that many companies in resource-intensive, high-pollution, and high-energy consumption industries struggle to secure credit, despite their ability or intent to transition. Even with viable technological pathways for transition, they often face credit restrictions. For instance, the eight major high-carbon industries included or soon to be included in the carbon trading market are power generation, petrochemicals, chemicals, building materials, steel, non-ferrous metals, paper-making, and aviation. Furthermore, other sectors with significant carbon emissions, such as older buildings and road transportation, also need to gradually decarbonize to meet dual carbon goals.

The failure to provide financial support for the transition of high-carbon industries to low-carbon alternatives could lead to several negative consequences.

First, the lack of funding could result in failed or delayed transitions, which are crucial for achieving the "30·60 decarbonization goal."

Second, the bankruptcy and closure of high-carbon businesses could pose financial risks to banks. If high-carbon companies go bankrupt due to insufficient financial support, it would lead to bad loans for banks and a sharp decline in the value of investment assets for equity investors.

Thirdly, closures and layoffs could destabilize social stability. The bankruptcy and subsequent layoffs in high-carbon industries, caused by a lack of financial support, could lead to social unrest.

In reality, the scale of transition activities far exceeds that of purely green initiatives, necessitating greater financial support. Currently, approximately 10% of all lending activities in China are classified as "green loans." Given that the banking system is the primary source of financing for the entire economy, this implies that only about 10% of economic activities are considered green, leaving the remainder as "non-green activities."

Non-green activities can be further categorized into transformable and non-transformable activities. Transformable non-green activities are those where entities have the intent, capability, and technological pathways to transition successfully, given adequate financial and policy support. Conversely, many non-transformable non-green activities involve entities lacking the intent and capability to transition and may exit the market in the coming years. For transformable non-green activities, establishing a framework for transition finance is essential. This includes defining clear standards, implementing disclosure requirements, and providing policy incentives to attract social capital toward achieving low-carbon and zero-carbon goals.

Market Practices of Transition Finance

In recent years, sustainability-linked loans (SLLs) have emerged as a prominent financial product in the international market. These loans are unique in that borrowers commit to achieving specific sustainability goals, such as reducing carbon emissions, with interest rates tied to their performance in meeting these targets. While there are no stringent rules on the allocation of funds, borrowers must adhere to strict disclosure requirements. This is primarily enforced through post-loan assessments, enabling financial institutions and the market to evaluate the borrower's ability to meet their pledges, thereby ensuring transparency.

Another prominent product is sustainability-linked bonds (SLBs), which operates similarly to SLLs. In this case, borrowers also commit to sustainability objectives, with interest rates linked to their success in achieving these sustainable goals. While the use of funds remains flexible, borrowers must undergo annual third-party verification of key performance indicators (KPIs). SLBs have a broader impact compared to SLLs. By 2021, global issuance of SLBs reached USD 135 billion, making up 4.8% of the total sustainable bond market, with participants including non-financial companies, financial institutions, and government-supported entities.

Additionally, the international market includes other transitional financial products like climate transition funds, though these are currently less common. These funds support transformation activities through equity investments.

Since 2021, transition finance products have been on the rise in China, including SLLs, SLBs, transition bonds, and low-carbon transition (linked) bonds. Recent examples include China Construction Bank's SLL to support green building projects, Postal Savings Bank of China's SLL for carbon reduction in power companies, and the SLB of China Guodian Corporation (Merged with China Shenhua Group to Become the China Energy Investment Corporation) to expand wind power capacity. Both the Bank of China and China Construction Bank have issued frameworks for transition bonds—the *Bank of China Limited Transition Bonds Management Statement* (January 2021) and the *China Construction Bank Transition Bond Framework* (April 2021)—clearly outlining eligible sectors and activities. In June 2022, the National Association of Financial Market Institutional Investors released a notice on pilot innovations related to transition bonds (NAFMII [2022] No. 93). Unlike SLBs, transition bonds specify how the funds must be used.

Despite the fast growth and high participation in transition finance, both domestically and internationally, several challenges remain.

First, the lack of a global standard for defining transition activities increases the risk of "greenwashing" (false claims of sustainability) and causes financial institutions to hesitate due to fears of such accusations.

Second, requirements for disclosing transition activities are unclear, with various entities adhering to different information disclosure frameworks.

Third, transition finance tools are still limited, primarily focusing on debt instruments with fewer options available in equity and insurance.

Fourth, there are insufficient policy incentives to promote further development in this sector.

Fifth, the concept of a just transition has not gained sufficient attention in market practices.

A Forward-Looking Framework for Transition Finance

The G20 Sustainable Finance Working Group (SFWG) has developed the G20 Transition Finance Framework (TFF) in 2023, which includes five core elements: identification standards, reporting of information, policy measures, financing instruments, and just transition.

1. **Identification Standards**

Identification of transition activities involves identifying their boundaries through two primary methods: the principles-based approach and the list-based approach.

The principles-based approach provides only general guidelines for transition activities, requiring entities to use science-based methods to formulate transition plans that align with the Paris Agreement and to obtain third-party certification. This approach is currently employed by organizations such as the International Capital Market Association (ICMA), the Financial Services Agency of Japan, and Bank Negara Malaysia. In essence, the principles-based approach does not specify which activities qualify as recognized transition activities, leaving it to organizations to invest significantly in specialized third-party certification.

On the other hand, the list-based approach defines qualifying transition activities through a catalog or list, detailing the technical pathways and outcome requirements for these activities. This approach is similar to China's Green Finance Directory and has been adopted by the European Union. The EU Taxonomy for Sustainable Activities explicitly includes "transition activities." When listed separately, these form a transition taxonomy. Currently, financial regulators in several countries are developing such taxonomies. Institutions like the Bank of China, China Construction Bank, and BDS Bank[1] have already created their own transition directories, identifying specific transition activities within key high-carbon industries to support financing. These directories typically list eligible transition activities, including requirements for technical pathways and outcomes.

The key objectives for identification of transition activity should include: reducing the cost of identifying transition activities and mitigating the risk of "greenwashing"; covering transition activities at both the company and project levels; allowing for dynamic adjustments based on technological advancements and policy changes; requiring organizations to have clear transition plans with both short-term and long-term action steps to achieve net-zero targets; ensuring that transition goals are scientifically formulated and aligned with the Paris Agreement; adhering to the "Do No Significant Harm" (DNSH) principle, ensuring no increase in environmental pollution or harm to biodiversity; clearly defining the conditions under which third-party certification is necessary.

2. **Reporting of Information**

The requirements for the reporting of information on transition activities encompass the following aspects: transition entity (enterprise) goals, plans, and timetables; science-based long-term transition pathway; Scopes 1 and 2 GHG emissions; Scope 3 emission data related to transition activities; governance mechanisms and specific measures for implementing transition plans, including systems for carbon emission

[1] Editor's Note: DBS Bank, originally known as the Development Bank of Singapore, is Singapore's largest commercial bank.

monitoring, reporting, and internal incentives; progress of transition activities and emission reduction effects; uses of transition funds and safeguard measures, including DNSH compliance.

3. **Policy Measures**

Policy measures encompass financial measures, carbon trading mechanisms, government-backed transition funds, financial policy incentives, and industry-specific policy levers. Specifically, financial policy incentives include instruments such as monetary policies, interest subsidies, and performance assessments for financial institutions. Industry policy levers might involve providing land for new energy projects, whereas fiscal measures include subsidies, tax breaks, and government procurement initiatives.

To boost green finance, the Chinese government has introduced various financial policy incentives. For instance, the central bank has implemented tools to support carbon reduction, local governments provide guarantees and interest subsidies for green loans, and there are government-backed funds at both national and local levels. Moving forward, these tools will be pivotal in supporting transitional finance.

Furthermore, industry policy levers play a crucial role. For example, many companies need to use green electricity to reduce carbon emissions, so the government must provide them with new energy quotas. If companies plan to build their own renewable energy facilities, the government can also grant them access to land. These incentive mechanisms collectively form a comprehensive policy framework to support sustainable development.

4. **Financing Instruments**

Currently, there are various debt financing tools in place. However, moving forward, China will vigorously promote equity financing instruments, including transition funds, private equity/venture capital funds, merger and acquisition funds, as well as insurance and other risk mitigation tools, and securitization. It is important for companies seeking financing with these transition instruments to clearly articulate their short-term, medium-term, and long-term transformation goals and plans. They should also disclose the content and impact of their transformation activities and establish KPIs linked to the outcomes of their transformation efforts.

5. **Just Transition**

A key concern is that certain transition activities might cause negative effects such as unemployment, energy shortages, and inflation that impact the economy and society. To mitigate these potential downsides, supportive measures should be put in place. Specifically, companies should be required to evaluate how their planned transitions will impact employment. If the transitions are likely to result in significant job losses and the social security system cannot provide sufficient support, those companies should develop countermeasures, including reemployment and retraining programs, to help affected workers secure new jobs. Companies should also disclose the employment impacts of their transitions and the steps they are taking to address them. Furthermore, financial terms of funding could be tied to KPIs that reflect these considerations.

Progress of Transition Finance in China

China has made significant strides in developing a transition finance framework.

First, the People's Bank of China is working on defining the standards and policies for transition finance.

Second, various government bodies, including the National Development and Reform Commission (NDRC), have issued several guiding documents related to transition pathways, which can serve as a foundation for creating a transition finance catalog.

Thirdly, the GFC has established a Transition Finance Working Group to bring together industry experts. This group focuses on researching standards, disclosures, and products associated with transition finance to support regulatory work.

Fourth, some financial institutions, including major banks, are developing transition finance systems to provide targeted support for high-carbon industries under controlled risks. This approach moves away from the previous practice of uniformly cutting loans to resource-intensive industries with high-pollution and high-energy consumption.

Fifth, at the local level, the Huzhou Municipal People's Government in Zhejiang Province has introduced China's first regional transition finance catalog and launched its initial batch of transition projects, providing incentives for these initiatives. Other regions are also compiling their own transition finance catalogs and promoting pilot projects.

Here are typical cases of transition finances, including the transformation paths and expected outcomes of the entities involved.

Case One: Emission reduction in City A's petrochemical industry. City A's petrochemical industry is on a mission to cut emissions through various strategies, including boosting energy efficiency, changing the energy mix, adopting low-carbon foreign energy, and using carbon capture, utilization, and storage (CCUS) technologies. Projections indicate that, within City A, carbon emissions from refined oil products have peaked by 2025, while the demand for basic fossil materials such as chlorine substitutes and ethylene is expected to peak between 2035 and 2040. The city aims to achieve carbon neutrality in its petrochemical sector by 2060.

Case Two: Financing for a coal-to-renewables transition company. A company currently relying on coal for about 90% of its electricity production plans to shift toward renewable energy and coal power equipped with CCUS, targeting 99% by 2050 and achieving carbon neutrality by 2055. Its transition plan includes retrofitting existing coal facilities, implementing CCUS technology, expanding solar and wind power generation, and developing energy storage solutions. The company's financing strategy outlines cumulative funding needs from 2022 to 2030, involving 40% equity financing and 20% transformation loans from commercial banks.

Case Three: Baowu Group's green transformation. China Baowu Steel Group Corporation Limited is committed to reaching carbon neutrality by 2050 through various technological innovations. They have also launched the Baowu Green Carbon RMB Fund, with a significant portion of the funds dedicated to supporting carbon reduction activities within Baowu Group's supply chain.

Recommendations for Local Governments

How can a local government drive financial transformation? Here are some key strategies to consider:

First, local governments may establish local standards or catalogs for transition finance projects in priority industries. Before the national-level catalog is released, local governments can take the lead by creating their own catalogs to jumpstart the implementation of transformation projects.

Second, local governments should integrate transition projects into the green project database and financial matchmaking platform. This involves enhancing the management system of the green project database to include transformation projects, which will support enterprises committed to transitioning in accessing financial resources, and utilizing the green finance platform to connect banks, insurance companies, funds, and other financial institutions with government incentive measures.

Third, local governments needs to launch demonstration transformation projects and establish transformation funds. Local governments can identify and implement demonstration projects in key high-carbon industries to showcase effective and low-cost transformation strategies and establish a dedicated fund to guide low-carbon transformation, providing additional capital to selected enterprises committed to transitioning.

Fourth, local governments should provide incentive mechanisms for transformation projects. This means leveraging existing green finance incentive mechanisms to develop innovative incentives tailored specifically for transformation projects, which can include guarantees, interest subsidies, new energy quotas, land use regulations, and even differentiated electricity pricing.

Background, Industrial Rationale, and Policy Principles of China's Dual Carbon Goals

Min Wang

Context of the Dual Carbon Goals

Basic Facts About Global Climate Change

In 2021, the Intergovernmental Panel on Climate Change (IPCC) released its sixth report, presenting these critical data points: the global temperature has risen by 1.1 °C since the Industrial Revolution, and carbon dioxide emissions have surged from 208 million tons in 1850 to 36.2 billion tons in 2019. This indicates that current atmospheric carbon dioxide levels and surface temperatures are the highest in 2 million and 120,000 years, respectively. An analysis of the global average temperature trend over the past two millennia reveals a sharp increase in global temperatures following the Industrial Revolution. The IPCC report predicts that

---

This article is based on the author's speech delivered at the 46th session of the MBA Forum organized by the National School of Development at Peking University on May 28, 2022.

M. Wang (✉)
Department of Economics, National School of Development, Peking University, Beijing, China

China Center for Environmental and Energy Economics, Peking University, Beijing, China

W. Xianqing (ed.), *Understanding China's Path to Modernization*,
https://doi.org/10.1007/978-981-96-7051-2_28

if global carbon dioxide emissions peak by 2050, global temperatures will rise by 2.1 °C to 3.5 °C by the end of the twenty-first century, reaching alarmingly high levels, which will have the following two significant impacts.

First, we are likely to experience more extreme temperatures and weather events. In recent years, various regions around the world have been hit by severe weather. A particularly striking case occurred in July 2021 when Zhengzhou, the provincial capital of Henan Province, China, was subjected to persistent heavy rainfalls. At the same time, Western Europe faced the worst flooding in recorded history, while the western part of North America recorded unprecedented high temperatures. Additionally, the Indian Meteorological Department reported that in April 2022, northwestern and central India experienced the hottest weather for the same period in 122 years. Temperatures in New Delhi reached 49.1 °C and 49.2 °C in two different areas, with the lowest recorded at 45.5 °C. Such extreme thermal conditions and high humidity in India may cause significant societal impacts.

Additionally, natural ecosystems and human economic activities will suffer significant consequences. Over the past 70 years, global glacier volume has decreased by about 33 meters. Climate change impacts every facet of human society and the economy, adversely affecting agricultural production, increasing mortality rates, reducing labor productivity and business investments, and slowing economic growth. These impacts are especially severe in economically vulnerable countries. Bill Gates has suggested that the effects of climate change could surpass those of pandemics. The primary driver of global climate change is the greenhouse effect caused by carbon emissions since the Industrial Revolution. Figure 1 depicts global carbon emissions since 1850, which have surged from 208 million tons to 36.2 billion tons by 2019, predominantly contributing to the 1.1 °C increase in global average temperatures over the past 150 years.

At present, China is the world's largest emitter of carbon dioxide. As shown in Fig. 2, in 2019, China's carbon dioxide emissions amounted to approximately 11 billion tons, while the United States emitted around 5.3 billion tons, the European Union around 2.9 billion tons, and India around 2.5 billion tons. China's emissions are equivalent to the combined emissions of these major economies, leading to significant international political pressure. Some argue that as a latecomer to industrialization, China's emissions after the Industrial Revolution have been primarily

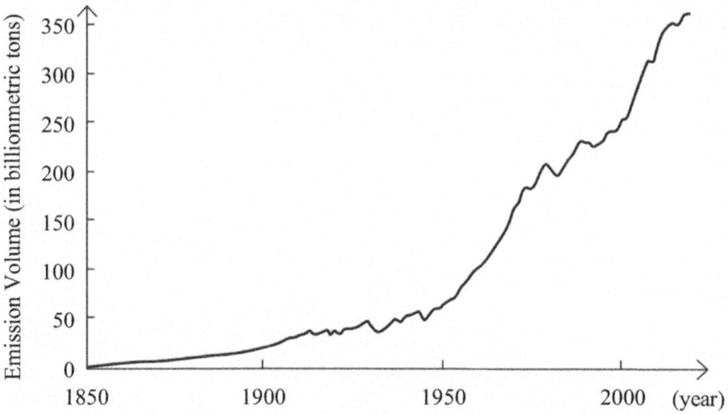

Fig. 1 Global Carbon Dioxide Emissions (1850–2019) (*Data Source* World Resource Institute [WRI]. Carbon emission data includes non-fossil energy carbon emissions from agricultural production, deforestation, and other sources)

contributed by developed countries. From 1850 to 2019, the cumulative carbon dioxide emissions of the United States, the European Union, and China were 433.2 billion tons, 301.2 billion tons, and 202.8 billion tons, respectively, accounting for 26%, 18%, and 14% of global cumulative emissions during the same period. Therefore, in terms of historical cumulative emissions, China is the third-largest emitter and faces considerable pressure. It is also evident that China's carbon dioxide emissions surged after its accession to the World Trade Organization in 2002, surpassing the United States in 2007 to become the world's largest emitter. Since then, China has faced significant international pressure regarding climate change.

2009 Copenhagen Climate Change Conference

At the Copenhagen Climate Change Conference in 2009, China made its inaugural international commitment to achieve a 15% share of non-fossil energy consumption and a 40–45% reduction of carbon intensity compared with 2005 by 2020.[1] To meet these targets, China has exerted

[1] Editor's Note: "Wen Jiaba's Speech at the Leaders Meeting on Climate Change" (Reference: http://www.gov.cn/ldhd/2009-12/19/content_1491149.htm).

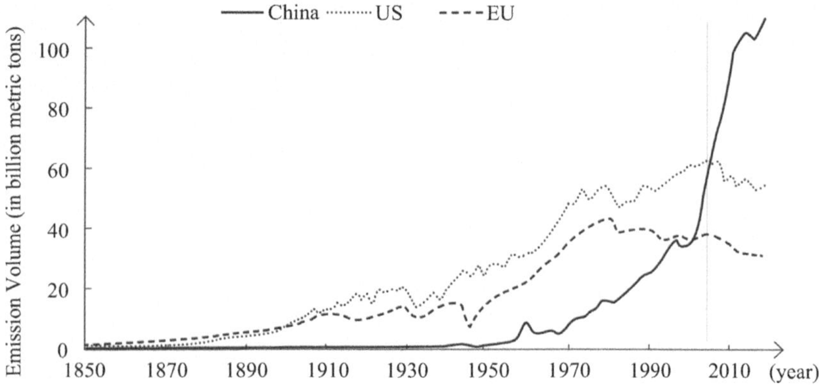

Fig. 2 Carbon Dioxide Emissions of the US, EU, and China (1850–2019)

considerable effort. Our research estimates that China has invested over RMB 2 trillion in subsidies for industries like wind power and photovoltaics, representing a substantial amount of funding.

75th Session of the United Nations General Assembly, 2020

The completion of the 2020 targets marks a significant milestone, but challenges remain with climate change and high carbon dioxide emissions. Looking ahead, President Xi Jinping's announcement of China's dual carbon goals at the United Nations General Assembly in September 2020 sets a crucial framework for the next phase. With carbon emissions still rising, President Xi Jinping emphasized the urgency by stating, "China will scale up its Intended Nationally Determined Contributions by adopting more vigorous policies and measures. We aim to have carbon dioxide emissions peak before 2030 and achieve carbon neutrality before 2060."[2] This ambitious target underscores the pressing need and substantial pressure ahead. In terms of 2020 US dollar, major developed economies such as the United States, Japan, and the European Union achieved their carbon peaks when their per capita GDP reached USD

[2] Editor's note: "Xi Jinping's Speech at the General Debate of the 75th Session of the United Nations General Assembly" (Reference: https://www.ccps.gov.cn/xxsxk/zyls/202009/t20200922_143558.shtml).

50,000 (in 2007), USD 46,000 (in 2007), and USD 19,700 (in 1979), respectively. According to our growth model, China's per capita GDP is projected to be around USD 14,000 (2010 USD) by 2030. This signifies that China faces considerable pressure to peak its carbon emissions at a relatively lower income level. The challenge is further magnified by China's substantial total carbon emissions and the worsening global climate crisis. In this context, China must implement proactive policies to tackle these environmental issues and effectively meet global climate goals.

China's Response to the Dual Carbon Goals

Since 2020, China has implemented two primary types of policies to achieve its dual carbon goals at the operational level. The first involves administrative directives, such as the power rationing observed in 2021. In China's centralized system, these policies are typically established through top-down targets set by the central government. Local governments then break down these targets and implement them using a one-vote veto mechanism. In 2021, many provinces resorted to power rationing due to difficulties in meeting energy consumption targets, partly attributed to issues with the electricity pricing mechanism. The second type of policy involves market-driven pricing strategies. For instance, in 2021, China launched a national carbon emissions trading market aimed at establishing a carbon price through the trading of emission permits. This market-driven approach incentivizes companies to reduce energy consumption and emissions. The initial phase included nearly 2400 coal-fired power plants, which contribute to about 40% of China's total carbon emissions.

The Relationship Between Economic Development and Carbon Emissions

In 2019, China's total carbon dioxide emissions amounted to around 11 billion tons, with fossil fuel emissions contributing approximately 9.9 billion tons. From an economic perspective, the total emissions from fossil fuels are primarily influenced by four key factors: economic aggregate, industrial structure, technological advancements, and energy mix. By projecting the development of these variables up to 2030, we can approximate the total emissions from fossil fuels expected by that time.

Economic Aggregate

Economic aggregate is the most crucial factor influencing carbon emissions. According to the "China 2049" project team at the National School of Development, Peking University, China's potential real GDP is projected to grow at an average annual rate of about 5% between 2021 and 2030. This suggests that by 2030, China's GDP will reach approximately RMB 170 trillion, which is 1.67 times the GDP in 2020. By 2060, the GDP is expected to soar to around RMB 420 trillion, 4.12 times the 2020 level. Assuming other three factors remain constant, these projections indicate that fossil fuel carbon dioxide emissions could rise from about 9.9 billion tons in 2020 to 15.2 billion tons by 2030, an increase of roughly 5.3 billion tons.

Industrial Structure

Industrial structure is also a significant factor affecting carbon emissions from fossil fuels. The industrial sector is a major consumer of fossil fuels, implying that with the same total GDP, a higher share of the industrial sector would lead to increased carbon emissions.

First, the evolution of industrial structure follows inherent patterns observed throughout history and economic development theories. As economies grow, the proportion of GDP derived from industry initially increases. This share peaks when a country's per capita GDP reaches approximately USD 15,000 to USD 20,000 (2017 international PPP dollars), constituting around 40% of the total GDP. After reaching this peak, the industrial share begins to decline. This transition occurred in the United States in the 1950s and in Europe in the 1960s. Currently, most developed economies have an industrial GDP share ranging from 15% to 20%. However, countries like Germany, Japan, and South Korea, known for their strong manufacturing capabilities, maintain a higher industrial share of about 25% to 33%. These changes in industrial structure can be attributed to two major factors. The first factor involve shifts in demand structure. At lower income levels, people focus on fulfilling basic needs such as food. As incomes rise, demand expands to include consumer goods like cars and homes. With further income growth, priorities shift toward high-quality education, healthcare services, tourism, and leisure activities. As a result, changing income levels in an economy lead to corresponding changes in the overall demand structure, thereby influencing the industrial composition. The second factor involves, changes in production costs. In the early stages of development, countries with lower per capita income benefit from competitive advantages in labor-intensive manufacturing sectors due to lower labor costs. However, as the economy grows and incomes rise, labor costs increase. In response, industries begin to adopt capital-intensive methods and automation technologies to replace labor. This shift not only achieves economies of scale but also drives rapid technological advancements, leading to a gradual decline in the prices of industrial products. For instance, today's laptops are considerably cheaper and of higher quality than those from decades ago. Conversely, the service sector relies primarily on labor, and its costs rise in tandem with economic growth and increasing labor costs. Consequently, even if the output of services and industrial products remains constant, relative price changes cause the share of services in GDP to increase, while the share of industry declines. Furthermore, these changes in production costs have implications for a country's comparative advantage in global trade, further influencing its industrial structure.

Second, China faces adjustments in industrial structure over the past decade. In 2011, China's per capita GDP was approximately USD 10,000 (2017 PPP dollars), with the industrial sector accounting for about 46.5% of GDP. By 2020, per capita GDP had risen to around USD 16,000 (2017 PPP dollars), while the industrial sector's share of GDP had decreased to about 37.8%. This nearly 9 percentage point drop in the industrial GDP share over just 10 years is notably rapid. In contrast, developed economies took roughly 30 years to achieve a similar reduction from their peak industrial GDP share. This phenomenon has sparked discussions about premature deindustrialization in China. Several factors contribute to this trend. The first factor relates to the change in the labor force. China's working-age population peaked between 2013 and 2014 and has been declining since. From 2014 to 2020, the labor force shrank by approximately 40 million people, which is evident in frequent news reports about robots replacing workers and rising wages for migrant workers. The decrease in the labor force has led to higher labor costs, which, in turn, have driven up service prices and altered the industrial structure. The second factor pertains to strong administrative policies, such as capacity reduction and environmental regulations, have constrained industrial growth, further impacting the industrial structure.

Third, carbon emissions vary significantly across different sectors. Currently, the sectors with the highest carbon emissions in China are thermal power, steel, cement, and transportation, accounting for 44%, 18%, 14%, and 10% of total emissions, respectively. Thermal power supports the entire national economy, while China's steel and cement production accounts for about 57% of global output. Despite the large production volumes, exports are minimal, with most production meeting domestic demand. Approximately 65% of steel production is consumed by the construction industry, and nearly all cement is used in construction. This indicates that the high production and carbon emissions in China's steel and cement industries are primarily driven by robust demand from the construction sector.

Fourth, China's unprecedented pace of urbanization has significantly boosted the demand for construction and transportation. To understand why the construction sector is experiencing such high demand, we need to consider the urbanization rate. China's urbanization rate underwent a dramatic rise between 1990 and 2020, climbing from around 26.8% to 63.80%. This represents an increase of nearly 40 percentage points over 30 years. Since 2000, China's urbanization rate has advanced at an impressive rate of about 13.6 percentage points per decade. This means that every ten years, more than 200 million people have moved to urban areas out of the total population of 1.4 billion. Such massive internal migration inevitably drives strong demand for both construction and transportation. In 2000, the total floor space under construction in China was around 660 million square meters. By 2020, this figure had soared to approximately 9.3 billion square meters, an increase of more than 13 times. Similarly, the number of vehicles in China grew from about 22 million in 2000 to 350 million in 2020. These statistics clearly indicate that China has entered a phase of rapid urbanization. Every developed economy goes through a stage of rapid urban development, but once the urbanization rate reaches the 70% to 75% range, the growth rate tends to slow down, leading to a significant decrease in construction demand. Currently, China's urbanization rate stands at 64%, suggesting that the country will enter a phase where the pace of urbanization slows down within the next decade.

In my opinion, China's urbanization trajectory closely mirrors that of South Korea, another rapidly developing country. South Korea experienced an exceptionally swift urbanization process, outpacing all previously developed countries. As illustrated in Fig. 3, from 1960 to 1992, South Korea's urbanization rate increased by an average of 1.5 percentage points annually for 30 consecutive years. However, after the urbanization rate reached 75% between 1991 and 1992, the growth rate began to decelerate. Over the next seven years, South Korea's urbanization growth rate dropped from an annual increase of 1.5% to around 0.2%. This experience underscores the fundamental principles of urbanization and provides valuable insights for China. I believe that China's urbanization inflection point may arrive even sooner. Figure 4 shows the growth of China's urbanization rate from 1991 to 2021. Between 1996 and 2016, it increased by approximately 1.5 percentage points annually, maintaining rapid growth for two decades. This pattern closely resembles that of South Korea. However, starting from 2016 or 2017, China's urbanization growth rate began to decline, with the urbanization rate increasing by only 0.8 percentage points in 2021.

The reasons behind this trend are multifaceted and warrant sustained observation. From my perspective, it is primarily linked to the response to the pandemic. Concurrently, the slowdown in urbanization might also signal significant shifts in China's population structure and size. Figure 5 illustrates the fluctuation in the number of newborns in China from 1991 to 2021. The relaxation of the two-child policy led to a surge in births in 2017 after consecutive years of decline. However, this upturn was swiftly followed by a sharp downturn, with just over 10 million new births in 2021.

Furthermore, China's overall population structure has undergone notable changes. In 2022, China's population growth turned negative for

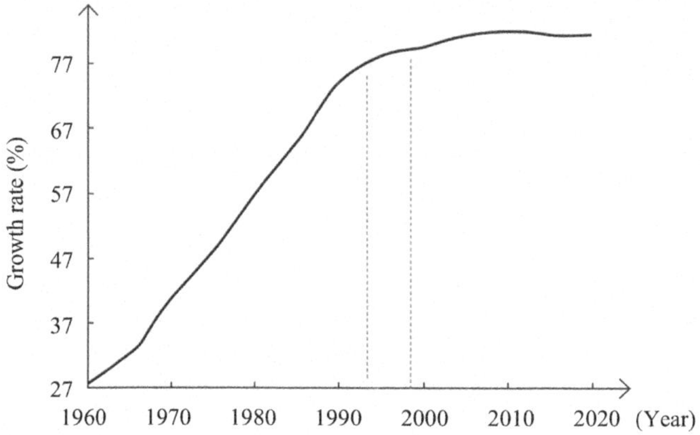

Fig. 3 Urbanization Rate in South Korea (1960–2020)

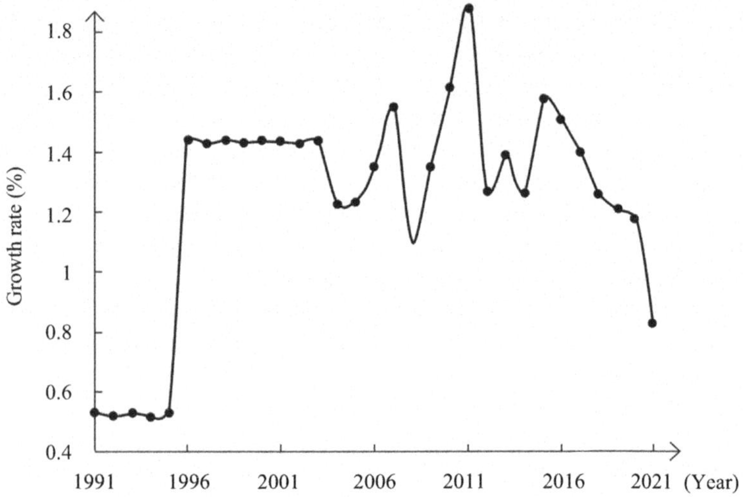

Fig. 4 Urbanization Rate in China (1991–2021)

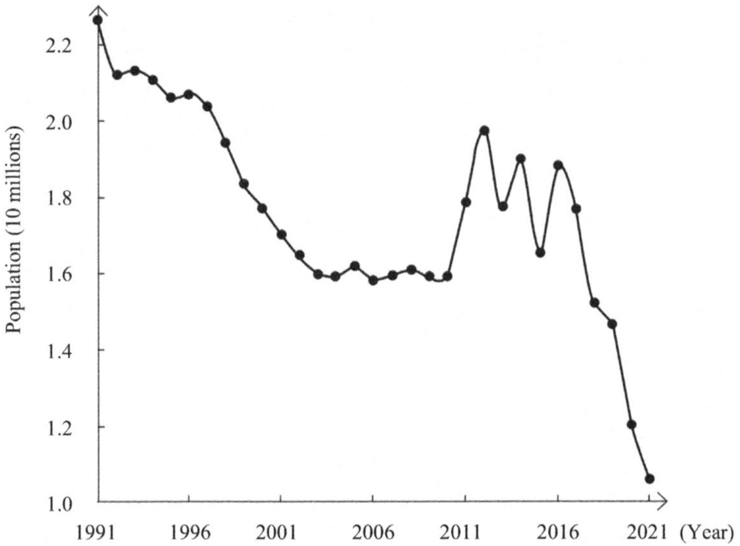

Fig. 5 Changes in China's Newborn Population (1991–2021)

the first time in four or five decades. This shift is crucial for understanding future economic development. As both the total population and urbanization growth rates decline, the demand for construction and transportation is expected to decrease. Over the next five to ten years, industries such as steel and cement may experience substantial shifts in demand. The sluggish real estate sales in 2022 can be attributed in part to macroeconomic deleveraging efforts, but are also likely a result of the significant slowdown in urbanization. While property prices remain robust in certain core areas and prime locations, the national real estate market may never return to its previous era of rapid growth, especially considering changes in urbanization rates and total population. Based on these factors, I anticipate that by 2030, the industrial GDP share will continue to decrease, potentially dropping from 38% to around 32%, conservatively speaking. This alone could lead to a reduction of approximately 1.8 billion tons in carbon emissions from fossil fuels.

Technological Advancements

Many of China's high-carbon-emission industries are actually at the forefront of global technological advancement. For example, the cement industry has largely adopted new dry-process production technology. As of the end of 2020, the nationwide implementation of ultra-low emissions for coal-fired units reached 9.5 billion kilowatts, accounting for 88% of the total installed coal power capacity. Key statistics show that the comprehensive energy consumption per ton of steel in steel enterprises decreased from 640 kilograms of standard coal in 2006 to 545 kilograms in 2020, a level comparable to that of Japan. Looking forward, China still has considerable potential for technological advancement. These high-carbon-emission industries all have potential technological alternatives. For coal-fired power generation, alternatives include natural gas, nuclear power, hydropower, wind power, and photovoltaics. The steel industry can adopt electric arc furnace steelmaking and hydrogen-based steelmaking, while the cement industry can use industrial waste, biofuels, and electricity as substitutes. In transportation, the development of new energy vehicles has surpassed expectations, with their sales volume in 2022 possibly accounting for around 20% of total vehicle sales. Many previous forecasts suggested this level might not be achieved until 2025, but it now appears attainable by 2022. Energy consumption per unit of GDP is determined by the economic industrial structure and technology.

Assuming a 24% reduction in energy consumption per unit of GDP by 2030 compared to 2020, and an annual GDP growth rate of about 5% over the next decade, the total consumption increment of primary energy will maintain an average annual growth rate of around 2.2%. Consequently, the reduction in fossil fuel carbon dioxide emissions resulting from industrial technological progress may be around 1.2 billion tons.

Energy Mix

Carbon emissions primarily originate from fossil fuels, making the share of clean or non-fossil energy in the overall energy mix especially critical. In 2020, China's coal, oil, natural gas, nuclear power, hydropower, wind power, and solar photovoltaics accounted for 56.6%, 19.6%, 8.2%, 2.2%, 8.1%, 2.8%, and 1.6% of its total primary energy consumption, respectively. Among these, China's non-fossil energy sources constituted 15.7%. Comparatively, nuclear power constituted 4.4% of global primary energy consumption, with higher shares of 8% in the United States and 11% in the European Union, while natural gas represented a substantially larger proportion, accounting for 25% globally, 34% in the United States, and 24.5% in the European Union. When compared to global levels, China's reliance on coal is disproportionately high, whereas its shares of natural gas and nuclear power are notably low. Transitioning the energy structure fundamentally involves shifting from fossil fuels to clean energy. Currently, renewable energy in China faces significant challenges due to generation instability. Hydropower, wind power, and solar photovoltaics can all experience disrupted supply during droughts and severe weather, making it difficult to support the entire power system in the short term. Consequently, the replacement of fossil fuels will depend on nuclear power and natural gas in the near future. To a certain degree, China possesses advantages in nuclear power, yet it lacks sufficient domestic natural gas reserves and relies heavily on imports. Presently, China's nuclear power technology, including third-generation advancements, is among the best globally. However, the sector faces significant policy challenges, Due to concerns over nuclear leaks, most of China's nuclear power plants, such as the Qinshan Nuclear Power Plant and Daya Bay Nuclear Power Station, are located along coastal areas. In contrast, France and the United States primarily place their nuclear plants inland. Given the high safety standards of Chinese nuclear technology, I believe we should consider the feasibility of deploying some nuclear power plants inland.

The energy structure is predominantly influenced by the relative prices among different energy sources, as they can often replace one another. This means that if the price of a particular energy source is low, its share in the overall energy mix will be higher. In China, we have abundant coal resources but relatively limited oil and gas reserves. As a result, coal prices are relatively cheap, leading to a higher share of coal in the energy mix. Traditional fossil fuels offer a stable energy supply but come with drawbacks such as pollution and high-carbon emissions. On the other hand, while nuclear power provides a stable energy supply as well, there are widespread concerns about nuclear safety, and it can be costly to produce.

Looking ahead, there is great potential for the development of new renewable energy sources. From 2010 to 2020, the costs of solar power plants, onshore wind power, offshore wind power, concentrated solar power, and electric vehicle batteries have all significantly decreased by 85%, 56%, 48%, 68%, and 89%, respectively. With continued technological advancements, these costs are expected to decline even further. Many research reports have already identified renewable energy as one of the primary energy sources to achieve carbon neutrality, indicating a promising future for renewables. Currently, one of the main challenges for new energy sources is their unstable performance, which will ultimately be resolved through technological advancements. Between 2010 and 2020, the proportion of non-fossil energy in China's energy mix increased by around 7 percentage points, in which nuclear power, hydropower, and wind/solar power contributed 1.56%, 1.67%, and 4%, respectively. The past decade has seen China's focus on the development of wind and solar technologies. Over the next decade, as these renewable technologies continue to advance and achieve further cost reductions, projections indicate that China's non-fossil energy share could rise substantially from 15.4% in 2020 to 25% by 2030, resulting in a reduction of approximately 1.3 billion tons of carbon dioxide emissions from fossil fuels.

Outlook for Carbon Emissions in 2030

Based on the aforementioned calculations, by 2030, China's economic aggregate could potentially add approximately 5.3 billion tons of carbon dioxide emissions. However, adjustments in the industrial structure might reduce emissions by 1.8 billion tons, and technological advancements in the industrial sector could further cut emissions by 1.2 billion tons. Additionally, changes in the energy mix are expected to result in a reduction of 1.3 billion tons of carbon dioxide emissions. Consequently, by 2030, carbon dioxide emissions from fossil fuels are projected to be around 10.9 billion tons. Considering trends in population and industrial structure, the macro environment for emission reduction in China by 2030 appears relatively favorable. However, it is crucial to highlight that achieving the dual carbon goals is a long-term mission. When implementing relevant policies, it is essential to adhere to the principles of economic development and adopt appropriate emission reduction strategies to minimize economic impact. The goal should be to harmonize economic growth with low-carbon living, avoiding any hasty measures.

Outlook for Carbon Neutrality in 2060

From my perspective, several important trends should be considered.

Firstly, as the rate of urbanization gradually slows, there will be a significant decrease in the growth of energy consumption after 2030. Between 1961 and 1979, rapid urbanization led to an average annual energy consumption growth of 4.14% in countries in the European Union and 2.94% in the United States. Over the following 40 years, these figures dropped to 0.58% and 0.83%, respectively. In China, the annual average energy consumption growth was 9.4% from 2001 to 2011, but it decreased to 2.9% between 2012 and 2020. Taking into account the background of slowing urbanization and a declining population, China's annual average energy consumption growth is not expected to exceed 1% after 2030.

Secondly, in the context of declining total energy demand, further reliance on three low-carbon technologies is essential: clean energy substitution, carbon capture technology, and agricultural and forestry carbon sinks. If we can effectively implement these three technologies, I believe China has the potential to achieve carbon neutrality by 2060. The strategic goal of targeting carbon neutrality by 2060 aligns with commitments made by developed economies, such as the United States and Europe, which aim to achieve carbon neutrality by 2050. Achieving carbon neutrality largely depends on technological advancements. If developed economies meet their targets on time, technologies such as energy storage, hydrogen energy, new energy vehicles, and carbon capture will have matured by then. Given China's strong industrial manufacturing capacity, it is entirely possible to scale up the production of these mature technologies within a ten-year span, thereby achieving carbon neutrality.

If developed economies fail to meet their carbon neutrality targets on time, they cannot reasonably expect China to achieve carbon neutrality by 2060.

Therefore, from any perspective, there is no need to hastily achieve the dual carbon goals in the short term, and it is unnecessary to control energy demand as a means to achieve these goals.

Policy Options

From an economic perspective, carbon emissions themselves represent an issue of externalities and market failure. The term "externality problem" refers to the fact that carbon emissions contribute to climate change, causing harm and costs to the entire human ecological system, health, and economic growth. However, the production sectors or individuals responsible for these emissions do not bear any of these costs. The "market failure" problem arises from the absence of a price on carbon emissions, leading to inefficient resource allocation in the market, which primarily relies on price mechanisms. Therefore, addressing carbon emissions necessitates government involvement or intervention. Theoretically, the optimal strategy for reducing carbon emissions across society as a whole is to adhere to the principle of marginal abatement cost. Specifically, economic entities or enterprises with lower marginal abatement costs should undertake greater emissions reductions, while those with higher marginal abatement costs should undertake fewer reductions. This process should continue until all enterprises have equal marginal abatement costs. This approach ensures that the resource allocation status with equal marginal abatement costs minimizes the overall social cost of emissions reduction. Achieving this principle primarily relies on two categories of policies: administrative directives and market-driven pricing policies. The pursuit of dual carbon goals follows the same logic.

Administrative Directives

In China, administrative directives predominantly depend on the central government setting policy goals, which are then broken down and executed at local levels. For instance, this might involve halting approvals or directly shutting down high-energy-consuming and heavily polluting enterprises, setting mandatory emission reduction targets, enforcing the installation of emission reduction equipment, and establishing emission standards. The advantage of these administrative measures is that they provide clear accountability and yield quick results. However, they fail to address the issue of information asymmetry. As previously discussed, the optimal emission reduction strategy is based on the principle of marginal abatement cost. However, since information is widely dispersed among enterprises, it is difficult for the government to gain a comprehensive understanding. When targets are subdivided and passed down to local governments, adhering to the principle of "lower-cost entities reducing more, higher-cost entities reducing less" becomes challenging. Consequently, local governments often resort to using tangible and concrete indicators to enforce reductions, such as installed capacity, steel furnace capacity, and enterprise size. This approach can lead to a uniform, one-size-fits-all method, which is crude and incurs high overall social costs. Research indicates that government environmental policies often disproportionately affect small private enterprises. The national economy, an organic system that has achieved significant success through market-driven division of labor and systemic synergy, can be disrupted by blanket administrative orders. Such one-size-fits-all administrative directives address only the symptoms rather than the root causes of environmental issues.

Administrative directives for control purposes typically employ three main types of measures. One is to achieve emission reduction through output control, such as reducing production capacity, limiting electricity, and suspending the approvals for energy-intensive and high-emission projects. The second is to reduce carbon emissions through energy use control, such as implementing "dual controls" on energy consumption. The third is to directly control carbon emissions, such as setting emission standards and mandatory reduction targets. Research in environmental economics has demonstrated that among three administrative measures—controlling production output, controlling energy consumption, and directly controlling carbon emissions—the latter is the most effective policy. Controlling production output yields the poorest results, followed by energy consumption control. The rationale is straightforward: within the realm of administrative directives, these policies offer increasing degrees of flexibility for emission reductions, thereby minimizing negative impacts on business operations in descending order of effectiveness. Therefore, if administrative directives are to be employed, direct control over carbon emissions is optimal. This sentiment was emphasized during the Central Economic Work Conference held in December 2021, which underscored the need to transition early from "dual controls" on energy consumption to "dual controls" on total carbon emissions and intensity. The conference also stressed accelerating the development of incentive and regulatory mechanisms for pollution and carbon reduction.

Market-Driven Pricing Policies

The core idea behind market-driven pricing policies is to assign a price to carbon emissions, shifting from cost-free emissions to priced emissions. This pricing mechanism allows companies to independently decide how to invest in emission reduction technologies, lower energy consumption, scale down production, or cease operations if necessary. The advantage of this system is that it encourages individual companies to reduce emissions optimally when the marginal cost of reduction equals the carbon price. When all companies face the same carbon price, their marginal reduction costs are expected to align, minimizing the overall cost of carbon reduction across society. This approach fosters a sustainable mechanism for long-term emission reductions. Additionally, carbon pricing can incentivize the adoption of clean energy and spur innovation in low-carbon technologies. There are two primary methods for setting a price on carbon: carbon taxes and carbon emissions trading. In practice, the European Union predominantly uses carbon emissions trading, supplemented by individual countries' carbon taxes due to the absence of an EU-wide carbon tax. Conversely, certain states in the United States have established their own carbon emissions trading markets. Both carbon taxes and emissions trading have their pros and cons. With a carbon tax, the government sets the carbon price, and the market determines the final amount of emissions. Emissions trading, however, involves the government capping total emissions, allowing the market to set the carbon price. Overall, the dual carbon goals, which aim to control total emissions, align more closely with emissions trading. Nevertheless, emissions trading can lead to issues such as data manipulation, high transaction costs, market monopolies, and a lack of motivation among local governments.

Summary

Based on analysis above and China's economic development around 2030, it appears that China has a relatively favorable macro environment for achieving carbon peaking. However, compared to developed countries like the United States, China's per capita GDP remains low. Implementing high-level emission reductions at this stage of economic development poses significant challenges, and it is crucial not to underestimate these difficulties. In my view, China should avoid a one-size-fits-all, cost-ignoring approach to emissions reduction. Instead, we should respect the natural progression of economic and carbon emission trends. The country's primary strategy should focus on leveraging market mechanisms and carbon pricing policies to manage the rapid growth of energy consumption and carbon dioxide emissions. If administrative directives are absolutely necessary, carbon emission control policies should take precedence over output control and energy use control policies, which should not be considered or implemented for emission reduction purposes.

First and foremost, we must reach a consensus and establish a policy framework centered on carbon emission trading and carbon pricing mechanisms, while creating a coordinated mechanism for policies of the dual carbon goals across various government departments. Currently, there is a lack of inter-departmental coordination in China's policies of the dual carbon goals. The accumulation of disparate policies from various departments has placed excessive burdens on enterprises. Effectively addressing carbon emission issues requires reliance on market mechanisms and carbon pricing. If we can achieve consensus at the central level, China should consider abolishing inefficient administrative policies, such as the approval of high-energy-consuming projects and energy consumption dual controls, which often disrupt market dynamics. Instead, the state should focus on market-based solutions like carbon emission trading and carbon taxes to achieve the country's dual carbon goals.

Second, we should gradually expand the national carbon emissions trading market and implement total emissions control when appropriate. By 2025, industries with high emissions, such as steel, cement, and petrochemicals, should be included in the carbon trading market. During the 15th Five-Year Plan period, sectors closely tied to public welfare, such as transportation and building heating, should also be incorporated. Additionally, it is advisable to include carbon sinks in the national carbon trading market as soon as possible. By around 2028, China should start implementing quota-based total emissions control for the national carbon trading market.

Third, for non-point source carbon emissions not covered by the trading market, we should consider implementing a carbon tax policy aimed at promoting carbon adaptation.

Fourth, we should deepen electricity market reforms to unlock the competitive advantages of renewable energy generation. In order to achieve the dual carbon goals, it is crucial to significantly increase the share of renewable energy. However, the instability of renewable energy supply must be addressed. Currently, this is mainly resolved through grid dispatching and energy storage solutions. It is recommended to introduce a market-driven pricing mechanism for the intermittency of electricity and establish pricing mechanisms for energy storage and peak load auxiliary services. Regional electricity trading markets can also be established across provinces to facilitate the scheduling and consumption of renewable energy within a broader grid framework.

Fifth, we should expedite the market-oriented reform of electricity pricing through the phased elimination of price controls and cross-subsidies. For a long time, China has kept prices of essential goods, such as electricity, artificially low to ensure public welfare. This practice has led to residential electricity prices being subsidized below the actual cost of supply through cross-subsidization. However, for carbon pricing mechanisms to be fully effective, a robust price transmission system is necessary. It is insufficient to simply set a price on carbon emissions; this price must be effectively transmitted to thermal power plants, generating companies, and ultimately, to every consumer and business. Only by doing so can we establish a society-wide mechanism that genuinely encourages electricity conservation and reduces carbon emissions. Without rationalizing the pricing mechanism, the effectiveness of the carbon tax and trading market will be significantly diminished.

The manufacturer's authorised representative in the EU is Springer
Nature Customer Service Centre GmbH, Europaplatz 3, 69115 Heidelberg,
Germany. If you have any concerns regarding our products, please
contact ProductSafety@springernature.com

Printed and bound by CPI Group (UK) Ltd, Croydon, CR0 4YY
01/10/2026
02225912-0014